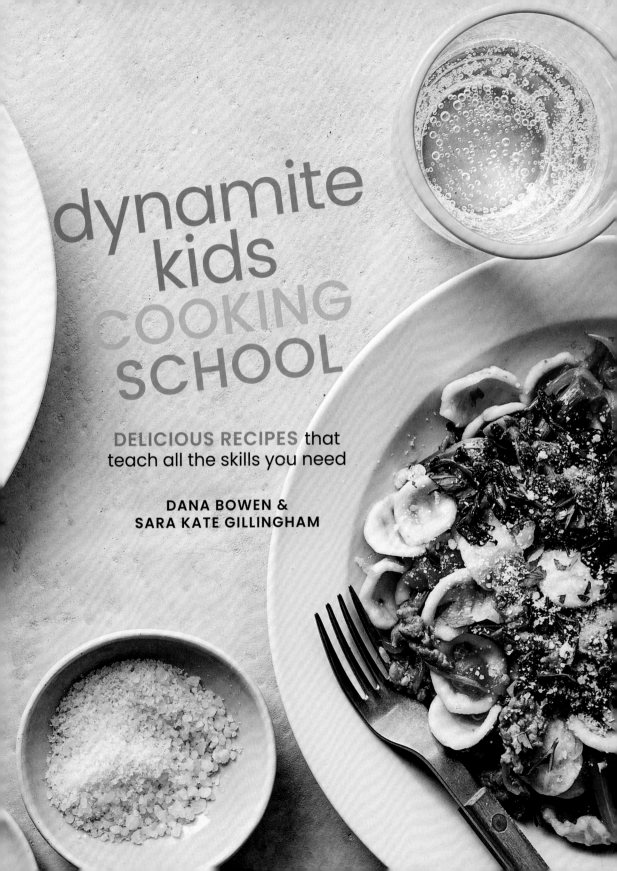

dynamite kids COOKING SCHOOL

DELICIOUS RECIPES that teach all the skills you need

DANA BOWEN &
SARA KATE GILLINGHAM

Published in the United States by Clarkson
Potter/Publishers, an imprint of Random House,
a division of Penguin Random House LLC,
New York.
ClarksonPotter.com
RandomHouseBooks.com

CLARKSON POTTER is a trademark and POTTER
with colophon is a registered trademark of
Penguin Random House LLC.

Library of Congress Cataloging-in-Publication
Data
Names: Bowen, Dana, author. | Gillingham, Sara
    Kate, author. | Pick, Aubrie, photographer.
Title: Dynamite kids cooking school / Dana
    Bowen, Sara Kate Gillingham, Aubrie Pick.
Identifiers: LCCN 2021058168 (print) | LCCN
    2021058169 (ebook) | ISBN 9780593138458
    (hardcover) | ISBN 9780593138465 (ebook)
Subjects: LCSH: Cooking. | Dinners and dining. |
    LCGFT: Cookbooks.
Classification: LCC TX714 .G5448 2022 (print)
    | LCC TX714 (ebook) | DDC 641.5--dc23/
    eng/20211230
LC record available at https://lccn.loc.
    gov/2021058168
LC ebook record available at https://lccn.loc.
    gov/2021058169

ISBN 978-0-593-13845-8
Ebook ISBN 978-0-593-13846-5

Printed in China

Photographer: Aubrie Pick
Photography Assistant: Nathaniel Yates
Downes / Timothy Evans
Production Assistant: Stephanie Murray
Food Stylist: Fanny Pan
Food Stylist Assistants: Allison Fellion / Cynthia
Bazan-Washington
Prop Stylist: Claire Mack
Prop Stylist Assistant: Alyssa Kreidt
Editor: Francis Lam
Editorial Assistant: Darian Keels
Production Editor: Joyce Wong
Production Manager: Kim Tyner
Compositors: Merri Ann Morrell / Dix / Zoe
Tokushige
Copy Editor: Kathy Brock
Indexer: Elizabeth Parson
Marketer: Andrea Portanova
Publicist: Kristin Casemore

Book and cover design by Stephanie Huntwork
Cover photographs by Aubrie Pick

10 9 8 7 6 5 4 3 2 1

First Edition

welcome to the dynamite shop!

We're glad you're here, and we're so excited to cook with you.

We're Dana and Sara Kate, two food writers and friends—and, most importantly, parents—who, in 2018, opened a cooking school for kids and families in an old Brooklyn pizzeria that now beams classes online to students all over the world.

We're all about empowering kids in the kitchen and helping them gain confidence by learning to cook. In our school, we host The Dynamite Dinner Club several times a week and walk the students through making a full meal for their family—it might be seasonal pasta one week, vegetable fried rice the next. We cook alongside them, they ask questions, we get close-ups of their cutting board. We also teach The Dynamite Baking Club, Weekend Workshops, weeklong summer camps, and a free Community Kitchen charity class where we invite guest chefs to teach us a dish to raise money for a social justice cause that's meaningful to them.

We're an inclusive and supportive community that revolves around food. Whether you're a parent of a budding cook or a young chef picking up your first very own cookbook, we're so happy you're here.

This book is a collection of our most popular recipes from all our classes—that means kids love to make them, eat them, and serve them! They're our greatest hits, with all the tips, tricks, lessons, and cooks' wisdom we impart to our students as we're cooking together. Our recipes are designed to teach kids how to think and act like confident home cooks.

We started The Dynamite Shop because we believe there are so many reasons to get kids in the kitchen early and often. As people who spend most days working with and thinking about food (Sara Kate has written three other cookbooks and started a popular food site called TheKitchn.com, and Dana is a food writer and former executive editor at *Saveur*, *Food & Wine*, and other culinary magazines), we could never find a cooking school that we would want to enroll our own kids in: most of them were too cutesy (you know, like "kidz" with a *z*) with infantilized recipes and instructions that talked down to kids and minimized their potential. Or, even worse, they taught cooking as a hyped-up sport, like cooking-show competitions with celebrity-chef bravura. They totally missed the point!

We wanted more for our kids in the kitchen. Cooking instruction has gradually disappeared from most of our lives without anyone ringing alarm bells. Most schools no longer teach home ec, and most households aren't set up as they used

to be, with multiple generations cooking together and passing down kitchen wisdom while preparing and sharing meals.

And as busy working parents, we also know that—let's face it—the mealtime hustle and challenge are real. So we created a program where empowering kids in the kitchen to get dinner on the table at least once a week was the solution to all that.

We signed the lease on a run-down pizzeria and transformed the dilapidated storefront space into a comfy teaching kitchen, with a cook's library, backyard garden, and neighborhood café up front. As soon as we opened, we were booked to capacity with our after-school program, which got dinner on one hundred families' tables each week, and our summer camps, which served thousands.

When we weren't teaching, we were a community hub: we hosted charity cookie swaps and PTA fundraisers, cooked for local shelters and assisted living residences, supported social action and food justice initiatives, made breakfasts for marches, and held election-year phone-bank events. It's crucial to us that we continue to make food spaces like kitchens and dinner tables places that are always welcoming young people to express themselves and to help one another.

In 2020, we switched to teaching cooking classes online so that kids could make dinner for their families in their own homes. Before we knew it, we were cooking with 500-plus families each week, all gathering remotely from around the world.

In the process of teaching online, we learned something important: teaching kids to cook in their *own* kitchens is the best way to help them build confidence and skills. They're more focused and in their comfort zone, and most importantly, they're cooking with a purpose—to feed the people they love. Our teachers can still see what they're doing and guide them safely and joyfully as they make a meal. And when class is over, dinner is on the table.

We developed this program—and now this book—to teach, support, guide, and cheer you on your path to becoming a dynamite cook.

why we cook

The obvious reason is that we need to eat! But there are so many meaningful benefits to cooking that don't show up on the plate. And there are lots of reasons why we should empower young people—and all people—to cook.

COOKING BUILDS COMMUNITY

Food is an uplifting way to connect, engage, and support the world around us and to celebrate its diversity. Whether it's understanding a different culture by exploring world cuisines or going to a picnic, barbecue, or potluck with neighbors, when people come together around food, good things happen. When we break bread together, we connect on a human level and bridge divides.

COOKING IS HOW WE SHOW LOVE

Whether it's the breakfast we make for our family, a meal we bring to a neighbor, or a birthday cake we bake for a friend, cooking is one way we show people we care. It's a real-world thing we can do to make people feel good.

COOKING IS CONFIDENCE AND CREATIVITY

Some of us are pastry artists, creating beautiful and elaborate desserts. Others like to make spice blends and are all about building flavor. Then there are the Cheese Whizzes and the Bread Queens and the Souper Stars. Cooking allows kids— anyone, really—to explore their creativity and express their identities through food. Dynamite Shop kids learn to customize dishes to their diets and tastes, and discover parts of their character along the way.

COOKING WORKS OUR BRAINS, HANDS, AND SENSES

Whether it's kitchen math (for example, scaling a recipe up or calculating volumes for pan sizes) or food science (such as learning about the Maillard reaction when searing and roasting or leaveners while baking), every Dynamite class touches on important STEM lessons.

COOKING IS HEALTH, BALANCE, AND WELL-BEING

By teaching kids how to make dinner or a new kitchen skill, we're helping them develop a healthy relationship with food and an understanding that the way we eat can benefit our well-being and that of the planet. The majority of our recipes are inherently healthy, vegetable-forward, and balanced—and, most of all, delicious!

how to use this book

In many of our recipes—even in their titles!—we encourage the cook to make the dish their way once they understand the basic formula or thinking behind it. We think that flexibility is the key to this book as well. What this means is that we're giving you the info and tools for success, but how you choose to use them, and what you ultimately make with them, are totally up to you.

1 You can use the contents or index to find the specific recipe or type of recipe you want to make. Say you want to cook mac and cheese or browse a bunch of soups—you can go directly to those pages. And while you're reading and cooking that recipe, you'll learn all the lessons we deliver when we teach it in class.

2 Use the contents page at the front of the book or index to find the lesson you want to learn. Say you want to learn about sauces or baking: go directly to those chapters, read the lessons, and then pick some recipes to make for practice.

3 Use this book as a guided course, working your way through as if we were teaching you in class: from kitchen safety and knife work, to seasoning and flavor, to eggs and the role they play in recipes, to vinaigrettes, and so on. If you want to do this, we suggest reading the first three chapters of the book before you get to the recipes. Then cook from the recipe chapters, picking a few recipes from each to make. As you read through the book, if you come across a food term you don't understand, refer to the glossary in the back of the book for an explanation.

In the spirit of choosing your own adventure, many of our recipes are written with lots of substitutions and swaps so you can cook your dish with what you have on hand or just prepare it with what you want to eat. So, for example, you can follow the Classic Mac and Cheese with Roasted Broccoli (page 122) recipe to a tee, and it'll be delicious . . . or you can swap in different cheeses or different roasted vegetables and take it in an entirely new and exciting direction.

Because that's the goal in learning to cook for anyone at any age: to look at a recipe for inspiration and make it your own. In that way, everything you do in the kitchen is a real adventure!

organizing your space

Have you ever noticed that the kitchen is always the most crowded room in the house? When people come over, no matter how you try to steer them to the living room or front porch, they always end up gathering, chatting, laughing, and, of course, nibbling in the kitchen. The energy of the kitchen and the magic that happens there have a gravitational force that pulls people together. It's no surprise it's often called the heart of the home.

One of the fun things we've found about cooking with kids online is that we get to see one another's very different kitchens: whether it's a tiny galley kitchen in an apartment in Manhattan or a sprawling one in a house in rural North Carolina, every cooking space reflects the way of life of the people using it. We have students who Zoom in from farmhouse kitchens and run outside to collect eggs from their chicken coops. One student joins us from her RV camper kitchen!

The things we bring into our kitchens have meaning and they tell stories: whether it's a recipe box passed down from your great-grandmother or a utensil you brought back as a souvenir from a trip.

It's not just the things we bring into the kitchen that are important, but how we organize the space to make cooking more enjoyable, efficient, and safe.

After making a meal or two, think about how you moved around and whether there are things you can do to change the space to make it really work for you. For example, if you find yourself walking all the way across the kitchen a bunch of times to put stuff in the garbage, maybe put a bowl on the counter that you can use as a container and dump it later. Or if you find yourself fishing through your drawers looking for tools, can you take them out before you start cooking and put them in a clean bin so you can get to them easily? Making your space work better for you will make you a more confident, capable, and creative cook.

the tools you need

When it comes to kitchen tools, we're big believers that less is more: there's no use in having unnecessary gadgets taking up precious space. In fact, most of the tools we suggest do double—or quadruple—duty in our kitchens. From our years of working in restaurants, and test kitchens, and developing recipes at The Dynamite Shop and at home, we've become evangelists about certain tools we can't live without and brands we swear by. But when it comes down to it, we could prepare most meals in this book with nothing more than just a few of the tools from the list below. And if we can reuse a tool in a recipe, even better—one less thing to wash!

KNIVES: Probably the most indispensable tools in the kitchen, we have a whole section in this book about knife work (see page 28), where we outline the three knives we believe every kitchen should have: a chef's knife, a paring knife, and a serrated knife.

CUTTING BOARDS: We love wooden cutting boards, but thick plastic boards are also great options and easy to clean and sterilize. Avoid thin, foldable plastic and glass cutting boards. We recommend having at least two cutting boards— one just for meat and another just for produce—

so we don't have to wash them between tasks.

PEELER: Our favorite is the easy-to-grasp OXO Good Grips swivel peeler.

CAN OPENER: A simple hand-cranked version.

WOODEN SPOONS: These are our go-tos for stirring everything in a pan or pot, and they look so pretty in a utensil holder! We love a flat-edged wooden spoon for scraping all the flavorful bits from the bottom of the pan.

LADLE: We prefer metal ladles because they are sturdy and don't melt or absorb flavors.

FISH SPATULA: This is one of our favorite tools in our kitchen—and not just for fish! It's thin enough to get under delicate pancakes or fillets to flip them, but also wide and long enough to transfer those items or anything else to or from a pan.

RUBBER SPATULA: These are great for gentle tasks, like folding batters and getting every last drop out of the bowl.

WHISK: A large metal balloon whisk allows us to whip up batters, eggs, sauces, and, of course, whipped cream. Make sure the wire is bendable but not flimsy.

METAL TONGS: For stirring or flipping ingredients in a hot pan, tongs are extensions of our hand.

INSTANT-READ THERMOMETER: It's the best $12 you'll spend to ensure that your meat is cooked correctly, that your water is just right for blooming yeast, and any other pressing temperature questions.

PASTRY BRUSH: We use this for basting meats while roasting, brushing beaten egg whites on dough for a glossy finish, or adding a rich coating of melted butter or flavored syrup to baked goods.

PEPPER GRINDER: Fresh-cracked peppercorns taste so much better than pre-ground pepper; you can smell it instantly. We can't complain about the prefilled plastic grinders you can buy for less than $5 at the supermarket.

SALT BOWL: Forget salt shakers or grinders; we reach into a bowl filled with salt and use our (clean) fingers to determine just how big or small of a pinch we want.

KITCHEN TOWELS: We use them for everything from cleaning up messes to doubling as a pot holder and stabilizing our cutting board so it doesn't slide around on the counter. We buy flour-sack cotton towels in bulk: We toss them into the washer and they're as white as new.

FINE-MESH STRAINER: We use a large one for straining stock and sauces and draining pasta. In fact, you don't really need to use a colander since a fine-mesh strainer does the trick!

CAST-IRON OR NONSTICK SKILLET: Our love for cast iron runs deep. These pans are indestructible and virtually nonstick once seasoned properly. If you don't have a well-seasoned cast-iron skillet, you'll need a nonstick one. With nonstick skillets, we're careful not to use metal utensils, which can scratch the cooking surface. So get some wooden or heatproof rubber or silicone spatulas, spoons, and tongs, too.

CAST-IRON DUTCH OVEN: A Dutch oven is a wide heavy pot that can be used for everything from sautéing greens to simmering soups to baking bread. Cast-iron ones retain heat beautifully to allow for steady, even cooking. We love the enameled versions: their finish is close to nonstick. Our go-to is a 5-quart version with straight sides from Le Creuset or Staub, but we also like the affordable nonenameled version from Lodge. If you take care of them, they'll last a lifetime and are beautiful heirlooms to pass down to future generations.

STOCKPOT: Every kitchen needs a big pot for boiling pasta water or cooking a lot of soup. Nothing fancy. Just big.

SAUCEPAN: Sometimes you don't want to take out your heavy Dutch oven to make sauce for your pizza or boil a few eggs. That's where a smallish (2- to 3-quart) saucepan comes in.

SHEET PANS: We love our aluminum sheet pans (also called sheet trays or baking sheets) and use them for everything: setting out ingredients for a recipe; toasting nuts; baking focaccia, cookies, or pizza; roasting vegetables; catching drips while baking pies; and cooking entire dinners in the oven. Our go-tos are a half sheet pan (about 13 × 18 inches) and quarter sheet pan (9 × 13 inches).

CASSEROLE DISH: We could never have too many of these in all shapes and sizes—from vintage oval enameled cast-iron beauties to rectangular glass versions. These are smaller than a roasting pan and what we reach for when we're making one-dish recipes, like lasagna.

MIXING BOWLS: We love stainless-steel nesting bowls that don't take up much space. The kind with nonskid rubber on the bottom makes tasks like whisking while drizzling in oil far easier (and safer!).

MEASURING CUPS AND SPOONS: Nothing fancy. Just sturdy stainless-steel tools that are easy to hold and clean.

LIQUID MEASURING CUP (4-CUP): We're picky about these: we want to be able to read the measurements from the side and above. The classic Pyrex is our fave.

SMALL PREP BOWLS: We use these for setting out ingredients or serving sauces on the side.

KITCHEN SCALE: We love digital scales for their precision, which is especially useful when baking breads or cakes.

STAND MIXER: You can use hand mixers, but a stand mixer makes mixing dough, whipping cream, and combining batters so much easier. Plus, we love the add-ons for rolling and cutting fresh pasta, making sausage, and more.

FOOD PROCESSOR: We still have our mothers' Cuisinarts and use them for everything from shredding cabbage and carrots to making pesto. If you don't have a full-size one, a more affordable mini food processor can get a lot of the job done.

BLENDER: We can't live without our morning smoothies! While a blender with a fierce motor like a Vitamix makes easy work of pulverizing nuts or ice, you don't need that much power (or to spend that much money) for most blender tasks.

KITCHEN TWINE: Our kitchen is never without a simple spool of cotton string for trussing meats or wrapping up gifts of baked goods.

PLASTIC ZIP-TOP FREEZER BAGS: For saving kitchen scraps or last night's dinner, we always have a stash.

PARCHMENT PAPER: This is paper with a nonstick coating that we use for everything: lining pans for baked goods, protecting our sheet pans, wrapping desserts.

PERMANENT MARKERS AND MASKING TAPE: For labeling foods before sticking them in the freezer.

MASON JARS: We use these (in all sizes) for storing leftovers, shaking up vinaigrettes, and making quick pickles. Plus, if you have flowers, it's an instant vase!

FINE GRATER: We like Microplanes for a fine shaving of cheese or zest.

BOX GRATER: For grating, shaving, and zesting.

PIE DISH: Glass, metal, or ceramic all work.

CAKE PAN: A 9-inch cake pan is great for simple cakes, and if you have two, you can bake a layer cake!

LOAF PAN: For pound cake, banana bread, chocolate-zucchini bread, and more.

MUFFIN TINS: We like to have two on hand for big batches of cupcakes and muffins.

the ingredients you need

These are the ingredients we keep on hand to prepare meals. When we shop for a recipe, we don't have to buy these ingredients because we make sure we always have enough!

NEXT TO THE STOVE

SALT: We keep kosher salt in a small bowl by the stove so we can season as we cook. It's our go-to because it has great texture and dissolves quickly. Diamond Crystal brand is our fave: It has a clean, not-too-salty taste. Whatever brand you use, try to keep to the same one so you'll learn how much saltier food gets with one pinch. Soon you'll start to figure out how much salt to add. For baking, we use fine salt because it measures more precisely. (But you can pretty much use the two interchangeably.)

BLACK PEPPER: Whether it's a grinder that you fill with peppercorns or a supermarket grinder that comes prefilled, practically everything we make gets a few fresh grinds before going out to the table for a . . . well, peppery finish.

EXTRA-VIRGIN OLIVE OIL: We love olive oil. It's healthful, there is so much to learn about how different it tastes depending on where it comes from, and, of course, we love its flavor. We use extra-virgin, the purest form, made from the first pressing of olives, because it has the most flavor and nutrients. The one thing to know about cooking with extra-virgin olive oil is that it has a low smoke point, which means it'll lose its flavor and burn if it gets too hot and starts smoking.

VINEGAR: Tartness comes from acids, and it's an important high note to balance the flavor of dishes. We lean on vinegar to do the trick. Apple cider vinegar, balsamic vinegar, red wine vinegar, and rice vinegar are the biggest players in our kitchen.

IN THE CUPBOARD OR PANTRY

NEUTRAL OIL: When we need an oil that doesn't add its own flavor or that has a high smoke point, we look to vegetable oil or canola oil.

GRANULATED SUGAR: The all-purpose sweetener.

BROWN SUGAR: For adding a depth of flavor to baked goods, sauces, and more. Dark brown sugar has a slightly richer flavor, but we believe the light and dark versions are mostly interchangeable. We'll note in recipes when one is preferred over the other.

POWDERED SUGAR: We sprinkle this over pound cakes and cookies and whip it into cream because of its quick-dissolving abilities.

HONEY: This sweetener has so many superpowers and, if you buy local honey, is a beautiful reflection of the season, made from the nectar of whatever blooms the bees feasted on.

MAPLE SYRUP: We love sweetening dishes with maple syrup. Its deep, caramelized flavor is as rich as it is sweet.

BAKING SODA AND BAKING POWDER: See our section on the science of baking (page 195); suffice it to say, our kitchen is never without both!

CORNSTARCH: For thickening sauces, puddings, and more, a little cornstarch goes a long way.

DRIED HERBS AND SPICES: We devote entire classes to seasoning with dried herbs and spices. Tasting them and understanding how they work in a marinade or sauce is a great way to unleash a cook's creativity and ability to create their own flavor profiles. The main rule of thumb for dried herbs, as compared to fresh, is to use them earlier in the cooking process and to use less since they are more concentrated in flavor. We tend to prefer making our own spice blends like

Creole seasoning instead of buying them—it's so easy to mix them up, and it doesn't take up more space in our spice rack. Here's a list of what we keep on hand.

Ground allspice

Ground cardamom

Ground cinnamon

Ground cloves

Ground cumin

Ground coriander

Ground ginger

Ground turmeric

Whole nutmeg

Crushed red pepper flakes

Paprika (sweet and smoked)

Oregano

Bay leaves

Garlic powder

VANILLA EXTRACT: We always use pure vanilla extract, as to us the imitation stuff has a slightly chemical flavor that can ruin a cupcake or whipped cream.

SEEDS AND NUTS: Not only are these a healthy source of fat, they also add great texture and flavor to dishes. We usually toast them before use to bring out even more of their flavor (see page 280). For a nut-free alternative, we love pepitas (shelled pumpkin seeds) instead.

PEANUT BUTTER: We always keep a natural peanut butter (without added sugar) on hand for quick snacks and stirring into sauces.

ALL-PURPOSE FLOUR: For the most common tasks, all-purpose is, well, all-purpose.

RICE: Short- and medium-grain brown and white rices are our go-tos: We love the texture and flavor as a base for everything from stir-fries to gumbo.

GRAINS: The more the merrier in our pantry! We eat our Rainbow Grain Bowl with Tahini Dressing (page 167) at least once a week, and we always make it with different grains: quinoa, wheat berries, farro, and barley are all delicious and good for you. See Cooking Grains (page 269).

YEAST: We keep a packet or two of active dry yeast on hand for pizza dough (see page 202) and Sleepover No-Knead Bread (page 199).

BEANS: We like to stock dried and canned beans of all kinds for chili, enchiladas, bruschetta toppings, sauces, and more. See Cooking Dried Beans on page 265.

WHOLE PEELED TOMATOES: For everything from pizza sauce to salsa, we go through many cans of whole peeled tomatoes each month. They're the most versatile canned tomatoes you can buy: Mash them by hand to leave them chunky or puree them; cook them down or leave them whole and uncooked. Italian San Marzano tomatoes have a sweet, concentrated flavor that's worth seeking out.

STOCK: You can use either store-bought or homemade stock or broth for our recipes; stock is usually richer than broth because it's made by simmering bones in addition to meat. We usually have a few quarts of homemade stock in our freezer from the last time we roasted chickens (see page 63), but as a backup, we like the organic soup base from Better Than Bouillon. We find it has a better flavor and is less salty than most canned or boxed broths. And it takes up less space!

IN THE FRIDGE AND FREEZER

GRATING CHEESES: We always have a hunk of Parmigiano-Reggiano or Grana Padano, and another of pecorino (a saltier sheep's-milk cheese) for grating over pasta, soups, bruschetta, and more.

CONDIMENTS: This list can grow very long! From Korean gochujang (fermented soy and chili paste) to good old-fashioned American ketchup, from Indian chutneys to Jamaican Scotch bonnet pepper sauce, we rarely go into a market without leaving with a jar of something sweet, salty, pungent, or bitter to add flavor to whatever we're whipping up.

ANCHOVIES: This is our secret-weapon ingredient for adding depth to dressings, sauces, and more. The funky fermented flavor dissipates, and the anchovy fillets dissolve in heat, so you won't see them in the final dish, but they'll make it taste so much richer.

KITCHEN SCRAPS: When we cook, we save many of our peelings and leafy root tops in a freezer bag to use the next time we make a stock (see page 264).

FROZEN BERRIES: Healthy fruits are always in our freezer. We buy them in bulk and use them for galettes, muffins, pancakes, smoothies, or a fancy compote or sauce to drizzle over parfaits.

YOGURT: It's our breakfast, our smoothie base, our marinade, our quick dressing. We use plain yogurt (ideally the thick full-fat Greek version that is higher in protein than other yogurts) for everything.

BUTTER: Our freezer is stocked with butter—we never want to be without enough unsalted for baking and salted for most everything else. We're cheerleaders for the deep yellow Kerrygold brand from a cooperative of Irish dairy farmers, which we think makes the most delicious butter on the planet.

ON THE COUNTER

ALLIUMS: Alliums refer to the flavorful plant family that includes onions, scallions, and garlic. We keep big bowls of different kinds within arm's reach: red, yellow, and sweet (Vidalia or Walla Walla) onions, shallots, and always lots of garlic. (But we store scallions in the fridge!)

ROOTS AND TUBERS: We use russet potatoes for baking, waxy Yukon Golds for roasting and boiling, and sweet potatoes for everything else.

CITRUS: We use the juice as well as the aromatic zest of limes, lemons, and oranges in everything from vinaigrettes to baked goods.

developing your skills

Now that the kitchen is stocked with all the tools and staple ingredients you need, you're ready to cook and to start really developing your culinary skill set. But there are a few other important lessons before you step up to the stove.

kitchen safety

As with any physical activity, there are risks involved with cooking. As good cooks, we do everything we can to minimize them and prevent any harm from happening. Here's how.

DRESS FOR SUCCESS

➜ Don't wear open-toed shoes (hot and sharp things fall down), crop tops (hot oil can splatter), or baggy sleeves (which can get in the way and catch fire).

➜ Take off any jewelry like bracelets, necklaces, rings, or earrings that can dangle or fall into food.

➜ If your hair is long, pull it back with a hair tie or tuck it under a cap.

KEEP IT CLEAN

➜ Wash your hands with soap and water often: before you start cooking, after using the restroom, if you touch your face or hair, and frequently between tasks, especially after touching raw meat.

➜ Tasting while you cook is a key step. But if you're cooking for other people, please taste with a clean spoon, not your fingers!

➜ Cover your face with the inside of your elbow when you sneeze or cough, then wash your hands.

STUDY UP ON FOOD SAFETY

➜ Separate raw meat from other ingredients and use a different cutting board to prevent bacteria from the meat from spreading to surfaces or other foods. If you put raw meat on a plate to season it with salt, for instance, put that plate in the sink once you're done so you don't use it for anything else.

➜ Store meat on the bottom shelf of the refrigerator so any juices that escape can't drip down onto other ingredients.

BREAK OUT YOUR THERMOMETER!

If you're wondering whether your roast chicken or grilled sausages are ready, there's an easy solution: take the temperature! Here are the internal temperatures the United States Department of Agriculture (USDA) recommends for meat, fish, and other foods. Once your food reaches the temperature provided below, you can be sure you've killed any potentially harmful bacteria.

BEEF, PORK, VEAL & LAMB STEAKS, CHOPS, ROASTS	**145°F** and allow to rest for at least 3 minutes
GROUND MEATS	**160°F**
GROUND POULTRY	**165°F**
HAM, FRESH OR SMOKED (uncooked)	**145°F** and allow to rest for at least 3 minutes
FULLY COOKED HAM (to reheat)	Reheat cooked hams packaged in USDA-inspected plants to **140°F** and all others to **165°F**
POULTRY	**165°F**
EGGS	**160°F**
FISH & SHELLFISH	**145°F**

➜ Cook meat and fish to the proper "safe" temperatures (see Break Out Your Thermometer! left).

➜ Use markers and tape! By that we mean label and date ingredients or leftovers so you can use ingredients the way cooks in restaurants do, with the FIFO system—first in, first out. That way, you'll always know how old something is before you cook or eat it, and you can be sure to use the oldest food first before it goes bad!

COMMUNICATE AND RESPECT

➜ Respect your cooking space—including the people you share it with—by communicating your movement. Tell someone when you are walking near them, especially if one of you is holding something sharp or hot!

➜ Always clean as you go and after cooking. Don't leave messes for other cooks to clean up! If you have something baking in the oven and it's going to be 20 minutes before you have to do anything else, use that time to tidy up the counter or get started on the dishes.

getting ready: mise en place

This French term (pronounced *MEEZ en plahs*), often just shortened to "mise," is used in professional kitchens to refer to the way cooks set up ingredients before they start cooking. It means "everything in its place," and it's all about keeping your tasks organized and easy to follow.

So when you cook any of the recipes in this book—or any recipe at all—first start by doing all your peeling, slicing, and dicing and neatly arrange the ingredients in small bowls or piles in the order you'll need to use them. It'll make everything so much easier! An orderly mise is one of the most important steps we can take to set ourselves up for success in the kitchen.

honing your knife skills

The very first lesson we teach, and one we return to again and again, is how to correctly and confidently use a knife. Knives are our most-used kitchen tools and learning to use them safely and effectively is key. Like learning to play a musical instrument, it takes a little time to get your hands comfortable with the motions, but once you get the hang of it, it'll feel totally natural.

And luckily, for most meals, the bulk of our mise en place is knife work, so we get plenty of opportunities to practice!

CHOOSING YOUR KNIFE

There are many different types of knives out there, each designed for a different kitchen task. In our kitchens, we have three knives in regular rotation.

CHEF'S KNIFE: This is the knife we use most, as it can get most jobs done. It has a long blade with a gentle curve from the base all the way to a sharp point. Slicing, dicing, mincing, and chopping—it does it all. Chef's knives come in a variety of lengths, and there's no right or wrong length, so find one that feels right in your hand. The standard is 8 inches, but smaller hands might prefer a 6-inch version.

PARING KNIFE: A paring knife usually looks like a mini chef's knife, with a slightly straighter blade. It's a good choice for small cuts or precise knife work. We use this for everything from coring fruits and vegetables to flicking out seeds.

SERRATED KNIFE: A serrated knife, often called a bread knife, has a long, straight blade with sharp teeth. Grab a serrated knife whenever you're cutting something with a tough exterior and a soft center, like a crusty loaf of bread or a juicy tomato. Using a serrated knife in a sawing motion allows you to get a clean cut without exerting a lot of force. Have you ever tried to cut a tomato with a regular knife? It squishes the tomato to bits! But a serrated knife will give you nice, even slices.

OTHER IMPORTANT TOOLS FOR KNIFE WORK

CUTTING BOARD: Choose a large cutting board that gives you plenty of space to spread out. If the board slips and slides around on your counter, lift it up and put a slightly damp kitchen towel (or even a few damp paper towels) flat underneath it. Give it a little nudge and see if it's sitting in place. If you are cutting both raw meat and produce, be sure to use two different boards, or cut the produce first, then the meat. Otherwise, be sure to thoroughly wash the board with soap and hot water after cutting any kind of animal product. Basically, you don't want raw meat juices touching the raw vegetables you're going to put into your salad!

SCRAP BOWL: Give yourself ample room to work by setting a small mixing bowl nearby to hold peels, seeds, cores, and any other scraps you'd otherwise push to the side of your board. This also makes for easy cleanup, and it's a great start to collecting scraps for a homemade vegetable stock (see page 264)!

HOW TO PROPERLY HOLD A KNIFE

Start with clean, dry hands. Hold your knife in your dominant hand (the one you write with), and wrap your fingers around the handle, close to where the blade starts. This is called "choking up on the blade." It gives you more control of your knife (think about when you write with a pencil—you wouldn't hold it near the eraser!), and you'll need to use less force every time you cut down.

Instead of picking up the knife and chopping down when cutting, you almost always want to keep the tip of the knife on the board and use a rocking motion to cut with the middle of the blade. (This is why the blade is curved!) This method is safer and keeps the edge of your knife sharp. The blade should be in constant contact with the cutting surface as you cut.

And your other hand has an important job, too! Use it to hold on to whatever it is that you're cutting to keep it from moving around on your board, but make sure you keep your fingers safe from the sharp blade. Do that by curling your fingers under in a bear claw and gripping what you're cutting with your fingertips as they're bent under your knuckles. Your fingers will be tucked out of the way, and your knuckles can act as a guide for your knife.

Whenever you cut something that is round or rolls (like an onion or a carrot), your goal with the first cut is to "find the flat" and stabilize it by placing the flat side down on your board. This helps turn something that could easily slip away from you into a stable object you can safely cut. Use the tunnel technique for this first cut: Place your thumb and index finger on either side of what you're cutting, creating a tunnel that you can slip your knife through, and cut down. You can also use the tip of your knife to make a small slit to rest the knife in and stabilize the blade, if your round object is particularly big. Once you find your flat, hold the item in place, cut-side down, with your bear claw.

Different parts of the blade also have different uses. (We told you this tool was made to do everything!) Use the tip of your blade when making a delicate or precise cut (like scoring an avocado). Leave tougher chopping or dicing (like cutting

through a large carrot) to the part of the blade closer to the handle.

KEEP IT SHARP!

This might seem odd, but a sharp knife is actually much safer to work with than a dull one! Sharp knives slide easily through what you're cutting without a lot of force. Dull knives force you to push down harder, which means there is more of a chance of the knife slipping off the food and cutting you.

So keeping your knives sharp is super important: with an adult's help, you can sharpen them on a whetstone (there are countless tutorials online) or using a knife sharpener, or bring them to a kitchenware store that offers knife-sharpening services. Once your knife is sharp, you can help keep it that way by honing the blade with a steel (that long metal rod with a handle that comes with most knife kits). Ask the person who helped sharpen your knives to show you how. Or, again, find a video of it online—some things are better seen than read!

Don't use your knife in ways that will dull it: Don't tap the sharp edge on your cutting board or use it to scrape together things you've cut or to clear scraps away. And opening boxes with your knife is out of the question!

vegetable prep 101

In lots of recipes—not just our own!—you'll see already prepped ingredients listed. Carrots are "peeled and diced," beans are "trimmed." For experienced cooks, a lot of times these things don't even need to be said. But if you're not super familiar, here's what those prep terms mean.

BEFORE YOU CHOP OR DICE

As a general rule, you always want to cut hard, round vegetables like carrots, yams, or squash into manageable pieces, then slice them in half and put the flat side down on the cutting board before slicing.

When a recipe calls for a peeled vegetable or fruit, hold your peeler in one hand and run it down the vegetable away from you to prevent the peeler from slipping and hitting the hand holding the vegetable. Turn the carrot, pear, or whatever and continue all the way around.

COMMON CUTS

DICE: Cut into small, even cubes, usually about ½ inch.

SLICE: Cut into thin strips, wedges, or rounds (such as onions to caramelize or pickle, or cucumbers for a salad).

ROUGH CHOP: Coarsely cut into roughly the same size (like herbs for a sauce).

JULIENNE: Cut into thin matchsticks (for example, vegetables for sushi).

CHIFFONADE: Stack leaves (such as fresh basil or mint to be used as a garnish), roll them into a tube, then cut the tube crosswise into thin ribbons.

BROCCOLI AND CAULIFLOWER

When a recipe calls for florets, it's referring to the flowers on the crown of the head. To remove them, hold the head upside down with the center stalk facing up. Cut each floret off the head where its small stem meets the center stalk. (Some cooks find this easier with a small paring knife; others like to use their big chef's knife.) When you are left with just the center stalk, chop or dice it to add to stir-fries or pasta sauce—it's sweet and delicious! You'll want to peel broccoli stalks until you get past any tough fibers. You can leave florets whole or cut them in half for faster cooking or to create more surface area for searing.

CITRUS

There are so many useful parts of a lemon, lime, orange, really any kind of citrus. Here's how we prepare all those parts.

PEEL: Use a vegetable peeler to remove the aromatic skin. Just be careful not to include much of the white part (called the pith), which is very bitter.

ZEST: Sometimes you just want the aromatic skin in small, grated pieces that are barely noticeable, aka the zest. To get the zest, use a fine grater or a zester, and run it along the skin until it's all removed, again avoiding the bitter white pith. Always zest *before* you juice!

JUICE: Before juicing, roll the fruit on the counter, pressing down on it as you roll; this pressure will help get the juices flowing by breaking the tiny membranes that hold the juice. Halve the citrus crosswise (not end to end) and place it in a handheld squeeze juicer with the cut side down. Squeeze it firmly over a cup or bowl to capture the juice. If you don't have a juicer, don't worry—you can use your hands and squeeze the citrus over a bowl, using your thumb or finger knuckle to get out as much of the juice as possible. Just be sure to remove the seeds!

GARLIC

A head of garlic is a cluster of cloves with papery skins. Here's how we prepare them for different uses.

PEELED: Using the side of a knife, press down on a clove to crack the skin. Peel off and discard the skin.

SLICED: Take the whole peeled clove and cut thin slices lengthwise across the clove.

SMASHED: Press down again on the peeled clove with the flat of a knife, if necessary, to crack open the clove. Cut away the hard root end. If the clove is too big, you can rough chop it before adding it to soups, stew, or ingredients about to be pureed.

CHOPPED OR FINELY CHOPPED: After you've peeled and smashed the garlic clove, just start cutting it into smaller and smaller pieces. "Chopped" usually means pieces no bigger than your pinkie nail, and "finely chopped" is about half as small as that.

MINCED: When you want to distribute garlicky flavor throughout a dish, mince it finely and evenly. Just chop it (see above) a whole bunch to make it super small!

ROASTED: Roasted garlic is a sweet, soft paste that's wonderful mixed into butter, whisked into mayonnaise to make aioli, and stirred into soups and stews. To roast garlic, cut the pointy end off an entire bulb, removing the tips of the cloves and exposing the flesh inside. Place the bulb on a piece of foil and drizzle with olive oil. Wrap it in the foil and roast at 350°F until the cloves are soft, about 30 minutes.

GINGER

This knobby root can seem hard to tackle and peel, but there's an amazing tool that makes it easy: a regular old spoon! Holding the spoon facing you where the bowl meets the handle, scrape off the skin with the side edge of the spoon, navigating around all the knobby twists and turns of the ginger with the tip and the side of the spoon. Once you peel away the skin, you can slice, smash, chop, or mince the ginger by following the same instructions as for garlic.

GREEN BEANS

Recipes often call for trimmed beans, which means snipping off the two ends (the pointy and the stem end). You can use your fingers to snap them off.

STEMMED GREENS AND HERBS

Many greens like kale, chard, and collards have a hard center stem that should be removed from the leaves. Hold a leaf in one hand with the leafy part hanging down, and use your other hand to strip away the leaves by running your fingers down along either side of the stem and pulling the leaves away. Once you have a stack of leaves, roll them lengthwise into a log and then cut the log crosswise into strips (aka chiffonade).

Use these same techniques for herbs: You can stem thyme by running your fingers along the center stalk. Or for leafy herbs like basil, stack, roll, and cut in chiffonade as described above.

LEMONGRASS

These long stalks have a beautiful citrusy aroma that adds amazing flavor to curries, marinades, and dressings. Start by removing the dry outer layers of the stalk, cut off the very bottom of the root end, and remove the firm tops (usually 6 inches or so). What you're left with is a pale yellowish-green stalk, the most aromatic part of the vegetable. It's very tough, though, so you'll want to make sure to slice it very finely or mince it if you're going to eat it. (It's fine to leave bigger chunks if it's going into tea or stock; you can strain the pieces out later.)

LETTUCE

Any head lettuce (versus loose-leaf lettuce), like iceberg, Bibb, or romaine, needs to be trimmed and thoroughly washed, as dirt can hide in its crevices. Trim and discard the root end, slice it in half lengthwise, and remove any hard center core or bitter yellow leaves.

Fill a big tub or a clean sink with water, swish the leaves in the water, then don't touch them for a few minutes while any dirt falls to the bottom. Lift out the leaves and dry them in a salad spinner or gently roll them in a clean kitchen towel.

TOMATOES

When cutting ripe, fresh tomatoes, use a paring knife or the tip of a chef's knife to carve out the center core and stem, then slice the tomato in half lengthwise from the stem end to tip. With the cut side down, use a serrated knife to slice the tomato into bite-size pieces.

When recipes call for crushed canned tomatoes, hold the tomato in your hand over a bowl and use your thumb to puncture a hole in the side. Gently squeeze out the juice, then use your hand to crush the tomato into pieces. This way the juice doesn't end up all over you or on the wall!

when to ask for help

We believe in kids' abilities to cook, but there are times when it's good to ask for help, no matter what your age. Some kids need to practice their knife skills before being left alone with slicing and dicing tasks. Some need help filling large pots with water and moving them to the stove or taking big, hot trays of food out of the oven.

If you are a young person reading this book, read the recipe first (see How to Read a Recipe, page 36), and if anything is confusing or seems a little difficult, ask someone. This is a good way to learn to trust your instincts. Listen to your gut!

If you are an adult looking to be an assistant to your young person, you probably know what their limits are; be on hand to assist when it comes to safety (hot handles, sharp knives, heavy pots), but also give them space to make their own choices and reassure them when their confidence might need boosting. In the kitchen, adults are usually needed more for the former than the latter, but being able to stand by for when the cook needs a hand is what parenting and partnering is all about. Knowing when to step back and let the kids surprise and wow us with their creations is also part of the gig.

setting the scene

At The Dynamite Shop, we don't just teach kids how to cook well; we teach them the importance of making the whole meal meaningful. The skills they learn are important, but what makes a meal special is more than getting good at cooking. It's also the way the table is arranged, the lighting, the music, and the conversation.

Setting the table thoughtfully is important. The table is the canvas for the artwork of your meal. It doesn't mean having silver or fancy plates; it does mean having a clean table with any homework and projects put away. You don't need to follow conventional charts about where the fork and knife are supposed to go, but we do encourage a neat and thoughtful arrangement of all the elements, whether you're using your grandparents' wedding dishes or just putting together a funky picnic table. And, of course, don't forget flowers and candles if you enjoy them! Little ways of elevating the scene are not just for special occasions. We consider *every* meal a special occasion, especially if you cooked it yourself.

One of our golden rules is *no electronics on the table at mealtime*! This not only makes for a prettier table (we like your hamburger-emoji phone case, just not at the table!), it encourages old-fashioned conversations. You can always start by talking about the food! What was it like to cook this dish? Does the meal remind your elders of anything they grew up eating?

What else makes a good vibe at mealtime? Music and lighting! We love making playlists for both cooking (upbeat!) and eating (mellow, but not sleepy). Cleaning up has its own playlist—that one is definitely energetic! Create your own or make it a group effort, inviting the whole family or guests at a dinner party to contribute their favorite tracks.

And even the light matters! Some people like low, moody lighting, some prefer it to be bright. Consider the way the room feels. Do overhead lights feel harsh? If you're using candles, is it a little dark? Play around and find what feels good to you.

how to read a recipe

Have you ever heard the expression "curl up in bed with a good cookbook"? No?? Well, it's a thing, and we do it all the time! It's not only essential to read a recipe before making it but it can be quite pleasant to page through a cookbook to understand how the author thinks and what kinds of flavor combinations they favor. No matter where you find a recipe—online, in a cookbook like this one, or in an email from a relative or friend—it's still important to read it through before making it. Not just once, but a few times, until you fully understand it. Ideally, you'll be able to picture each step in your head before you actually get in the kitchen!

The most obvious reason to read a recipe before cooking is to check the ingredients and make a shopping list. You also need to be sure you have the right tools and equipment. The other reason is to calculate whether you have enough time to move through all the steps. There's nothing worse than starting on dinner and then realizing you need to let something marinate for 48 hours!

There are a few standard parts to a recipe: title, yield, ingredient list, and method. Often authors will add bonus elements, like how much time it takes to prepare (we don't, because we want everyone to work comfortably at their own pace—no pressure!) and headnotes, which are little introductions to each recipe with helpful info.

YIELD

This tells you how much food the recipe makes. This is important, because you want to make the right amount of food! For instance, some recipes have large yields ("serves 10 to 12") because it is a dish meant for a crowd or it keeps or freezes well. If you are cooking only for a few people or don't have room to store leftovers, consider cutting all the ingredient amounts by half; if you have more people to feed, you can increase the amounts instead. (And you can test your math skills!) Keep in mind that often, less food cooks in less time, and more food cooks in more time—so you'll have to keep an eye on how long things are cooking. Sometimes there are items that are not as easily divided— one egg, for example. Maybe this will be a fun game for you, or maybe it's a good time to ask for some help.

RECITE TITLE

This is self-explanatory!

SERVES 4 TO 6

summery one-pot mac and cheese

1 pound dry **short-cut pasta**, such as rigatoni, macaroni, penne, or cavatappi

3 tablespoons **extra-virgin olive oil**

2 teaspoons minced **garlic** (about 2 medium cloves)

1 cup (8 ounces) **whole-milk ricotta cheese**

1 cup (3 to 4 ounces) freshly grated **Parmesan cheese**

1 cup lightly packed **fresh basil leaves**, sliced into very thin strips (chiffonade)

1 tablespoon **freshly grated lemon zest** (from 1 small lemon)

¼ cup **freshly squeezed lemon juice**

A few cracks of **freshly ground black pepper**

Crushed red pepper flakes (optional)

Here's a classic way to get dinner done in one pot without a lot of fuss but with a lot of flexibility. Instead of making a full-on cheese sauce, we like to "sauce" the mac with ricotta cheese mixed with Parmesan and lots of basil ribbons. It comes out creamy but light—perfect for warm weather! You can also add another cheese, like fontina, asiago, or Gouda, for a sharper flavor. The real secret here is adding a cup or so of starchy water reserved from cooking the pasta; the heat helps melt the cheese and the starch in the liquid gives the sauce a little heft.

1. Bring a large pot of heavily salted water (it should taste like the ocean) to a boil over high heat. Add the pasta and cook to a firm al dente, about 2 minutes shy of the package directions. Using a mug, scoop out and reserve about ½ cup of the pasta water. Drain the pasta in a colander and set it aside.

2. Work quickly! Set the same pot over medium heat, add the olive oil and garlic, and sauté until the garlic softens but does not brown, about 1 minute. Add the reserved pasta cooking water, the ricotta, and the Parmesan and stir until the cheeses melt.

3. Stir in the pasta, tossing well to coat. Add the basil, lemon zest, and lemon juice and season to taste with salt, black pepper, and a pinch of red pepper flakes (if using). Remove from the heat and serve immediately.

121

HEADNOTE

Look here for tips, tricks, or the story behind the recipe.

MARK IT UP!

We encourage cooks to mark up the pages of recipes as they read them (assuming it's your book!). Make notes in pencil while you cook where you changed quantities (like "less red pepper flakes!") or doubled or halved the quantities, or go back after making the dish to adjust things, like finding your oven led to a different cooking time or whether the dish was too salty. This way the recipe becomes yours. This is truly learning to cook.

METHOD

Read through this section (also called the directions or steps) to make sure you have enough time to make the dish and that you have the equipment to get it all done.

INGREDIENTS

Definitely read through this before you start cooking, and probably before you go shopping, to make sure you have everything you need!

how to build flavor

We spend about as much time in our classes *tasting* as we do *cooking*, and it's not just because we love to eat!

Learning to taste and talk—and really think—about flavor helps give us the tools and the vocabulary we need to build meals. Which flavor combinations work really well, and which ones don't work at all? If it's bland, what can we do to make it better? And what does it mean to say a dish tastes "balanced"?

Understanding flavor and how to control and change it in a dish—by using different ingredients or different techniques—is a key step in any cook's journey.

In this chapter, we share all the tips and even some of the food *science* (yes!) we wish we had known when we were first dabbling in the kitchen. Of course, everything in this chapter is just the tip of the iceberg. You could spend years studying techniques at culinary school, reading books, and even just watching YouTube videos.

Think of this chapter as an informed shortcut: Knowing these flavor-building skills will help us make decisions on the fly when we're conceiving or cooking a dish. They allow us to understand recipes and why the instructions are written a certain way. They'll bolster your confidence and help you become a creative, think-for-yourself cook.

The first thing to know is *how* we perceive taste. To tune into *taste*, we primarily use our tongues, which are covered in taste buds, to detect sweet, salty, sour, and bitter. But the experience of *flavor* is actually the coming together of several senses. Smell obviously plays a big part. We can "almost taste" something when we smell it, long before it hits the tongue. Do you think your other senses (touch, sight, and sound) influence your perception of flavor? How? If you really pay attention to your experience with food, you might find that all your senses are activated.

We all know the four main tastes that our taste buds perceive: sweet, sour, salty, and bitter. Then there's umami, otherwise known as savoriness; it's the aftertaste of a really good piece of cheese, or meat, or mushrooms, or soy sauce, or a thousand other things. The interplay of these five tastes is what makes a meal interesting. If your food was all just one-note—just sweet or just sour, for example—the meal would be, well, one-note and boring. Food is at its most delicious when these tastes are mixed, contrasting with or balancing each other, like salted caramel. Here's what you need to know about each.

salty

Salt is the spotlight that shines light on a dish: Just adding a pinch can enhance flavors and other seasonings that are hiding in the mix. That's why we sprinkle a bit on our brownies (see page 229) and our meatballs (see page 89). It's not because we want to taste the salt *itself*; it's because we want to taste more of the great flavors that are already there.

You need to be careful: you can always add more, but you can't take it away! Whenever we can, we salt "to taste," which means we add a little bit, taste, and season again if needed.

Salt also draws moisture out of foods. Whether it's cucumber we're salting for a salad, eggplant pre-frying, or turkey before roasting, a little salt affects the texture as well as the flavor.

You can look to ingredients other than salt to get saltiness. Soy sauce, olives, capers, and cheeses like Parmesan and pecorino all lend salty notes to a dish.

sweet

Not all sweetness comes from sugar, honey, agave, or maple syrup. Some natural sweetness comes from caramelized onions, roasted vegetables, fruit juice, or vinegar (think sweet, oaky balsamic vinegar or sweet-tart pomegranate molasses). As with salt, start with a little sweetness and add more to taste.

bitter

You might think this would be an unpleasant flavor, but a little bitterness is a great foil for something sweet—just think of chocolate! Or bitter greens with a sweet vinaigrette. If something is too bitter, adding a salty ingredient—like olives or grated pecorino—will help round it out.

sour

Pucker up! The tart flavor we associate with limes, lemons, pickles, and vinegars is one of the most important flavors in a cook's tool kit: a squeeze of lime in a rich taco, lemon over roasted chicken, or kimchi alongside fried rice, acts as a high note. If you think of rich food as "heavy," a little sourness (also called acidity) can help balance and lift it up.

umami

The ingredients that pack a punch of intense umami give dishes a super-satisfying depth. Parmesan cheese, cured meats, smoked fish, pickled anything, mushrooms (fresh or dried), caramelized onions, ketchup, and most things that are fermented, aged, smoked, or pickled—all add savoriness. A cheeseburger (see our version on page 98) with caramelized onions, pickles, ketchup, and sautéed mushrooms is about the most umami-fied dish we can imagine—which is why everyone loves it so much!

flavor pairings that work

One of the wonderful things about learning to cook is discovering what flavors you like to eat together. This is where personal taste comes into play. (We've had students insist there is no better pairing than chocolate and wasabi, much to the skepticism of everyone around them.) But there are also some classic pairings that can be a helpful jumping-off point as you begin experimenting with your own combinations. Think about these tried-and-true combos as seasonings in a sauce, spice mix, dry rub, or vinaigrette.

- Garlic, tomato, basil
- Butter, herbs, lemon
- Cumin, coriander, black pepper
- Fresh ginger, lime, lemongrass, cilantro
- Olives, capers, onion, anchovies
- Bacon, onion, mushrooms, thyme
- Cinnamon, nutmeg, cider, maple syrup
- Chipotle, orange, oregano

your own spice blend

In a small bowl, combine 5 tablespoons of mixed ground spices, such as **cumin**, **coriander**, **smoked paprika**, **cinnamon**, **cayenne**, **chili powder**, **dry mustard**, and/or **black pepper**, with 2 tablespoons of **kosher salt**. Blend well, store in an airtight container, and apply it as a dry rub or mix it into marinades before using.

spice is nice

While the five tastes are the building blocks of meals, spices are often the specific seasonings that bring colors and nuance to a dish. Maybe it's a hint of warming nutmeg in your Cheesy Cauliflower Gratin (page 134), or some bay leaves and cardamom pods to add fragrance to rice, or a spicy rub of paprika and cayenne for Skillet-Roasted Whole Chicken (page 63). These spices will mix with whatever ingredients you're cooking, meld with the melting fat and pan juices, and create a delicious sauce.

And here we can start with a fun experiment and lesson: you can make your own spice mix! This is how we introduce kids to recognizing different spices and experimenting with the concepts of flavor balance.

Go get into your kitchen's spice collection. We encourage you to smell and then taste individual spices. First put a teeny-tiny pinch on the back of your (clean) hand and taste it. Then add the spices you like to a bowl, mixing gradually, until you have a blend you like!

There are sometimes hiccups along the way (figurative and literal) when something is too spicy or someone takes the cinnamon too far, but with experimentation comes a priceless skill: knowing how to make a well-balanced flavor-enhancing spice blend to keep on the kitchen counter and use on everything from kebabs to roasted potatoes to compound butter.

fat is flavor

Though it gets a bad rap in our diet-obsessed culture, fat plays an important role in cooking, and we're big cheerleaders for it (in moderation). Whether it's a vegetable-, dairy-, or animal-based oil or fat, it adds a rounded mouthfeel and satisfying richness to dishes.

Equally as important, fat helps carry flavor across a dish. Some recipes start by heating oil or fat with some flavorful ingredients like garlic or spices—we often use the word "blooming" to describe this process. That fat then acts as a vehicle of flavor, traveling to each and every bite.

embrace aromatics

We often start a dish by slowly sautéing aromatics, which are ingredients that become the flavor base in a dish. Maybe it's a classic mix of carrots, onions, and celery (called mirepoix; see page 283); or a sofrito of tomato, onion, garlic, green pepper, and cilantro; or a curry paste made with ginger, garlic, and spices (see page 152). These provide a strong foundation of flavor in the pan onto which you can add other layers of flavor, such as browned meats, stock, and sautéed vegetables.

We often cook onions slow and low until they're deep brown, completely caramelized, and supersweet; these go into risotto (see page 95), baked pastas, enchiladas (see page 135), and more. We also pickle onions (see page 274) to add a bright, sharp pop of flavor on top of salads and soups. Or we slice onions raw for a refreshing, astringent garnish.

With garlic, we often add it after we've cooked the onions, since we don't want the garlic to burn. Or we'll roast it until sweet and soft (see page 32) and mix it with butter or mayo. But we also love it fresh and raw, mashed with fresh herbs and other seasonings for a quick pesto (see page 109) that adds flavor to other dishes.

dress it up

One of the surest ways to amp up flavor in many dishes is to add a condiment. Taste them on their own, think about what flavors they have, and imagine how they might improve something else. If a food feels a little too light or tart, maybe something sweet or rich would help. If a food feels too heavy, maybe it needs a little kick from something tart.

One of our absolute favorite flavor enhancers is vinaigrette. It's not just for salad! Vinaigrette dressings are simply a mix of oil and vinegar with other seasonings that you can drizzle over salad greens or other foods to make them more flavorful. We love vinaigrettes tossed with leftover meats, as a dip for raw vegetables, or drizzled over grains like rice. You can choose a neutral oil (like vegetable oil) to let the flavor of the vinegar come forward, or use a mild-flavored olive oil or a specialty oil (like walnut or sesame oil, in which case, you'll want to use less) to add another layer of flavor. For vinegars, the sky's the limit! We love apple cider, white wine, and balsamic vinegar for classic dressings, and rice vinegar or even citrus juice for something tangier.

We start with a 3 to 1 ratio of oil to vinegar, and then often add a binder (an ingredient that helps the oil and vinegar blend together, or "emulsify"). In the recipe below, the mustard does this job. From there, we'll season and adjust the flavors, adding things like fresh or dried herbs, ground spices, garlic, or shallots. This recipe is so easy to make, you'll never want to buy bottled dressing again. Shake it up in a mason jar (or the mustard jar after you empty it!), serve it from the jar, then just pop it in the refrigerator and use it all week long!

let it marinate

A marinade is a liquid seasoning that infuses flavor into meats or vegetables before cooking. Fat is needed in many cases to carry flavor, so it's often essential to mix the seasoning with a bit of oil or yogurt. Acid (from citrus or, again, yogurt) is also helpful in tenderizing the ingredients. See our Spiced and Marinated Kebabs (page 77) for a great lesson in working with marinades.

customizable vinaigrette
MAKES ABOUT 1 CUP

¾ cup **neutral** or **mild flavored oil** (or add 1 to 2 tablespoons of a stronger specialty oil, like walnut or toasted sesame, along with the neutral oil)

¼ cup **vinegar** (we love apple cider vinegar or balsamic vinegar)

1 tablespoon **Dijon mustard** (other types of mustard, honey, agave syrup, or applesauce work as binders, too)

1 teaspoon **kosher salt**

¼ teaspoon **freshly ground black pepper**

Combine all the ingredients in a lidded mason jar, cover, and shake until fully blended (emulsified). The dressing will probably separate into oil and vinegar eventually; just shake it up again if it does.

beyond basic vinaigrettes

Add these ingredients to your dressing to take it up a notch:

1 teaspoon very finely minced **garlic**

1 teaspoon **honey** or **maple syrup**

Herbs: 1 teaspoon chopped fresh oregano, basil, rosemary, thyme, or marjoram, or ½ teaspoon dried

Spices: ¼ teaspoon smoked paprika, ground cumin, or ground sumac

Freshly squeezed **lemon juice** (swap 1:1 for the vinegar)

1 teaspoon **freshly grated citrus zest**

a guide to vinegars

Vinegar is a fermented liquid containing acetic acid, which occurs naturally in ingredients containing alcohol and/or sugar, like wine and cider. It's an essential ingredient for balancing flavor with its sour tang, but we also use it to marinate, preserve, and more.

And while we love trying vinegars made or infused with endless flavor combinations, there are a few essentials that our pantries are never without.

DISTILLED WHITE VINEGAR: This is pretty one-note in flavor, but that's not necessarily a bad thing in our eyes. We use distilled white vinegar for pickling, baking, and adding a dash of pure acidity without other flavor.

APPLE CIDER VINEGAR: A light and "sweeter" vinegar (it's not really sugar-sweet, but it should be a bit less sharp), we reach for ACV to add a touch of sweetness to our pickles, for a light salad dressing, or to balance the flavor of our favorite soups or stews (see Vegetarian Three-Bean Chili with All the Toppings, page 146).

RED WINE VINEGAR: Bolder in flavor, red wine vinegar is our go-to when we need an acid to pair with other salty, bold flavors, like in an Antipasto Salad (page 178).

BALSAMIC VINEGAR: Rich, sweet, and syrupy, balsamic vinegar is made from grape must (a by-product of the wine-making process). It gets its signature oaky flavor from the barrels it's aged in. We pair balsamic vinegar with dishes that are loaded with fruits, cheeses, and nuts, such as Apple Cranberry Salad with Balsamic Vinaigrette (page 173).

RICE VINEGAR: Sweet and subtle, rice vinegar perfectly balances dressings, marinades, and sauces with lightness and freshness, without overwhelming them (see Iceberg Wedge Salad with Carrot-Ginger Dressing, page 174).

4 more ways to amp up flavor

As good cooks, it's our job to always be on the lookout for ways to make food more flavorful. Here are some of our other favorite tricks, many of which aren't about adding ingredients, but simply doing something to them.

BROWN IT

No matter what you're cooking, it'll probably benefit from searing in a hot pan and creating a flavorful, charred crust, or broiling in the oven until nice and crispy on top. The Maillard reaction (see page 97) is the scientific explanation for why browning food creates flavor. But whether you know the chemistry or not, you can definitely taste the difference between a burger with a nice browned crust and one that's soft and pale-colored, or the difference between a crisp golden brown french fry and a soft tan one. Once you understand that heat makes a difference, you'll give everything from chicken thighs to broccoli stems the sear treatment.

DEGLAZE

You know all those browned bits left in the pan when you're done cooking, searing, or roasting? They're all concentrated flavor! And they shouldn't go to waste. Add a bit of liquid—stock, a juice, or even water—and scrape them off the pan while simmering, and you'll have an intensely flavorful liquid to add to a soup or sauce.

REDUCE

One of the easiest ways to bump up the flavor in a dish is to simmer it until the water in the ingredients evaporates, leaving behind a more concentrated liquid. This works for a quick jam or compote, a soup or stew, or even marinara sauce.

Depending on what you're cooking, be careful not to take your reduction too far, or you may end up with a syrup!

GARNISH

This term gets overused, but we don't want to overlook it! A garnish is like tying a pretty bow on your dish just before it's done; sure, it's probably fine without it, but why not scatter on some fresh, bright-tasting herbs at the end, or some aromatic zest, or some garlicky, crunchy bread crumbs? It will make your dish prettier . . . and tastier!

1

eggs

Eggs are so important in many cultures across the world. They signify birth, renewal, and new life. Many religions feature them during spring holidays like Easter and Passover. And in the kitchen, they're even more magical.

Cooked on their own—fried, scrambled, or boiled—they give you a high-protein dish that you can serve with all kinds of accompaniments, from hot sauce to fresh herbs. Just a few additions can make simple eggs into a great meal—and not just for breakfast!

They are a key ingredient in fresh pastas and batters; we especially love the thin pancakes called crepes that you can make sweet or savory. And when used in baking, eggs are an invaluable culinary tool that lifts and lightens things from cakes to soufflés to quick breads.

In this chapter, you'll find a few recipes that highlight the versatility of eggs, but of course you will find eggs in other dishes throughout the book. This is just the tip of the iceberg; we could write a whole book about eggs. In fact, maybe we will.

boiled eggs

6 large **eggs**

1 tablespoon **distilled white vinegar**

½ teaspoon **kosher salt**

What's a perfect boiled egg? It's a trick question! Because the perfect boiled egg is the boiled egg you like best. But we can figure out how to make them the way you like them every time.

In our Cook Like a Pro camp, we devote an entire day to eggs, and we start with the exercise of boiling them for different amounts of time to compare the results. We write different time stamps on the shells, set a timer, then remove them one by one with a slotted spoon. We peel them, taste, weigh in on the texture and flavor of each, and talk about our favorites. Our ideal boiled egg has firm whites and a soft center, but you can use the method below to figure out your favorite.

We make big batches of boiled eggs and keep them in the fridge for snacks or to add to salads, avocado toast, breakfast sandwiches, and more.

1. Place the eggs in a single layer in a saucepan and add enough cold water to cover by 1 inch. Add the vinegar and salt to the water; this helps prevent the shells from cracking, but if they do, it will help keep the whites from running out.

2. Put the pot on the stove, turn the heat to high, and bring the water to a boil (that means really active bubbles).

3. Once the water boils, remove the pot from the heat, cover it, and set a timer. Let the eggs sit in the hot water for 6 minutes for a softer soft-boiled egg (with a runny yolk), 7 minutes for a more firm soft-boiled egg with a slightly congealed yolk (our favorite), and 10 minutes for a fully hard-boiled egg with a solid yolk. Meanwhile, make an ice bath by putting a handful of ice cubes in a bowl of cold water. Remove the eggs with a slotted spoon and gently place them in the ice bath.

4. When they've cooled, peel the eggs by cracking them on your counter and removing the shells under cold running water. Use the peeled eggs immediately or store unpeeled eggs in a covered container in the refrigerator for up to 5 days.

fried egg

1 teaspoon **extra-virgin olive oil** or **butter**

1 large **egg**

1 teaspoon **cold water** in a little bowl

Pinch of **kosher** or **flaky salt**

Freshly ground black pepper to taste

If you've cooked a batch of bacon for breakfast, save that precious fat! You can replace the butter or oil in this recipe with bacon fat and have a super-smoky fried egg. You can also pour it into a glass or metal jar and use it to add flavor to most anything: roasted vegetables, potatoes, risotto, and more.

It's the simplest, and one of the most satisfying, things: a perfectly fried egg with the yolk just the way you like it, and the whites set firm with crisp edges. Whether you're frying an egg to sit atop a plate of Up-to-You Fried Rice (page 84) or a Rainbow Grain Bowl with Tahini Dressing (page 167), or to eat it on its own with a piece of toast, knowing this basic technique will help you get it right every time. The secret is a spoonful of water added to the pan before it gets covered with a lid: this creates steam so the pan acts more like an oven and the heat cooks the egg from all sides. This recipe is for one egg, but if you have a large enough pan, you can make two or even three at the same time, adding another teaspoon of oil or butter for each additional egg. (You might need to cook them a little bit longer, too, depending on your pan and stove.)

1. In a nonstick or well-seasoned cast-iron skillet with a lid (or something you can use as a lid), heat the oil over medium-high heat until shimmering. (If you're using butter, it will bubble up; the butter's hot enough when the foaming stops.)

2. Crack the egg into the skillet, aiming for the middle of the oil, then reduce the heat to low. Cook for a few seconds, until the white is opaque, then pour the water alongside (not over) the egg. Cover the skillet and cook for 1 minute. Lift the lid to see if the white is firm (or "set") and the yolk is soft and liquidy but contained under a thin, cooked skin (for a more set yolk, cook it about 30 seconds longer). Season with a pinch of salt and a few cracks of pepper and serve immediately.

scrambled eggs

2 large **eggs**

1 tablespoon **whole milk** (optional)

Pinch of **kosher salt**

1 tablespoon **butter**

Freshly ground black pepper to taste

Mixing the eggs well incorporates air, which will make them light once they're cooked. Be careful to remove the pan from the heat when the eggs get fluffy and are still moist. The longer they're exposed to the heat, the drier and firmer they'll become, so knowing that, you can choose how you like your eggs.

1. In a small mixing bowl, whisk the eggs, milk (if using), and salt with a fork until foamy.

2. In a medium to large nonstick or well-seasoned cast-iron skillet, melt the butter over medium heat. Once the butter melts, pour in the egg mixture. Use a rubber spatula to stir the eggs until they've clumped together softly. Take them off the heat now or keep cooking to make them firmer. Transfer to a plate and sprinkle with a few cracks of pepper.

poached egg

1 teaspoon **distilled white vinegar**

1 large **egg**

Kosher or **flaky salt** and **freshly ground black pepper** to taste

Nothing says "fancy brunch" quite like a poached egg. We put them on everything from sautéed greens to avocado toast—basically anything that will benefit from a runny yolk. Plus, they're so much fun to make! Poaching means to cook in liquid over low heat. Adding a touch of vinegar and swirling the water helps keep the egg whites together in a neat bundle around the yolk. It takes practice, so don't be discouraged if the first one isn't picture-perfect! You can use the same pan of simmering water to poach multiple eggs one at a time.

1. Fill a medium saucepan with at least 4 inches of water. Add the vinegar and heat over medium or medium-low heat to a very gentle simmer; there should be only the tiniest of bubbles. Crack the egg into a small shallow bowl, then swirl the water with a spoon and carefully slide the egg out of the bowl and right into the water—don't drop it in from too high up!

2. Let the egg cook undisturbed until the white has set, 3 to 4 minutes. Using a slotted spoon, remove the egg and place it on a plate. Season with a small pinch of salt and a few cracks of pepper. Serve immediately.

totally adaptable frittata

12 large **eggs**

½ cup **heavy cream**

1 teaspoon **kosher salt**

½ cup (about 2 ounces) shredded or crumbled **cheese** (optional, but we love Cheddar, mozzarella, Monterey Jack, or goat cheese)

3 tablespoons **extra-virgin olive oil**

1 large **onion**, thinly sliced (optional)

2 to 3 cups sliced or chopped **vegetables,** such as mushrooms, asparagus, bell peppers, potatoes, zucchini

2 cups packed chopped **leafy greens,** such as kale or spinach

1 to 2 teaspoons chopped **fresh herbs**

½ cup chopped **cooked meat**, such as bacon, ham, or sausage (optional, but this is a great use of leftovers!)

Kosher salt and **freshly ground black pepper** to taste

A frittata is basically a mix of delicious things—like vegetables, cheese, and meats—baked into eggs, sliced into wedges, and served.

It's satisfying any time of day, and it's a great recipe for customizing and perfect for transforming leftovers in creative ways. You can use all the ingredients below or mix and match the fillings however you want.

You can serve a frittata hot, cold, or at room temperature, so it's also a great make-ahead meal to cook for a crowd. You can be a brunch superstar by hosting a frittata party, featuring several versions that people can try with a big salad alongside, and have it all prepared hours or even a day ahead.

1. Preheat the oven to 375°F.

2. In a large mixing bowl, whisk together the eggs, cream, and salt until well combined. Stir in the cheese, if using.

3. In an oven-safe 12-inch skillet, heat the olive oil over medium heat. Add the onion (if using) and cook, stirring occasionally, until fragrant and caramelized to a deep golden color, 10 to 12 minutes. Add the sliced/chopped vegetables and cook until softened and any water they release has evaporated. Add the leafy greens and stir until wilted and bright green. If the greens release any water, cook until it has evaporated.

4. Remove the pan from the heat, mix in the fresh herbs and the cooked meat (if using), then season generously with salt and pepper.

5. Pour the egg mixture over the cooked vegetables and transfer the pan to the oven. Bake for 30 to 40 minutes, until the eggs are just set. (When you gently shake the pan, the frittata should just slightly shift back and forth.) Remove the pan from the oven and let rest for 10 minutes. Use a rubber spatula to free the frittata from the pan and invert it onto a plate. Slice into wedges and serve.

frittata fillings

Once you know the basic recipe (and it really is basic!), you can make frittatas in countless ways that are entirely your own. Here are some of our favorite combos, but it's up to you to decide how much of each item to add!

- Spinach, dill, feta cheese

- Sausage, red peppers, onions, mozzarella

- Tomatoes, basil, ricotta

- Bacon, mushrooms, onions, Cheddar cheese

- Chorizo, cilantro, green peppers

- Ham, Swiss cheese, mushrooms

sweet and savory crepes

*10-inch crepes

2 cups **all-purpose flour** (or a gluten-free substitute, such as Bob's Red Mill 1:1)

2 cups **whole milk**

⅔ cup **lukewarm water**

4 large **eggs**

6 tablespoons (¾ stick) **butter**, melted (see Note), plus more for cooking

2 tablespoons **granulated sugar**

Large pinch of **kosher salt**

NOTE: Melt the butter in a pan over medium-low heat or in a microwave-safe bowl in the microwave for a few seconds until just liquefied.

These thin French pancakes may seem like a fancy restaurant dish, but they're easy to make. Unlike standard pancakes, crepes don't call for a leavener like baking soda or baking powder to rise (see Understanding Leaveners, page 195), so their light lift comes from nothing more than eggs.

While we make this recipe by hand with a whisk, you can also use a blender. Either way, it's important not to skimp on the resting time, so the gluten in the flour relaxes and the flour can fully soak up the liquid. Then the crepes will be light and airy instead of dense and firm.

A nonstick pan and a super-thin rubber spatula for flipping will make your crepe-making job easy.

Crepes can be sweet and savory. Make our spinach-and-cheese version (see page 56) for lunch or dinner, then finish with a sweet version for dessert! See our grid on page 57 for filling ideas, or get creative and design your own!

1. In a large mixing bowl, whisk together the flour, milk, and water until smooth. Beat in the eggs, then add the melted butter, sugar, and salt. (Alternatively, combine all the ingredients in a blender and blend until smooth.) Cover the bowl and refrigerate for at least 30 minutes or up to 2 days.

2. When you're ready to make the crepes, bring the batter to room temperature and beat it again to recombine everything.

3. In a large nonstick skillet, melt a small knob of butter (about a teaspoon) over medium heat. Fill a ¼-cup measuring cup by dipping it into the batter, then pour the batter into the center of the hot pan; lift the pan and use your wrist to tilt it, swirling the batter around so it covers the entire bottom surface of the pan.

4. As soon as the batter appears to have dried (we're talking less than a minute), use a thin rubber spatula to flip the crepe over and cook it until buttery spots appear

(RECIPE CONTINUES)

on the underside, about 30 seconds. Transfer the crepe to a plate and cover with foil. Repeat the process, stacking the crepes, until all the batter has been used.

5. The crepes can be served as is with something to top them (powdered sugar and a big squeeze of lemon juice is classic) or filled, with either sweet or savory fillings (see below). To fill, place about 3 tablespoons of the desired filling on the bottom half of the crepe, and roll it into a tight cylinder, or spread the filling over half the crepe and fold it in quarters.

spinach and cheese crepes

makes enough filling for 12 crepes; serves 4 to 6

2 tablespoons **extra-virgin olive oil**

2 medium **yellow onions**, thinly sliced (about 2 cups)

2 pounds **fresh spinach leaves**, or 16 ounces **frozen spinach leaves**, thawed (about 3 cups)

½ teaspoon **dry mustard**, or 1½ teaspoons **jarred mustard**

¼ teaspoon **freshly grated nutmeg**

Kosher salt and **freshly ground black pepper** to taste

3 cups (12 ounces) shredded **Swiss cheese**

1 batch **crepe batter** (see page 55)

6 slices **ham**, halved (optional)

1. In a large skillet, heat the olive oil over medium heat. Add the onions and cook, stirring occasionally, until they are deeply golden but not fully browned, 10 to 15 minutes. Add the spinach, mustard, and nutmeg. Use tongs to toss the spinach and cook until all the leaves are wilted, 3 to 4 minutes (cook thawed frozen spinach just long enough for it to break apart and mix with the onions). Remove from the heat and season with salt and pepper. Let cool, then add the cheese and toss until well mixed. Set aside.

2. Preheat the oven to 200°F. Place a sheet pan on the middle rack.

3. Make a crepe following the directions on page 55. Immediately after the first flip, scatter ¼ cup of the spinach-and-cheese filling across the bottom half of the crepe. Place half a slice of ham (if using) across the top of the spinach-and-cheese mixture. Once the crepe is done (you'll see buttery brown spots on the underside) and the cheese has begun to melt, use a spatula to fold the empty half over the filling and then carefully press the crepe down into the pan. Use the spatula to fold the crepe in half one more time (it will now be a quartered circle) and press down once more into the pan. Transfer the finished crepe to a plate and serve immediately or hold on the sheet pan in the warm oven until you're ready to eat.

crepe fillings

These are some of our favorites, but get creative and invent your own combos!

SWEET

Ricotta cheese mixed with marmalade

Nutella

Bananas cooked in brown butter

Cottage cheese mixed with lemon zest, basil, and powdered sugar

Strawberry-rhubarb compote with mascarpone cheese or softened cream cheese

Fig jam or roasted figs with Gorgonzola Dolce or other mild blue cheese

Poached pears with crystallized ginger

Blueberry compote (see page 245 for our homemade compote) or syrup with crumbled goat cheese

Melted chocolate

SAVORY

Sautéed mushrooms with fresh herbs and goat cheese

Scrambled eggs (see page 51) with roasted potatoes and peppers

Roasted asparagus with lemon zest and fresh ricotta

Fresh mozzarella, tomatoes, and pesto (see page 109)

dutch baby

2 large **eggs**

½ cup **whole milk**

½ cup **all-purpose flour**

1 teaspoon **granulated sugar**

½ teaspoon **salt**

2 tablespoons **butter**

FOR SERVING

Lemon wedges, powdered sugar, fresh berries, and/or **maple syrup**

It's a good idea for cooks of any age to be able to prepare something impressive for their friends and loved ones at the drop of a hat with easy-to-find ingredients, preferably from memory. This way you will always be a treasured guest at other people's houses and can whip up nourishment in a flash at your own home. Topping that list of recipes is the Dutch baby, a whimsical oven-baked pancake that contorts itself into a wavy, puffed popover thanks to the rise it gets from the whisked eggs in the batter. Eggs are amazing at capturing air, and when the batter bakes, that air gets hot and puffs the pancake. You can serve this for breakfast or brunch with fresh fruit or even as a savory meal with sautéed vegetables and grated cheese.

1. Preheat the oven to 425°F.

2. In a large bowl, whisk together the eggs, milk, flour, sugar, and salt until a batter forms. Let this stand at room temperature for at least 15 minutes.

3. Place the butter in a 9- or 10-inch cast-iron skillet, pie pan, or Pyrex dish. Set the pan in the oven until the butter melts. Using mitts or towels to protect your hands, remove the pan and carefully swirl the butter to coat the bottom and sides. Pour the batter into the pan and quickly return it to the oven.

4. Bake until the Dutch baby is golden brown and the edge rises high above the sides of the pan, 12 to 15 minutes.

5. Cut the pancake into wedges and serve with a squirt of lemon juice, a dusting of powdered sugar, and berries, or simply some maple syrup.

2
roasting

Nothing's more impressive than a beautiful roast coming out of the oven and being carried to the holiday table, but roasting isn't a technique that's reserved just for special occasions. You'll find us roasting dinner on a sheet pan many nights a week, because it's one of the more hands-off and forgiving cooking techniques: once you've done the chopping and seasoning, the oven does the rest!

When you roast, hot air inside the oven surrounds and cooks the ingredients. Lower temperatures mean longer cook times but more even cooking; if you cook the same ingredient at a higher temperature, the outside will brown—and maybe burn—before the inside is done. This means you may want to cook big cuts of meat, like a turkey or a roast beef (or our Cheater's Porchetta on page 66) at a lower temperature, but crank it up for smaller pieces or diced or sliced vegetables and meat, like our Spiced and Marinated Kebabs (page 77). Smaller cuts will cook much faster, which is a bonus in our book!

In this chapter, we'll explore all kinds of roasting and learn how we make the oven our best friend.

skillet-roasted whole chicken

1 tablespoon **kosher salt**

1 teaspoon **freshly ground black pepper**

1 tablespoon **freshly grated lemon zest**

1 tablespoon packed **light** or **dark brown sugar**

One 3- to 4-pound fresh **whole chicken**

Lemon halves, garlic cloves, and **fresh sturdy herbs** (like thyme, rosemary, or sage), for stuffing the bird (optional)

A few tablespoons **chicken stock** or **apple cider**, for making a pan sauce

> We have roasted many chickens over the years and find that a 3- to 4-pound bird not only fits perfectly in the skillet, but it also cooks most evenly. Because a bigger bird might require more time for the legs and thighs to be done, you'll risk overcooking the lean breast meat.

Knowing how to roast a chicken is pretty simple. Knowing how to roast a chicken that your friends and family will remember for years to come isn't much harder! And it qualifies as one of our back-pocket recipes, which are recipes you want to keep readily available—maybe even memorize—so that you can always whip up a meal without much fuss.

Here we start with a whole bird, which looks great and gives everyone a choice of either white meat (wings and breasts) or dark meat (thighs and legs). A whole chicken is also much more economical than buying individual parts.

We season it with salt, pepper, lemon zest for a little bit of citrusy flavor, and just a spoonful of brown sugar that gives it a nice brown shellacked skin. (The sugar literally turns to caramel!) The trick is to flip the chicken midway through its cooking time, which gives the skin an even crisp. Once you get good at the method, try seasoning the chicken with Your Own Spice Blend (page 40).

1. Preheat the oven to 450°F degrees. Place a heavy 10- to 12-inch ovenproof skillet, preferably cast iron, on the middle rack.

2. In a small bowl, mix together the salt, pepper, lemon zest, and brown sugar. Set aside.

3. Working in a clean sink free of any dishes, remove the packaging from the chicken and pour any juices down the drain. Reach inside the chicken's body cavity and remove the bag of giblets, if it has one. The giblets can be discarded, saved for stock, or used to make gravy later. Carefully discard all other packaging, taking care not to drip juices anywhere.

4. Pat the chicken dry very thoroughly with paper towels. Make sure to dab any liquid behind the wings or legs. Blot inside the body cavity, too, patting the chicken as dry as you can, inside and out.

5. Place the chicken on a sheet pan or large platter and set aside. Immediately clean the sink and your hands using soap and hot water. Sprinkle the outside of the

(RECIPE CONTINUES)

chicken with the sugar mix and rub it into the skin. If desired, stuff the inside of the chicken with halved lemons, whole garlic cloves, and fresh herbs.

6. Reduce the oven temperature to 375°F. Gently pat the chicken dry again with paper towels.

7. Using oven mitts or dry towels, remove the hot skillet from the oven and place it on top of the stove. Place the chicken breast-side up (so the flat side lies down) in the skillet. You should hear it sizzle. Transfer the skillet back into the oven and roast for 20 minutes.

8. After 20 minutes, carefully take the skillet out and look; the skin should have started to bubble and blister. If the chicken appears to be burning or smoking, reduce the oven temperature to 350°F before returning the chicken to the oven. Roast for another 10 minutes.

9. Remove the skillet from the oven and place it on a burner. Carefully turn the chicken over onto its breast side, taking care not to tear the skin. You might ask a partner to help, one person gripping the chicken with tongs—one tong in the cavity and the other tong on the middle of the breast—and the other person turning the chicken over across its side.

10. Return the chicken to the oven and roast for another 10 to 15 minutes, depending on its size. Finally, turn the chicken again to lie flat on its back and roast another 5 to 10 minutes to recrisp the breast skin.

11. Check the chicken for doneness by inserting a meat thermometer into the innermost part of the thigh and the meatiest part of the breast. It should register at least 165°F degrees. Return it to the oven if it is not done, covering it with foil if the skin is browned.

12. When the chicken is cooked, transfer it from the skillet to a plate and tent with foil. Pour off the clear fat from the skillet and reserve it for another use. Deglaze the pan by adding a few spoonfuls of stock, and use a spoon to scrape up any crusty brown bits on the bottom of the pan, stirring to dissolve them for a sauce.

13. Let the chicken rest for 10 to 15 minutes. Serve the chicken with the pan sauce.

a quick guide to roasting vegetables

Suggested roast times (for vegetables cut into 1-inch pieces)

ASPARAGUS
5 to 10 minutes

BROCCOLI
10 to 15 minutes

BRUSSELS SPROUTS
20 to 30 minutes

CAULIFLOWER
20 to 30 minutes

ROOT VEGETABLES (radishes, turnips, carrots, parsnips, beets)
20 to 30 minutes

SOFT SQUASH (summer squash or zucchini)
20 to 30 minutes

POTATOES (ANY TYPE)
25 to 40 minutes

PEELED HARD SQUASH (butternut or winter)
30 to 40 minutes

spiced roasted vegetables

2 to 3 pounds **sturdy vegetables** (see chart at left for suggestions), trimmed and cut into 1-inch pieces

1 large **onion** (any type), sliced into ½-inch wedges

Extra-virgin olive oil

2 to 3 teaspoons **Your Own Spice Blend** (page 40) or your favorite store-bought **spice blend** (use 1 teaspoon per pound of vegetables)

Freshly ground black pepper to taste

OPTIONAL SEASONINGS

Smashed **garlic cloves**, chopped **fresh sturdy herbs** (like rosemary, sage, and/or thyme) or **dried herbs** (like tarragon or oregano), and/or **citrus wedges** and **freshly grated zest**

We love vegetables every which way, but roasting them on a sheet pan is our favorite cooking method because it really brings out their sweetness. Food science flash: The vegetables meeting the pan and becoming crispy and extra flavorful is an example of the Maillard reaction (see page 97) at work. This recipe is our go-to for all kinds of sturdy vegetables, from carrots to squash. Seasoned with warm spices and onion, they're delicious alongside main dishes or on their own, topped with a fried egg or drizzled with pesto or tahini. We always make big batches (see the photograph on page 60!) so we have enough leftovers for our Rainbow Grain Bowls (page 167).

1. Preheat the oven to 425°F.

2. In a large mixing bowl, toss the vegetables that require the longest cooking time with the onion and enough olive oil to evenly coat them. (See suggested roast times for specific vegetables at left.) Sprinkle with the spice blend, pepper, and any optional seasonings you're using. Using your hands, toss until the vegetables are well coated.

3. Spread the seasoned vegetables on a large sheet pan in a single layer so each piece makes contact with the pan. Add the faster-cooking vegetables to the mixing bowl and toss with a bit more oil, spices, and pepper.

4. Roast according to the guide at left, adding the faster-cooking vegetables when appropriate partway through, until the edges of the vegetables are browned and caramelized and the centers are tender when tested with a fork. Using a spatula, toss the roasted vegetables to meld their flavors, and transfer them to a serving bowl or serve straight from the pan.

cheater's porchetta

1½ pounds **pork loin**

2 teaspoons **kosher salt**

Freshly ground black pepper to taste

½ cup **pesto**, homemade (see page 109 or 110) or store-bought

2 tablespoons chopped **fresh sage**, plus a few leaves for garnish

4 to 6 slices **bacon**

Extra-virgin olive oil, for drizzling

SPECIAL EQUIPMENT

Kitchen twine

> One of the useful lessons here is tying the meat up with twine (called trussing) so it will hold its shape and trap its juices while cooking. Of course, some of those juices do seep out, creating the most delicious pan sauce, which we then toss with pasta to round out this meal.

Porchetta is an Italian slow-roasted pork that's seasoned with herbs and spices and cooked until fragrant and fall-apart tender. The traditional recipe uses different kinds of pork and takes hours and hours, but our cheater's version uses lean pork loin, which we split open, slather with pesto, and roll up into a cylinder that showcases beautiful pinwheels of seasoning when sliced. Since pork loin is lean, it cooks quickly, but we wrap it in strips of bacon so the smoky fat melts into the meat as it roasts.

We've scaled this recipe for a smaller dinner, but if you're feeding a bigger group, double or triple the quantities and use a whole pork loin. Butterflying it will be a bit trickier, and you'll need to add more cooking time (the thermometer will be your guide to when it's ready). Get ready to wow the crowd when the roast comes out of the oven!

1. Preheat the oven to 400°F. Place the pork loin fat-side down on a large cutting board. Use a chef's knife to cut lengthwise down the center of the meat, but do not cut all the way through—leave about ½ inch attached along the bottom, like a hinge, to keep the meat in one piece.

2. Now you'll butterfly both sides. Using your hand to pry open the loin, start at the cut in the center of the meat and continue to cut through the meat, keeping the knife parallel to the cutting board, unrolling the loin as you go, maintaining the ½-inch thickness. Repeat on the other side, so you have a relatively flat and even slab of meat.

3. Place a layer of plastic wrap or a gallon-size zip-top bag on top of the meat and use a meat mallet, rolling pin, regular hammer, or the side of an unopened can to pound the meat and even out the thicker parts to make the slab as evenly thick as possible.

4. Using a sharp knife, lightly cut slits about ⅛ inch deep in a grid pattern (called crosshatching) all over the meat, but be sure not to cut all the way through the meat. (This helps the seasonings flavor the pork.)

5. Season the pork on both sides with salt and pepper. Rub the pesto into the cut side of the pork, and sprinkle

the sage on top. Roll up the loin lengthwise in a tight cylinder and wrap it with the bacon.

6. Cut 3 or 4 long pieces of kitchen twine and use them to tie a knot every 2 inches or so around the roast to help keep its shape. Slip a few sage leaves under the twine on top of the roast.

7. Place the loin on a sheet pan and drizzle with olive oil to coat it. Roast for 30 to 35 minutes, until a meat thermometer inserted into the thickest part of the loin registers 145ºF. Remove from the oven and let rest for 10 minutes. Transfer to a cutting board and cut the porchetta crosswise into ½-inch-thick slices. Serve immediately, drizzled with the pan juices.

whole-roasted sweet potatoes
with maple spice compound butter and all the toppings

This is a side dish that could easily be a meal in itself. The lesson here is that while roasting smaller ingredients at a higher temp helps caramelize the sides (see page 61), roasting larger ingredients whole at a lower temp (and in this case protected by foil) lets you cook them evenly throughout (and is more like baking; see Roasting vs. Baking, below). When you do that with a sweet potato (or a regular potato), you create a fluffy interior that's perfect for holding whatever topping you want to stuff—or overstuff!—it with. Set out a toppings bar on the counter, give each person their own potato, and let them customize their ideal meal!

A compound butter is butter that's been mixed with seasonings; when you melt it on something, all the flavors come along with it!

FOR THE SWEET POTATOES

4 to 6 medium **sweet potatoes**

Chopped **fresh parsley** and thinly sliced **scallions**, for serving

FOR THE COMPOUND BUTTER

½ cup (1 stick) **butter**

1 tablespoon **freshly grated orange zest**

1 tablespoon **maple syrup**, plus more to taste

1 teaspoon **Your Own Spice Blend** (page 40) or your favorite store-bought **spice blend**, plus more to taste

1. **Roast the sweet potatoes:** Preheat the oven to 400°F.

2. Prick the sweet potatoes all over with a fork; wrap each in foil and place on a sheet pan. Roast for 45 to 60 minutes, depending on size, until soft.

3. **Meanwhile, make the compound butter:** Let the butter sit out on the counter until softened. In a mixing bowl, mash together the butter, orange zest, maple syrup, and spice blend until well combined. Taste and adjust the seasoning with more maple syrup and spice blend if you'd like.

4. When cool enough to handle, slice the tops of the potatoes lengthwise, and open them a bit. Top with compound butter, parsley, and scallions and serve.

Don't skip the skin! Sweet potato skins have lots of nutrients, from potassium to vitamins A, C, and E—and a perfect texture for holding another round of toppings and eating them folded up, taco-style!

roasting vs. baking

While roasting and baking both take place in the oven, there are important differences between them. Roasting is usually done at a higher temperature so the exterior of the food cooks faster than the interior, creating a caramelized and crispy surface. Think roasted meats like chicken and turkey, or roasted vegetables like potatoes. Baking is usually at a lower temperature, and this gentler method cooks foods evenly throughout, which is why it's ideal for batters you want to cook into cake with a uniform crumb, evenly cooked casseroles, or delicate fish fillets.

butternut squash pasta
with goat cheese and caramelized onions

2 pounds **butternut** or other hard **winter squash**

Kosher salt and **freshly ground black pepper** to taste

3 tablespoons **extra-virgin olive oil**, plus more for drizzling

2 large **onions**, thinly sliced

1 pound **dry pasta**, such as ziti, rigatoni, penne, or fusilli

2 tablespoons chopped **fresh sage leaves**

4 cups chopped **kale** (we used lacinato)

¾ cup (about 2½ ounces) grated **Parmesan cheese**

3 ounces **goat cheese**, at room temperature

Zesty Bread Crumbs (page 277), for garnish (optional)

When winter squash is in season, we're always slicing or dicing big batches and roasting them on sheet pans until sweet and creamy, just like the Spiced Roasted Vegetables on page 65. They're a great thing to make ahead and keep in the fridge to create meals later.

We add roasted squash to lots of stuff, but one of our favorite uses is this comforting pasta.

It all starts on the stovetop with a sauce made simply by slow-cooking onions and sage until they're caramelized. Then we add the roasted squash, kale, and other ingredients. And then the great lesson: You can make all that goodness into a sauce just by adding some of the water you cooked the pasta in! That liquid helps release the oniony browned bits from the bottom of the pan; scrape up all that flavor and stir it right into your sauce! The water also helps wilt the kale before it's all tossed together with the cheeses, and since it contains some starch from the pasta, it adds some body and flavor.

The toasted bread crumbs are a fancy finishing touch that adds crunch.

1. Preheat the oven 350°F.

2. With a sharp knife, carefully cut the squash in half lengthwise. They can be very hard, so be careful. One of the safer ways to do this is by using the point of the knife to cut straight down into the middle of the squash, and then pull the handle toward the board to cut down through the squash, almost like half a scissor. Then turn the squash around and repeat on the other side.

3. Using a spoon, scoop out all the seeds and stringy bits and put those in your trash bowl or compost.

4. Place the squash cut-side down on a sheet pan and roast in the oven until tender when pierced with a fork, about 1 hour. Remove it from the oven and let cool.

5. Once cool enough to handle, scoop the squash flesh from the skin into a bowl. Season with salt and pepper. (All this can be done up to 2 days in advance.)

6. Heat 3 tablespoons oil in a very large skillet (12 inches is ideal) over medium heat. Add the onions and a generous pinch of salt and cook, stirring occasionally, until deep golden and caramelized, 12 to 15 minutes.

7. Meanwhile, bring a large pot of heavily salted water (it should taste like the ocean) to a boil over high heat. Add the pasta and cook until al dente (about a minute shy of the package instructions). Using a mug, carefully scoop out and reserve a cupful of the pasta cooking water. Drain the pasta in a colander, drizzle with olive oil, toss, and set it aside. When the onions are caramelized, add the sage and stir over medium heat until its aroma starts to bloom. Add the squash, stirring until well combined. Add the kale and a nice splash of the reserved pasta cooking water, and stir to release any browned bits from the skillet. Cook, stirring, until the kale is slightly wilted. Add more water, if necessary, to keep the vegetables moist.

8. In a large bowl, mix together the cooked pasta, vegetable sauce, and cheeses until well combined. Season with salt and pepper to taste and top with toasted bread crumbs, if desired.

why we love sheet pans

Take a peek into our kitchen cupboards and you'll find a large stack of sheet pans in various sizes. Also called baking pans or rimmed cookie sheets, these simple, essential kitchen tools are just a flat sheet of metal with rimmed sides about an inch tall. They're great for everything from roasting dinner (Spiced Roasted Vegetables, page 65) and baking cookies (Brown Butter Chocolate Chip Cookies, page 230) to creating a hot, flat surface for crispy pizza crust (Sheet Pan Pizzas, page 204).

The size we use most often is the half sheet pan, measuring about 13 × 18 inches. They are large enough to cook an entire dinner, which we do many nights a week. We use smaller quarter sheet pans (13 × 9 inches) for small batches of cookies and heating up leftovers. We use eighth sheet pans (6 × 9 inches) for toasting nuts, making individual pizzas, and even as plates for casual gatherings!

herbed hasselback potatoes

½ cup (1 stick) **butter**

2 tablespoons grated **Parmesan cheese**, plus more for sprinkling

2 tablespoons **fresh thyme leaves**

1 tablespoon minced **fresh chives**

1 teaspoon **kosher salt** (or ½ teaspoon, if using salted butter)

½ teaspoon **freshly ground black pepper**

6 medium **Yukon Gold potatoes**

Extra-virgin olive oil, for drizzling

SPECIAL EQUIPMENT

2 chopsticks

When we're looking for something special to serve alongside a great steak or platter of roasted vegetables, these thinly sliced, fanned-out, and baked-till-crispy Hasselback potatoes are our go-to. By slicing the potatoes super thin and rubbing them down with herbed butter, each thin layer roasts quickly and soaks up the seasoning. Count on one potato per person: They're too good and too much fun to share!

So far in this chapter we've roasted vegetables whole (Whole-Roasted Sweet Potatoes with Maple Spice Compound Butter, page 69) and in pieces (Spiced Roasted Vegetables, page 65); this recipe shows us what can happen when we do both at the same time!

1. Preheat the oven to 425°F. Line a sheet pan with foil.

2. Let the butter sit on the counter until soft. In a medium mixing bowl, thoroughly combine the butter with the Parmesan, thyme, chives, salt, and pepper.

3. On a cutting board, tuck two chopsticks along the long sides of a potato to nestle it a bit. When you start to slice the potato crosswise, the chopsticks will prevent your knife blade from going all the way through, so the pieces remain attached. Starting at one end of the potato, slice across at ⅛-inch intervals all the way down to the chopsticks. Repeat with the remaining potatoes.

4. Place the potatoes cut-side up on the prepared sheet pan. Using clean fingers, carefully rub the butter on top of the potatoes, making sure it gets in between the slices; sprinkle a bit more Parmesan on top. Bake for 50 to 60 minutes, drizzle with oil if the tops look dry, until the potatoes are golden brown and the tops are crispy. Serve right away.

spiced chicken thighs
with brussels sprouts and orange zest

6 to 8 **chicken thighs** or **drumsticks** (about 2 pounds)

2½ tablespoons **Your Own Spice Blend** (page 40) or your favorite store-bought **spice blend**

1½ to 2 pounds **Brussels sprouts**, trimmed and halved (or your favorite vegetable!)

Zest of 1 orange (about 1 teaspoon; reserve the orange flesh for another use—or just eat it!)

4 **garlic cloves**, smashed

1 teaspoon **kosher salt**

½ teaspoon **freshly ground black pepper** to taste

Extra-virgin olive oil, for drizzling

Whenever you're roasting something large with lots of surface area and skin, place it cut-side down on the sheet pan so the exposed surface doesn't dry out.

This spiced chicken-and-vegetable dinner is a weeknight winner because it comes together so quickly all on a single sheet pan. The chicken pieces (we use thighs and legs, but you can also do chicken breasts cut in half crosswise) cook faster than a whole bird, the skin crisps up beautifully, and the cooking juices meld with the spices, Brussels sprouts, and citrus, creating a delicious pan sauce we love to sop up with good bread.

The vegetables and seasonings you use can change with the seasons. In winter and fall we love it like this with Brussels sprouts; in the spring we might roast artichokes and new potatoes, and in the summer, eggplant and peppers (see A Quick Guide to Roasting Vegetables, page 64). Whatever you use, the process for cooking this is the same, but the times may vary. Part of the fun is figuring out which spices we like best with different vegetables!

1. Preheat the oven to 400°F.

2. Using a paper towel, pat the chicken dry. Sprinkle the spice blend over the chicken, making sure the pieces are evenly coated.

3. In a medium bowl, toss the Brussels sprouts, orange zest, and garlic with the salt and pepper and enough olive oil to just coat it all.

4. On a sheet pan, place the the chicken pieces skin-side up in a single layer. Cover the pan with foil and roast in the oven for 15 minutes.

5. Carefully remove the pan from the oven, add the Brussels sprouts around the chicken pieces, and roast, covered, for another 10 minutes. If you're putting the chicken and vegetables on a platter, don't forget to also serve the juices left on the pan!

spiced and marinated kebabs

Kebabs rank high on the kid-friendly chart: They're fun to skewer, they're endlessly customizable when it comes to ingredients and seasoning, and they cook quickly. They also offer a great lesson in seasoning with marinades before cooking. You'll notice that many marinade recipes contain oil, fat, or an acid (something tart), because oil carries flavor and acid helps break down the texture of the ingredient so it can soak up all that flavor. In this case, we use a full-fat yogurt, both fat *and* acid! You can use lemon juice and olive oil, or even a vinaigrette dressing, if you'd like to make it dairy-free.

FOR THE MARINADE

1 tablespoon **Your Own Spice Blend** (page 40) or your favorite store-bought **spice blend**

½ cup (4 ounces) **plain whole-milk yogurt**

3 tablespoons **extra-virgin olive oil**

1 teaspoon **kosher salt**

½ teaspoon **freshly ground black pepper**

2 pounds boneless, skinless **chicken thighs** and/or **breasts**, cut into 1¼-inch cubes (see Note)

1 large **yellow onion**, cut into 8 wedges, root end left intact

2 large **red, yellow,** and/or **orange bell peppers**, stemmed, seeded, and cut into 1-inch pieces

SPECIAL EQUIPMENT

Ten (10-inch) wooden skewers

NOTE: For a vegetarian alternative, substitute mushrooms and/or zucchini, plus a second onion.

1. Soak ten 10-inch wooden skewers in water for at least 20 minutes (to prevent burning). Line a large sheet pan with foil and top it with a baking rack.

2. **Make the marinade:** In a large bowl, mix the spice blend, yogurt, olive oil, salt, and pepper together. Add the chicken and toss to coat completely. For the most flavorful results, cover the bowl and refrigerate for at least 1 hour or up to overnight.

3. **Assemble the kebabs:** Alternate threading the chicken with the peppers and a few slices of onion (not the entire wedge) on the skewers, leaving no space between them. Do not skimp on the skewers but leave a 1-inch space at the bottom end so you have something to hold.

4. Preheat the oven to 450°F.

5. Place the skewers on the rack of the prepared sheet pan, making sure they don't touch. Roast for 15 minutes, then flip the skewers over and roast for another 10 to 15 minutes. Test a few pieces of the chicken to make sure they are done by slicing into the center; there should be no shininess to the meat and the juices should run clear. (Alternatively, the temperature on an instant-read thermometer should read 165°F.) If the chicken is not completely cooked, roast for an additional 5 minutes, then check again.

6. Remove the kebabs from the oven and let cool a few minutes before serving.

3
sautéing & searing

If standing at the stove is your happy place (it is ours!), then searing, stir-frying, and sautéing are the techniques for you. These are hands-on recipes that are all done in a pan on the stove and engage all our senses: we need to look for the oil to start shimmering (an indication that it's hot enough to start adding ingredients), smell that the aromatics are becoming fragrant but not about to burn, taste if the dish needs more salt or balance. When we use all our senses, we're fully present in the meal we're cooking—and that's the best way to learn.

Whether it's our seared Perfect Cast-Iron Steak (page 96) or our sautéed Lemony Broccoli Rabe (page 88), these stovetop techniques are some of the most satisfying to us as cooks.

laab moo lettuce wraps

FOR THE DRESSING

⅓ cup **freshly squeezed lime juice** (from about 3 medium limes)

2 tablespoons **fish sauce** (optional)

1 tablespoon packed **light brown sugar**

½ teaspoon **sriracha sauce** (optional)

1 tablespoon **vegetable oil** (optional, if you're cooking with tofu)

1 teaspoon **soy sauce** or **tamari** (optional, if you're cooking with tofu)

The Thai and Laotian genre of dishes known as laab (sometimes spelled laap or larb) inspired this recipe, which has become a house favorite among our students and families. Essentially a salad made of fragrant minced meat (this version calls for pork, or use tofu for a vegetarian version), it's a great first lesson in sautéing because it doesn't require super-high heat; most of its flavor comes from gently cooking the filling with aromatics like garlic, lemongrass, makrut lime leaves, and chile, and then it gets another flavor boost with a sweet and tangy dressing. Laab is traditionally quite spicy, but we present it simply as a dish loaded with all kinds of flavors and encourage kids to be daring. Maybe try a little more spice than usual or understand that the fish sauce in the dressing (optional for vegetarians) may smell pretty strong, but a small amount really pumps up the flavor of the dish. Traditionally laab is served with sticky rice, but we serve it with a choice of rice and with lettuce leaves for wrapping bites.

1. **Make the dressing:** In a small jar, combine the lime juice, fish sauce (if using), brown sugar, and sriracha (if using; also add the oil and soy sauce, if cooking tofu). Shake up the dressing to blend the ingredients and set aside. (Reshake the dressing before using.)

2. **Make the filling:** Heat the oil in a large skillet over medium heat. Add the red onion, garlic, and chile (if using) and cook, stirring constantly, until fragrant, about 2 minutes. Add the ground meat or tofu, lemongrass, makrut lime leaves, and fish sauce (if using) and cook, stirring occasionally, until the meat or tofu is cooked through (or the tofu is starting to brown), 5 to 6 minutes.

3. Transfer the filling to a large serving bowl and stir in the cilantro, mint, and scallions. Toss with the shaken dressing. Top with the slivered onion. Serve at any temperature you like (laab is often served at room temperature) with the lime wedges, lettuce leaves for wrapping, and rice on the side.

FOR THE FILLING

1 tablespoon **vegetable oil**

½ cup chopped **red onion** (about ½ small onion)

4 teaspoons minced **garlic** (about 4 medium cloves)

1 **Thai red chile**, minced, or a pinch of **Thai chili powder** (optional)

1¼ pounds **ground pork** or **chicken** or **firm tofu** (one and a half 14-ounce packages, drained and diced)

2 tablespoons chopped **lemongrass** (about 1 inch)

2 or 3 **fresh makrut lime leaves**, minced, or 1½ teaspoons freshly grated **lime zest** (from 1 medium lime)

2 teaspoons **fish sauce**, or to taste (optional)

8 to 10 whole sprigs **fresh cilantro**, chopped

Leaves from 2 sprigs **fresh mint**, very thinly sliced

4 **scallions** (white and green parts), thinly sliced

FOR SERVING

½ small **red onion**, sliced into very thin slivers

1 **lime**, sliced into wedges

1 large head **Bibb lettuce**, leaves separated and kept whole

Coconut Rice (page 270) or **Sticky Rice** (page 271)

crispy sesame orange chicken or tofu

2 pounds boneless, skinless **chicken breasts** or **thighs** or **extra-firm tofu** (from two 14-ounce packages, drained)

2 tablespoons **toasted sesame oil**

2 teaspoons **freshly grated orange zest**

¾ teaspoon **kosher salt**

A few cracks of **freshly ground black pepper**

½ cup **freshly squeezed orange juice**

2 tablespoons **soy sauce** (substitute tamari for gluten-free)

2 tablespoons **rice vinegar**

1 tablespoon **granulated sugar**

⅓ cup plus 2 teaspoons **cornstarch**

1 large **egg**, beaten

3 tablespoons **vegetable oil**, plus more if needed

2 teaspoons minced **garlic** (about 2 large cloves)

3 **scallions** (white and green parts), thinly sliced on the diagonal

1 tablespoon **sesame seeds**, toasted (see page 280)

Cooked rice (see page 269), for serving

A big reason for starting The Dynamite Shop was to hand kids the keys to dinner. So often parents are tapped out by the end of the day, and we (yes, even the two of us!) turn to ordering in. Here in New York City, the iconic ordered-in dinner is Chinese takeout, so we decided to teach the kids what we call "takeout fake out."

1. Pat the chicken or tofu dry with a paper towel. Trim away any excess fat and cut the chicken into 1-inch cubes (or cut the tofu into ½-inch cubes). In a large mixing bowl, combine the chicken or tofu pieces, sesame oil, 1 teaspoon of the orange zest, the salt, and the pepper.

2. In a small mixing bowl, combine the orange juice, soy sauce, vinegar, sugar, 2 teaspoons of the cornstarch, and remaining 1 teaspoon orange zest.

3. Add the beaten egg to the chicken or tofu mixture and mix well. Add the remaining ⅓ cup cornstarch and toss.

4. In a large nonstick skillet, heat the vegetable oil over medium-high heat until shimmering. Using tongs, arrange the chicken or tofu pieces in a single, even layer in the pan. (You may need to work in batches to make sure everything is in one layer.)

5. Cook the chicken or tofu without moving it until the bottom turns golden, about 2 minutes. Using tongs, flip the pieces to brown the other sides. Remove from the heat and transfer the chicken or tofu to a large paper towel–lined plate to cool for 2 to 3 minutes.

6. If there is a lot of oil left in the pan, hold some paper towels in the tongs and use them to wipe most of it out, but leave about 1 teaspoon in the pan. Place the pan over medium heat, add the garlic, and stir for just a few seconds. Meanwhile, stir the sauce to ensure there are no lumps of cornstarch, then add it to the pan and stir constantly until thickened.

7. Return the chicken or tofu to the pan and stir to mix well. Transfer to a plate and scatter with the scallions and sesame seeds. Serve with rice.

garlic-ginger blistered green beans

2 tablespoons **vegetable oil**

1 pound **green beans**, trimmed

1 tablespoon minced **garlic** (about 3 medium cloves)

1 tablespoon peeled and minced **fresh ginger** (a 1- to 2-inch piece)

2 tablespoons **soy sauce** (substitute tamari for gluten-free)

1 tablespoon **rice vinegar**

1 tablespoon **sesame seeds**, lightly toasted (see page 280)

This is our favorite way to cook green beans: quickly, in a sizzling hot pan so they keep their crunch but soften inside and blister on the outside. The fragrant sauce comes together in the pan in a flash. Just be careful not to cook the garlic and ginger too long before adding the soy sauce and vinegar, or that garlic will burn and turn bitter. This same method works well for other sturdy green vegetables, like broccoli, okra, and snow or snap peas, and vegetables prepared this way are one of our favorite things to serve with our Panfried Dumplings (page 86) or Up-to-You Fried Rice (page 84). The toasted sesame seeds add a fancy finishing touch and toasty flavor.

1. Heat the oil in a large skillet over medium heat. Once it's shimmering, add the green beans so that as many of them are touching the bottom of the pan as possible. Let the beans sit undisturbed in the pan for 30 to 60 seconds to get some nice browning on them, then cook, tossing often, until they begin to shrivel and are slightly blistered, about 5 minutes more.

2. Add the garlic and ginger and sauté until fragrant but not burnt, about 1 minute. Add the soy sauce and vinegar; toss well to coat. Sprinkle with the sesame seeds and serve immediately.

up-to-you fried rice

4 tablespoons **neutral oil**, such as canola

1 large **onion**, chopped (about 2 cups)

2 to 3 cups **mix-ins** (see Note on page 85)

Kosher salt and **freshly ground black pepper** to taste

1 tablespoon peeled and minced **fresh ginger** (a 1- to 2-inch piece)

2 teaspoons minced **garlic** (about 2 large cloves)

5 cups **cold cooked rice** (preferably day-old; see page 269)

¼ cup **soy sauce** (substitute tamari for gluten-free)

1 tablespoon **toasted sesame oil**, plus more to taste (optional)

SPECIAL EQUIPMENT

Wok or large skillet (at least 12 inches)

> NOTE: Garnish with chopped cilantro, basil, or chives. Drizzle with sriracha, gochujang, hot mustard, or chili oil. Top with toasted sesame seeds (see page 280), peanuts, or a fried egg.

If you're like us, you'll usually have some odds and ends in your fridge: a piece of roasted chicken, an unused carrot, a handful of herbs. Fried rice is one of our favorite ways to pull these bits and bobs together into a meal. Sometimes we make it with bacon and scallions with a fried egg on top; other times, it's leftover chicken or wilted greens. It's always the ultimate comfort food!

This recipe is a great one for teaching stir-frying over high heat. With a recipe that moves as quickly as this one, having your mise en place ready (see page 27) is essential to things going smoothly.

The other thing to keep an eye on is your skillet size. You'll need a big one (12 inches) or a wok to cook this recipe. But the good news is, if you don't have a big pan, you can just do some kitchen math and prepare half the recipe at a time! Since it comes together in a flash, you can cook multiple batches quickly.

1. In a wok or large skillet, heat 2 tablespoons of the neutral oil over high heat until shimmering. Add the onion and cook, stirring constantly, until just translucent, about 3 minutes. Add any raw vegetable mix-ins and cook until crisp-tender, 1 to 3 minutes, depending on their firmness. If you're using tofu or cooked meat, add it now and stir to combine and heat everything through. Season with salt and pepper and transfer everything to a bowl.

2. In the same pan, heat the remaining 2 tablespoons neutral oil over medium-high heat. When it starts to shimmer, add the ginger and garlic and stir until aromatic, about 30 seconds. Add the rice, stir to combine and heat it through, then add the reserved mix-ins and the soy sauce, quickly stir-frying in a circular motion so as much of the rice as possible touches the bottom of the pan. Drizzle with the sesame oil (if using) and stir-fry for 1 to 2 minutes more, until the rice is evenly coated and heated through. (If you like crispy bits of rice, you can press it against the pan and leave it to cook until a crust forms, then start stir-frying again.)

3. Remove the pan from the heat and garnish with herbs, drizzles, and toppings (if desired).

NOTE: Cut everything into bite-size pieces: chopped raw or cooked vegetables (carrots, mushrooms, broccoli, cauliflower, asparagus, bean sprouts), frozen and thawed peas, cooked leafy greens (kale, chard, spinach), kimchi, diced firm tofu, and/or chopped or shredded cooked meat (chicken, ham, roast pork). This recipe is a great way to use leftovers!

panfried dumplings

Every culture seems to have its own version of a filling wrapped in dough, from Polish pierogi to Japanese gyoza to Italian ravioli. This version, hailing from the southern region of China around Hong Kong, was adapted from a recipe shared with us by chef Chris Cheung of East Wind Snack Shop in Brooklyn, New York.

We start by seasoning a big bowl of ground pork (or finely chopped vegetables for vegetarian dumplings) with ginger, garlic, soy sauce, and scallions, then we wrap our dumplings, practicing different folds and shapes. The more hands, the better! Like many foods that require manual assembly, dumplings are a dish that friends and family often make together, and when we teach it, we love seeing multiple generations lending a hand, chatting as they go.

When it comes to cooking, we make these potstickers the way our other resident dumpling expert, former *Gourmet* magazine editor Lillian Chou, taught us: crispy on the bottom, chewy on the top. And don't forget the dipping sauce! You can also simply steam or boil these dumplings if you prefer them that way.

FOR THE PORK OR CHICKEN FILLING

12 ounces **ground pork** or **chicken**

¼ cup chopped **scallions** (white and green parts)

1½ teaspoons minced **garlic** (about 2 medium cloves)

1½ teaspoons peeled and minced **fresh ginger** (a ½- to 1-inch piece)

2 tablespoons **soy sauce** (substitute tamari for gluten-free)

FOR THE VEGETARIAN FILLING

½ cup shredded **napa cabbage**

¼ cup finely grated **carrot**

¼ cup chopped **scallions** (white and green parts)

¼ cup chopped **white button mushrooms**

1 tablespoon chopped **fresh basil leaves**

1 tablespoon chopped **fresh mint leaves**

1 tablespoon chopped **fresh cilantro leaves**

2 teaspoons peeled and minced **fresh ginger** (about a 1-inch piece)

2 teaspoons **toasted sesame oil**

2 teaspoons **soy sauce** (substitute tamari for gluten-free)

1. **Make the filling:** In a medium bowl, mix together all the ingredients for either the meat or the vegetarian filling.

2. **Assemble the dumplings:** On a clean work surface, lay out a few dumpling wrappers, leaving the rest in a stack, and set a small bowl of water nearby. Place about a teaspoon of the filling in the center of each wrapper. Dip your finger in the water and wet the edges of the wrappers. Fold the wrappers into half-moons, pressing the edges to seal. (At this point, if you want, you can embellish your dumplings by crimping the edges accordion-style, making 5 to 7 folds in each.)

3. **Panfry the dumplings:** In a nonstick skillet, heat 2 teaspoons of the vegetable oil over medium-high. Once it's hot, carefully arrange the dumplings flat-side down in a circle around the edge, filling in the center area with a smaller circle of dumplings, and cook uncovered for about 2 minutes, until the bottoms are browned. Reduce the heat to medium, add ½ cup

30 store-bought round
wonton/dumpling wrappers

Vegetable oil or **all-natural
cooking spray**, for the pan

Dumpling Dipping Sauce
(recipe follows)

water, cover the pan, and cook until the dumplings are
fully steamed, about 6 minutes. Remove the lid and
allow all the liquid to evaporate, another minute or
two. Shake the pan gently to ensure the dumplings do
not stick. Turn off the heat.

4. To serve, transfer the potstickers to a plate. (Or, for a
pretty upside-down presentation, ask for help from an
adult: Get a plate large enough to cover the entire pan
and flip it right-side down over the pan, with one hand
holding it in place. Then carefully flip the pan and the
plate together so the dumplings turn out onto the
plate.) Serve immediately with dipping sauce.

dumpling dipping sauce

makes 1 cup

¾ cup **soy sauce** (substitute
tamari for gluten-free)

3 tablespoons **rice vinegar**

1 tablespoon peeled and
minced **fresh ginger**
(a 1- to 2-inch piece)

Whisk together all the
ingredients in a small
bowl and serve.

lemony broccoli rabe

1 large bunch **broccoli rabe** (about 1 pound)

2 large **garlic cloves**, thinly sliced

2 tablespoons **extra-virgin olive oil**

1 small **lemon**

Kosher salt and **freshly ground black pepper** to taste

We're broccoli rabe cheerleaders, and we think a lot more people would be, too, if they knew how to cook (not overcook) this assertive-in-a-good-way vegetable. Blanching it first softens its characteristic bitterness and makes it easy to cook ahead, cool, then quickly sauté with garlic and lots of bright zest right before dinner. We cook regular broccoli the same way, and you can use this same method for all kinds of leafy greens—try Swiss chard, kale, mustard greens, or beet greens.

This side dish is our go-to for roasted meats or pasta dinners. We tuck leftovers into sandwiches, grain bowls, or any meal that can use an extra boost of vegetables.

1. Fill a large pot with enough water to submerge the broccoli rabe (but don't add that yet!); set it over high heat. Fill a large bowl with ice water (this is your ice bath) and place it next to the stove.

2. When the water in the pot comes to a boil, add the broccoli rabe, stirring to make sure it's submerged. Cook until bright green, about 1 minute. Use a slotted spoon to scoop the broccoli rabe out of the boiling water and plunge it into the ice bath. (This process is called "shocking," which immediately stops any further cooking.) Let the broccoli rabe cool in the ice bath, then drain it in a colander. Press out as much water as possible, then transfer the broccoli rabe to a cutting board. Chop the broccoli rabe into bite-size pieces.

3. In a large skillet, heat the garlic and olive oil over medium-high heat until the garlic starts to brown, about 1 minute. Add the broccoli rabe and sauté, stirring occasionally, until crisp-tender and heated through, about 2 minutes.

4. Meanwhile, zest the lemon over the pan, then cut it in half and squeeze the juice in—make sure you catch any seeds! Stir to combine. Season with salt and pepper and serve.

vegetarian meatballs

Who says you need meat to make a delicious meatball? Our vegetarian meatballs swap the meat for cooked lentils, which get mixed with plenty of fresh herbs, dried spices, and tangy cheese. The trick here is to mash and break up some of the lentils into a paste, which helps bind (or hold) the balls together. It's really important to drain the lentils well and really pack the balls tightly while shaping, so they don't fall apart in the pan.

2 cups **vegetable stock**, store-bought or homemade (see page 264)

1 cup **dried green lentils**

1 **bay leaf**

1 teaspoon **kosher salt**, plus more to taste

½ cup **dried bread crumbs**

⅓ cup (about 1 ounce) grated **Pecorino Romano** or **Pecorino-Parmesan blend cheese**, plus more for topping

4 teaspoons minced **garlic** (about 4 medium cloves)

3 tablespoons chopped **fresh flat-leaf parsley**, plus more for garnish

1 teaspoon **Italian seasoning**

½ teaspoon **fennel seeds**

½ teaspoon **crushed red pepper flakes**

Freshly ground black pepper to taste

1 large **egg**

1 tablespoon **extra-virgin olive oil**, plus more as needed

3 cups **marinara sauce**, store-bought or homemade (see page 117)

Cooked polenta, pasta (see page 116), or **bread**, for serving

1. Preheat the oven to 425°F. Combine the stock, lentils, bay leaf, and salt in a saucepan. Bring to a boil over high heat and then lower the heat until there are a few slow bubbles. Cook until the lentils are just tender, 12 to 15 minutes. Remove the bay leaf, drain the lentils in a colander, and let them cool.

2. In a large mixing bowl, combine the cooled lentils, bread crumbs, cheese, garlic, parsley, Italian seasoning, fennel seeds, and red pepper flakes. Using your fingers, mix the ingredients, breaking open some of the lentils to form a semi-sticky paste. Season the mixture with more salt and black pepper to taste. In a small bowl, beat the egg and drizzle it over the lentil mixture. Using your fingers, mix well to evenly combine and form into twelve 1½-inch balls (about the size of a Ping-Pong ball), packing them tightly with your hands. Transfer to a sheet pan.

3. In a cast-iron or nonstick skillet, heat the olive oil over medium-high heat. Sear the lentil balls, turning them with a spoon so they brown all over, about 5 minutes. Do this in batches if the balls won't all fit comfortably at once, adding more oil if needed.

4. Unless you're working in a cast-iron or oven-safe skillet, transfer the balls to a 9 × 13-inch baking dish, evenly spacing them apart. Pour the marinara sauce around and over the lentil balls; season with salt and black pepper and sprinkle with more cheese. Bake for 15 minutes, until the cheese has melted and the sauce is bubbling. Garnish with fresh parsley. Serve over pasta or polenta, or with lots of crusty bread.

meatballs and sauce

1 pound **ground beef** (preferably 80% lean)

½ pound (2 or 3 links) **sweet Italian sausage**, casings removed (for a pork-free version, substitute the same amount of ground beef)

⅓ cup (about 1 ounce) grated **Pecorino Romano** or **Pecorino-Parmesan blend cheese**, plus more for topping

¼ cup (about 2 ounces) **whole-milk ricotta cheese**

½ cup **dried bread crumbs**

2 teaspoons minced **garlic** (about 2 large cloves)

3 tablespoons chopped **fresh flat-leaf parsley**, plus more for garnish

1½ teaspoons **Italian seasoning**

Kosher salt and **freshly ground black pepper** to taste

1 large **egg**

1 tablespoon **extra-virgin olive oil**, plus more as needed

3 cups canned **crushed tomatoes** or **Basic Marinara Sauce** (page 117)

Cooked pasta (see page 116), **polenta**, or **bread**, for serving.

When it comes to comfort foods, it's hard to beat Italian American–style meatballs in red sauce. There are countless ways to make them, but we like adding pork sausage to the usual beef/pork blends (a shortcut that adds flavors like fennel, garlic, and pepper to the mix). We also add ricotta cheese, which helps make the meatballs light and tender. The bread crumbs keep the meatballs moist by absorbing juices, and the egg acts like a glue to keep everything stuck together.

You could form your balls and bake them in the sauce, but the reason we put this in the sautéing chapter is that we suggest browning them in the pan first, giving them a super flavorful exterior.

This recipe introduces students to the Maillard reaction (see page 97), the science behind searing that turns the proteins brown and makes them taste delicious. And it's not just for the meatballs themselves; you get lots of browned bits in the bottom of the pan that will flavor the sauce. Serve this the classic way, with spaghetti or polenta—or just with some great bread and a big salad.

1. Preheat the oven to 425°F.

2. In a large mixing bowl, combine the beef, sausage, both cheeses, bread crumbs, garlic, parsley, Italian seasoning, 1 teaspoon salt, and a generous grind of pepper. In a small bowl, beat the egg, then drizzle it over the meatball mixture. Using your fingers, mix well to evenly combine. Form the mixture into twelve 2-inch balls (a bit larger than a golf ball) and transfer to a sheet pan.

3. In a cast-iron or nonstick skillet, heat the olive oil over medium-high heat until shimmering. Add the meatballs and cook without touching them until they are well browned, about 3 minutes. (If the meatballs don't all fit comfortably in the pan, do this in batches, using more oil between batches if needed.)

4. Turn the meatballs with a spoon so they brown all over, cooking another 3 minutes or so. If your skillet is not oven-safe, transfer the meatballs and pan juices to a 9 × 13-inch baking dish, spacing them evenly apart.

5. Pour the tomatoes around and over the meatballs; season with salt and pepper and sprinkle with more pecorino. Bake for 20 minutes, or until an instant-read thermometer inserted into the center of a meatball registers 165°F. (Or you can just cut a meatball in half to make sure the center is cooked through with no pink.) Garnish with fresh parsley. Serve over pasta or polenta or with lots of crusty bread.

healthy greens quesadillas

3 tablespoons **extra-virgin olive oil**

½ **red onion**, diced (about ⅔ cup)

8 cups shredded **kale**, **collard greens**, or **spinach** (if you're using spinach, use 10 or more cups)

¼ teaspoon **kosher salt**

A few cracks of **freshly ground black pepper**

Ten 10-inch **flour tortillas** (or 20 corn tortillas for gluten-free)

3 cups (12 ounces) shredded **Monterey Jack cheese**

Salsa Fresca (page 104) and **Classic Guacamole** (page 105), for serving

Quesadillas rank pretty high on the list of crowd favorites. We're all for showing kids how to make their favorite dishes, but we also like to throw in some twists, such as some sautéed greens for flavor and extra nutrition. That's how these healthy quesadillas came to be. And while we suggest greens like kale, collards, or spinach, students have been known to go off-road with their additions. Once you get the process, you can add whatever fillings you want!

The lesson here is that after you've sautéed the greens, you don't then have to stand at the stove searing one quesadilla after the next: placed on a sheet pan in the oven, they get just as crispy on the outside with molten cheese in the center, and best of all, they all cook and are done at the same time so you can bring them to the table all at once for dinner.

1. Preheat the oven to 375°F.

2. In a medium skillet over medium heat, warm 2 tablespoons of the oil until shimmering. Add the onion and sauté until softened and just starting to brown, about 3 minutes. Add the greens and sauté until completely wilted, about 3 minutes. Season with the salt and pepper.

3. On a flat work surface, lay out the tortillas. Evenly distribute the cheese over half of each tortilla and top with the greens mixture, dividing it evenly. Fold the empty half over the cheese and greens to form a half circle. Lightly brush the tops with some of the remaining 1 tablespoon oil. Place the quesadillas oiled-side down on a large sheet pan (you may have to use more pans, depending on the quesadillas' size). Lightly brush the tops with more oil.

4. Cover with foil and bake for about 10 minutes, until the cheese is melted. Uncover and return the quesadillas to the oven to crisp for another 2 to 3 minutes.

5. Serve with salsa and guacamole.

summer squash and herb risotto

2 quarts **chicken** or **vegetable stock**, store-bought or homemade (see page 262 or 264)

¼ cup **extra-virgin olive oil**, plus more for drizzling, if desired

3 tablespoons **butter**

1 medium **yellow onion**, diced (about 1½ cups)

2 teaspoons minced **garlic** (about 2 medium cloves)

2 cups **short-grain rice**, such as Arborio, Vialone Nano, Carnaroli, or even sushi rice

1 to 1½ pounds small **yellow squash** or **zucchini**, quartered lengthwise and thinly sliced

1 cup packed mixed chopped **fresh herb leaves**, such as basil, dill, parsley, thyme, sage, and fennel fronds, plus more for garnish

¾ cup (about 2½ ounces) grated **Parmesan cheese**, plus more for garnish

Kosher salt and **freshly ground black pepper** to taste

Risotto is a saucy northern Italian rice dish, and we think of it as a seasonal canvas: we make it with zucchini and herbs when gardens are overflowing in summer, in the fall we turn to butternut squash or Brussels sprouts, and in the winter, when things are spare, we may just make it with caramelized onions, Parmesan, and sage. It's one of those recipe formulas you should keep in your back pocket to whip up meals with whatever ingredients you have on hand or are inspired to bring together in a dish.

You start by toasting the rice in a little butter and oil in the pan. Then you start to add stock, little by little, and stir (and stir and stir!). The rice soaks up the liquid, and its starches add body to the sauce. That's why risotto seems creamy even though there's no cream added!

1. In a medium saucepan, bring the stock to a simmer over medium heat.

2. In a Dutch oven or large saucepan, heat the oil and 1 tablespoon of the butter over medium heat until the butter melts. Add the onion and cook, stirring, until translucent, about 5 minutes. Add the garlic and stir until aromatic, about 1 minute.

3. Add the rice and stir until all the grains are toasty and coated in oil. Using a metal or glass measuring cup, scoop up about a cup of the hot stock and add it to the rice, then cook, stirring constantly, until fully absorbed, about 2 minutes. Add the squash and another cupful of stock, stirring until fully absorbed, another 2 minutes. Keep stirring and adding more stock, a cupful at a time, making sure the stock is fully absorbed between additions and before adding another, about 15 minutes total.

4. When the rice is al dente and the squash is cooked, stir in the herbs and the Parmesan and another cupful of stock and cook until the mixture is creamy. Shut off the heat, stir in the remaining 2 tablespoons butter, and season with salt and pepper. Serve immediately, garnished with more Parmesan, chopped herbs, and a drizzle of olive oil, if you like.

perfect cast-iron steak

2 pounds **boneless beef steaks** (1 to 3 steaks, depending on cut, such as strip, rib eye, flank, flat iron, sirloin, or hanger), 1 to 1½ inches thick

2 teaspoons **kosher salt**

1 tablespoon **butter** per steak

A few cracks of **freshly ground black pepper**, or to taste

SPECIAL EQUIPMENT

10-inch cast-iron skillet or heavy-duty frying pan

NOTE: When shopping for steak, the general rule is to purchase ½ pound of boneless steak per person. One 2-pound sirloin or two 1-pound strip steaks will feed 4.

Treat your family to a special occasion meal . . . while brushing up on your searing chops!

Cast-iron pans retain heat very well, which is great for getting the flavorful char on your steak, but if you don't have cast iron, use a sturdy, heavy sauté pan or skillet. The other pro move here is to constantly flip the steak as it cooks, which helps develop that crust and cook the steak more evenly and quicker. Because the pan will get very hot, make sure you're protecting your hands with kitchen towels or oven mitts when touching the handle, and ask an adult to help if need be.

This recipe is also a great lesson in controlling temperature as we cook. We always take steaks out of the refrigerator to come to room temperature before cooking; otherwise, the inside will be too cold while the outside cooks quickly. We also take the steak off the heat just shy of our desired internal temperature, because it will continue cooking from its residual heat after you take it out of the pan.

For the full steak-house effect, serve this with Herbed Hasselback Potatoes (page 72), Lemony Broccoli Rabe (page 88), and bottomless Shirley Temples (page 259).

1. Line a sheet pan with paper towels. Pat the steaks dry with more paper towels, set them on the sheet pan, and sprinkle them all over with the salt. Let the steaks sit for 30 minutes and continue to pat them dry every few minutes. The steaks should lose a lot of their ice-cold chill before going into the pan.

2. Heat a heavy 10-inch or larger cast-iron skillet over high heat. When the pan is smoking hot, 1 to 2 minutes, add the butter. When it's melted, use sturdy metal tongs to place one of the steaks in the center of the pan. Let the steak sit undisturbed in the pan for 1 minute. Then, using the tongs, lift the steak up, flip it, and set it raw-side down in the middle of the pan. Cook, flipping the steak every 30 seconds. After 2 minutes, add a few cracks of pepper.

3. When the steak has a brown, crackly crust, 5 to 6 minutes total, start to check for doneness. Take the pan off the heat for a moment and insert an instant-read thermometer into the side of the steak. For medium-rare, aim for 125°F; for medium, 140°F; and for well-done, 160°F—keep in mind that the steak will continue cooking slightly off the heat. Transfer the steak to an elevated rack or cutting board.

4. Repeat the whole cooking process with any remaining steak(s) and butter, wiping out the pan between steaks.

5. Let the steak(s) rest for 5 to 10 minutes, depending on their thickness. Cover them loosely with foil if the room is cold.

6. Using a very sharp knife, slice the steak(s) against the grain and serve immediately.

the maillard reaction

The Maillard reaction is the name for the chemical process that happens when simple proteins and sugars (such as those found in meat, fish, poultry, mushrooms, and lots of other foods) are seared with high heat. It's a reaction that creates complex flavors (nutty, savory, umami) and changes the color and texture of the food. Basically, it's what we call "browning," because, well, it turns food brown.

When we talk about the Maillard reaction, we're talking about cooking with high or medium-high heat and—this is key—keeping the heat dry. That means browning doesn't happen in a pot of liquid—you can't boil something until it browns—and it means the food has to be very dry when it hits the hot pan. That's why you see lots of recipes telling you to pat food dry with paper towels before searing or roasting it.

Often, searing or browning is the first step of cooking, since it adds flavor, before you continue with lower, indirect heat or cooking in liquid—for example, browning meatballs before adding them to a pan of sauce.

Think of the crunchy brown crust on a perfectly seared steak or the savory charred edges on a roasted potato. That's the Maillard reaction at work!

smash burgers

1 pound **ground beef** (preferably 80% lean)

1 teaspoon **vegetable oil** or **canola oil**

2 teaspoons **kosher salt**

¼ teaspoon **freshly ground black pepper**

4 slices **cheese**, such as Cheddar or American (optional)

4 **potato buns**, sliced and toasted, if you wish

OPTIONAL TOPPINGS

Ketchup, mustard, mayonnaise, caramelized onions, sautéed mushrooms, cooked bacon, pickles, shredded **lettuce, tomatoes**

Who among meat eaters doesn't love a juicy burger? They come in all shapes and sizes and can be grilled, seared, baked, or even steamed!

This cooking method is hands-down our favorite: we roll the meat into a ball and smash it thin against a hot skillet so it cooks quickly and forms lots of crispy, flavorful edges. Top with cheese and some pickles and sandwich it in a squishy potato roll—you couldn't do better at a fancy burger shack!

1. Divide the beef into 4 equal portions and shape them into balls.

2. Coat a large cast-iron skillet with half the oil. Heat over high heat until very hot and starting to smoke, then place 2 balls of meat in the skillet and smash them flat (about ¼ inch thick) with a spatula. Season each with ¼ teaspoon of the salt and a pinch of the pepper.

3. Cook undisturbed for 2 minutes, until they are seared brown and crisp on the bottom. Use the spatula to flip them, season each with another ¼ teaspoon salt and a pinch of pepper, and top with the cheese (if using). Cover the pan and cook until the cheese melts, about 1 minute more. Transfer the patties to the bottom buns, add any toppings you desire and the top buns, and serve immediately. Repeat with the remaining 2 burgers.

4

sauces

Oh, how we love a good sauce! A sauce can take a bowl of plain pasta or rice from side-dish status to full-on nourishing flavor-packed meal. Some sauces—like marinara (see page 117) and pesto (see page 109)—can be made in bulk with hardly any extra work and frozen, so they'll be available to you for months. Some sauces, like Salsa Fresca (page 104), heat things up. Other sauces, like Tzatziki (page 102), cool things down. When we teach many of the sauces in this book, students marvel at their ability to make something from scratch so easily that they may have only experienced store-bought or in restaurants. We know we've succeeded when a young cook not only gets their first homemade pasta sauce on the table for dinner but says they'll never buy the jarred stuff again.

In every sauce we teach are lessons on customizing flavor; whether it be in salting, spiciness, acidity, or garlic, getting a sauce "right" is about balance and, really, about what you like most.

tzatziki

½ small **cucumber** (3 to 4 ounces), peeled if skin is tough or waxy

½ teaspoon **kosher salt**

½ cup **plain Greek yogurt**

1 tablespoon **extra-virgin olive oil**

2 teaspoons chopped **fresh mint leaves**, plus more to taste

2 teaspoons chopped **fresh dill**, plus more to taste

2 teaspoons **freshly squeezed lemon juice**, plus more to taste

1 teaspoon minced **garlic** (about 1 medium clove)

Kosher salt and **freshly ground black pepper** to taste

This creamy Greek cucumber-and-herb yogurt sauce is our go-to with grilled meats, spiced vegetable kebabs, and other rich foods that benefit from a cooling counterpoint. Go ahead and put a big dollop on your plate as a dip for your food, or even just for bread.

It's also a great lesson in salting vegetables (in this case, the grated cucumber) to make the sauce extra flavorful. The salt draws out excess water from the cucumber that would otherwise dilute the sauce, and we pour it off before mixing the cucumber into the yogurt.

1. Using the large holes of a box grater, grate the cucumber into a colander or fine-mesh strainer set over a medium mixing bowl. Toss with the salt. Leave it in the colander for about 5 minutes, then press the grated cucumber against the colander to release the excess moisture. Squeeze the cucumber in your fists to remove any remaining moisture. Discard the water from the bowl and place the cucumber flesh in the bowl.

2. Add the yogurt, olive oil, mint, dill, lemon juice, and garlic to the bowl and stir to blend. Let the mixture rest for 5 minutes to allow the flavors to come together. Season with salt and pepper.

3. As with all sauces, season it to taste with a little more herbs, lemon juice, salt, and pepper, if needed, just before serving.

4. Serve immediately.

romesco

2 large **garlic cloves**

½ cup chopped canned or jarred **roasted red peppers** or **pimientos**, drained

⅓ cup diced ripe or canned **tomatoes**, or ¼ cup canned **crushed tomatoes** or **tomato puree**

⅓ cup slivered **almonds** (you can substitute walnuts), toasted (see page 280)

2 tablespoons chopped **fresh flat-leaf parsley**

1 teaspoon **smoked paprika**

1 teaspoon **red wine vinegar** or **sherry vinegar**

⅓ cup **extra-virgin olive oil**

Kosher salt and **freshly ground black pepper** to taste

This Spanish pureed red pepper sauce spiked with garlic and toasted almonds is traditionally made in the spring to eat with grilled leeks.

We make it year-round and serve it every which way: it goes on platters with roasted vegetables, but it's also wonderful slathered on toasted bread, passed alongside grilled meats, and dolloped into frittatas. It's *that* good.

Making romesco allows us to break out our blender or food processor and teach students how to use them, both to puree the ingredients and to emulsify the sauce by slowly streaming in olive oil.

1. In a food processor or blender, combine the garlic, roasted peppers, tomatoes, almonds, parsley, paprika, and vinegar. Pulse (turn the machine on and off in short bursts) until a chunky sauce forms.

2. With the food processor on low speed, gradually add the oil in a slow, steady stream. The sauce will look creamier as the oil combines and emulsifies. (You can leave the romesco chunky or process it until totally smooth; we like it both ways!) Season with some salt and pepper, then turn off the motor. Taste for seasoning and adjust with more salt and pepper as needed. Buzz to combine and taste again.

3. Serve immediately or transfer to an airtight container and store in the refrigerator for up to 5 days. Allow to come to room temperature before serving.

salsa fresca

1 pound **vine-ripened tomatoes**, chopped, or 1 can (14 to 16 ounces) **diced tomatoes**, drained

1 small **red onion**, finely chopped (about 1 cup)

1 **jalapeño pepper**, seeded and chopped (optional)

¼ cup chopped **fresh cilantro leaves**

2 teaspoons minced **garlic** (about 2 medium cloves)

Juice of 1 to 2 **limes** to taste

Kosher salt to taste

Salsa fresca is best made with fresh, ripe in-season tomatoes, but when tomatoes are not at their peak, the lime juice should help punch up the flavor. In the middle of winter when there are no fresh tomatoes, we satiate those salsa cravings by making this recipe with canned tomatoes.

In a medium bowl, mix together the tomatoes, red onion, jalapeño (if using), cilantro, and garlic. Season to taste with the lime juice and salt.

classic guacamole

½ small **red onion**, chopped (about ½ cup)

1 **jalapeño pepper**, chopped (optional; seeds removed if you want less heat)

2 ripe **Hass avocados**, halved and pitted (see below)

2 tablespoons chopped **fresh cilantro leaves**

1 tablespoon **freshly squeezed lime juice**, or to taste

½ teaspoon **kosher salt**, or to taste

Since every amount of every ingredient in guacamole is about balancing flavor, the amounts here are merely suggestions.

Our seasoning mantra is "You can always add more, but you can't take it out," so we encourage you to taste (just a little, and always with a new, clean spoon!) as you go. Start with a small amount of salt and lime juice, then increase as desired. See how much the salt and lime make the whole thing pop? If you want more, add just a little bit, mix, taste, and see if you want even more than that!

In a mixing bowl (or, if you have one, using a molcajete, which is like a mortar and pestle but made from volcanic rock), mash the onion and jalapeño (if using) with a wooden spoon or fork to a chunky paste. Scoop the flesh from the avocados into the bowl, add the cilantro, and stir to combine. Season with the lime juice and salt.

how to choose and cut an avocado

Most avocados at grocery stores are not ready to eat; they are picked while still unripe. So when you want to make guacamole, make sure your avocados have a day or two to ripen first. A perfectly ripe avocado is firm but yields slightly to pressure, but won't feel mushy, and the tiny piece of stem at the top will flick off easily. You may luck out at the store and find a ripe one, but otherwise, let the avocado sit on your counter for a couple days and test it to determine when it's ready for showtime!

STEP 1: Halve the avocado. Using a chef's knife, cut into the side of the avocado until you feel resistance from the pit. Rotate the avocado on the knife until you've made a full circle. Remove the knife and use your hands to twist the two avocado halves and pull them apart.

STEP 2: Hit the pit. To remove the pit, protect your hand with a kitchen towel and hold the avocado pit-side up in the palm of your hand. Carefully give the pit a gentle whack with the knife, so that it sticks into the pit. Twist the knife and lift the pit out of the avocado. Cover your hand with a towel or oven mitt to protect it, then grab the pit and pull it off the blade.

STEP 3: Remove the flesh. Use the tip of your knife to score the avocado flesh (press through until you feel resistance from the skin) into strips or cubes, then use a spoon to scoop out the presliced or diced avocado!

how to fix a "broken" mayo

A mayonnaise "breaks" (meaning the ingredients separate, looking almost curdled) when the mixture isn't properly emulsified, and it happens to all of us! It usually happens when the oil is poured in too quickly. Mayonnaise takes time; you really have to be patient when whisking the oil into the yolks.

To fix it, you need one more egg yolk. Place the yolk in a clean bowl, then very gradually whisk the broken mayo into the yolk, starting with a small spoonful and adding a bit more after it's fully incorporated. Whisk constantly as you gradually add the rest of the mayo.

If you don't have another egg yolk, you can try the same thing with a teaspoon or two of hot water in a clean bowl, slowly adding and whisking in a bit of the mayonnaise at a time. This method produces a slightly thinner sauce.

mayonnaise and aioli

1 large **garlic clove** (optional; for making aioli)

Pinch of **kosher salt**, plus more to taste

1 large **pasteurized egg yolk**, at room temperature

2 teaspoons **freshly squeezed lemon juice**

½ teaspoon **Dijon mustard**

¼ cup plus 2 tablespoons **extra-virgin olive oil**

¼ cup plus 2 tablespoons **neutral oil**, such as vegetable or grapeseed oil

A fun part of the journey to becoming a good cook is learning to make something people are used to buying at the store. Making mayo gets extra fun when we bump up the fanciness level and ask, "Have you ever heard of aioli?" And then the big reveal comes: It's just mayonnaise with garlic!

So this recipe is about learning to DIY a condiment-aisle favorite but also how the addition of one ingredient takes the recipe into a whole new zone. Physically it's a workout to emulsify these sauces, but we feel there is no better way to learn than to do it by hand, watching the oil and egg come together gradually. These sauces are great on everything from burgers and hot dogs to steamed artichokes and roasted vegetables.

1. If you're making aioli, mince the garlic, then sprinkle it with a pinch of salt right on the cutting board. Using the flat side of a chef's knife, mash it into a smooth paste.

2. Put a damp kitchen towel on the counter and place a large mixing bowl on it. (The towel helps keep the bowl from sliding around.) Add the egg yolk, lemon juice, and mustard and whisk until well combined.

3. If you're making mayonnaise, whisk in a pinch of salt (aioli will get its salt from the garlic paste).

4. In a measuring cup or bottle with a spout, combine the oils. While whisking continuously, very slowly pour the oil into the egg mixture. This might be good to do with a partner: One person pours very slowly while the other whisks quickly. Do this until you use all the oil and the mixture thickens and emulsifies into mayo! If making aioli, whisk in the garlic paste now.

5. Season to taste with salt. Serve immediately or transfer to an airtight container and store in the refrigerator for up to 3 days.

any-herb pesto

4 cups lightly packed **fresh herbs** or **greens** (see Note)

4 teaspoons minced **garlic** (about 4 medium cloves)

½ cup (about 2 ounces) grated **Parmesan cheese**

Zest and **juice** from 2 **lemons** (2 to 3 tablespoons juice)

⅔ cup **extra-virgin olive oil**

Kosher salt and **freshly ground black pepper** to taste

Crushed red pepper flakes to taste (optional)

NOTE: We recommend a mix of any of the following: fresh basil, parsley, mint, chives, dill, and fennel fronds (the frilly tops from a fennel bulb). You can also use minced baby greens, like spinach or kale, as well.

Pesto is an uncooked pasta sauce typically made from basil, olive oil, pine nuts, and Parmesan cheese. We like to take the traditional formula and mix it up with a wide range of herbs and/or greens, from basil or parsley to spinach or kale.

There are so many ways you can use pesto. We stir it into our Up-To-You Vegetable Soup (page 142) and serve it with roasted vegetables, and, of course, it's one of the best ways to sauce pasta, especially fresh pasta. You can also spread it on sandwiches or serve it with simply cooked chicken, pork, or seafood—it will make pretty much anything into a delicious meal.

We encourage you to taste and adjust the seasonings to your own preference. Some want more salt, some prefer less lemon. We like to chop the ingredients for this pesto by hand (the old-fashioned way!), because we're usually making small batches to use fresh, and the chopped version yields a looser, chunkier pesto. But you can use a food processor or blender instead.

1. In a large mixing bowl, combine the herbs, garlic, Parmesan, and lemon zest and juice. Using a wooden spoon, mash the ingredients to thoroughly combine. While stirring and mashing, slowly add the olive oil in a thin stream to form a chunky paste. Season with salt, black pepper, and red pepper flakes (if using) to taste.

2. Alternatively, this can be made in a food processor or blender by pureeing the herbs, garlic, Parmesan, and lemon zest and juice together. Then, with the motor running, slowly pour in the olive oil until the sauce comes together. Turn off the food processor or blender, season to taste, buzz to combine, and taste again.

3. Pesto will stay fresh in the refrigerator in an airtight container (press a piece of plastic wrap directly against the top of the pesto before putting on the lid) for about a week. You can also freeze it in a zip-top freezer bag, squeezing out the air, for up to 3 months. Sometimes the pesto darkens in storage, but this is just oxidation; it hasn't gone bad!

kale and toasted pepita winter pesto

3 to 4 cups tightly packed chopped **curly kale leaves**

3 or 4 medium **garlic cloves**

½ cup (about 2 ounces) grated **Parmesan cheese**

½ cup **pepitas**, lightly toasted (see page 280)

2 tablespoons **freshly squeezed lemon juice**

⅔ cup **extra-virgin olive oil**

1 teaspoon **kosher salt**, or to taste

Freshly ground black pepper to taste

> Make this in batches—it is a lot of kale! Try not to blend it into oblivion; a little texture is nice.

A truly seasonal winter recipe is not easy to come by in New York City, where we live. At some point, we get tired of potatoes and turnips and start craving the vibrant flavors of summer. Enter this completely adaptable, nut-free pesto. (We make it with pepitas—pumpkin seeds—instead of the traditional pine nuts.)

We love this rich, wintry sauce as written, but we encourage you to see this as a kind of formula that you can play with! Swap kale for basil when it's plentiful, or spinach . . . or even roasted broccoli! Pretty much anything green works. Skip the Parmesan cheese for dairy allergies, or add more if you love it, or use any grateable hard cheese. And sub another kind of nut or seed in place of the pepitas if pumpkin seeds aren't your thing. Soon you'll be making your own flavors, whatever season it is!

1. In a blender or food processor, pulse the kale, garlic, Parmesan, pepitas, and lemon juice until combined. Drizzle in the oil while the motor is running and blend until smooth.

2. Turn off the blender. Season with the salt and pepper and adjust as needed. Buzz to combine and taste again.

10 things to do with pesto

TOSS WITH YOUR FAVORITE PASTA. Try it with fresh pasta. Save a bit of the pasta cooking water to thin your pesto and create a sauce that will coat the noodles.

SPOON IT INTO SOUP. A big dollop of fresh pesto is a great addition to our Up-to-You Vegetable Soup (page 142).

USE IT TO SEASON ROASTED VEGETABLES. Toss zucchini, potatoes, mushrooms, and more veggies with pesto after roasting (see page 65).

PAIR IT WITH PROTEIN. Our Cheater's Porchetta (page 66) calls for slathering pork loin with fresh pesto, but also consider pairing pesto with your favorite roasted chicken, steak, or fish.

USE IT AS A SANDWICH SPREAD. Combine it with fresh mozzarella and some ripe tomatoes for a summer caprese sandwich.

DOLLOP IT ON YOUR PIZZA. Swap it in for (or add it to) a tomato-based pizza sauce the next time you make Sheet Pan Pizzas (page 204).

FILL A CREPE. Make a batch of crepes (see page 55) and fill with pesto, salty cheese, and your favorite sautéed vegetables (we love mushrooms!).

SHAKE IT INTO DRESSING. We love adding a few spoonfuls of pesto to our Customizable Vinaigrette (page 43) for some extra herby flavor.

WHISK IT INTO MAYO. Make a quick dip or spread by whisking some pesto with mayonnaise (see page 107).

MAKE A COMPOUND BUTTER. Mix and mash pesto with some softened butter to use in a pan sauce (see page 112) or spread on fresh-baked bread or biscuits.

pan sauces and mounting with butter

Some of the simplest techniques we teach students are pro moves that define experienced cooks. The ability to make a delicious pan sauce to serve with seared meat or fish is one of them. Compared to gravy, which is thickened with flour, a pan sauce requires not much more than some minced aromatics, like shallot or garlic, fresh herbs, and liquid to unlock all the flavorful browned bits at the bottom of the pan. Finish things off with a knob of butter to add a glossy, rich sheen to your sauce, then drizzle it over your sliced steak, pork chop, or seared salmon for a restaurant-worthy meal.

FOR THE COMPOUND BUTTER

2 tablespoons **butter**, at room temperature

1 tablespoon minced **shallot**

2 teaspoons minced **garlic** (about 2 medium cloves)

1 to 2 teaspoons chopped **fresh herbs**, such as parsley, rosemary, thyme, or tarragon

FOR THE SAUCE

1 cup **vegetable**, **chicken**, or **beef stock**, store-bought or homemade (see page 264 or 242)

Kosher salt and **freshly ground black pepper** to taste

1. **Make the compound butter:** In a mixing bowl, mash the butter with the shallot, garlic, and herbs. Adjust the quantities to taste. Set aside.

2. **Make the sauce:** After removing seared meat or fish from the pan, turn the heat to medium-low. Pour in the stock and use a wooden spoon to scrape up any browned bits stuck to the bottom of the pan. Add the compound butter and whisk until melted. Turn the heat to medium and cook, stirring, until the sauce comes to a simmer and thickens slightly. Season with salt and pepper and serve at once.

béchamel sauce

2¼ cups **whole milk**

3 tablespoons **butter**

3 tablespoons **all-purpose flour** (or a gluten-free substitute, such as Bob's Red Mill 1:1)

Pinch of **freshly grated nutmeg**

Kosher salt and **freshly ground black pepper** to taste

> Extra credit! Add melted cheese to béchamel and it becomes another sauce, called Mornay sauce.

One of the best ways of learning how to cook—and one of the joys of cooking!—is knowing the building block recipes you can use to pull together lots of different dishes from scratch.

Béchamel, one of the classic "mother sauces" in traditional French cooking, is one of those recipes. You might know it or one of its close relatives as "white sauce" or "cream gravy," but it's a simple, creamy sauce made by whisking together a flour-and-butter mixture called a roux and cooking it with milk until thickened. Melt cheese into it, and it's the base for our Classic Mac and Cheese with Roasted Broccoli (page 122). Or you can use it to coat vegetables in a gratin or to fill arancini (rice balls) or crepes. You can flavor it with cheese, herbs, and tomatoes . . . What will *you* do with it?

1. Warm the milk in a saucepan over medium-low heat until warm to the touch but not superhot.

2. In a heavy-bottomed saucepan over medium-low heat, melt the butter. Whisk in the flour and cook, whisking constantly, until a paste forms, taking care to not let it brown, about 2 minutes. This is your roux.

3. Continuing to stir or whisk, add a little of the warm milk so it can mix evenly with the roux. Add more milk, a little at a time, still whisking, until the mix looks well combined. Keep stirring as the mixture thickens and comes to a boil.

4. Add the nutmeg and salt and pepper. Lower the heat and cook, stirring, for 2 to 3 minutes more. Remove from the heat.

5. Use immediately, or cool for later use: cover it with plastic wrap or wax paper or pour a thin layer of milk over it to prevent a skin from forming. Reheat the sauce in a saucepan over low heat, stirring.

5

pasta

For many young cooks, pasta is their first toe-dip into the world of cooking, often because it's their number one favorite food on the planet. Pasta with pesto or marinara? Yes, please! Bring it on! Enthusiasm aside, there are so many great culinary lessons to be learned when working with pasta, whether it's boiling store-bought pasta just right or making silky egg noodles from scratch (see page 118). Pasta is the ultimate canvas for our creativity in the kitchen, and many dishes, like our Up-to-You Seasonal Pasta (page 124) or Up-to-You Lasagna (page 128), are infinitely customizable based on our cravings and the ingredients we have on hand. Others have tried-and-true lessons baked in: if you know how to make Classic Mac and Cheese with Roasted Broccoli (page 122), you can apply the same formula to whatever shape of pasta, type of cheese, and vegetable you like. That's the end goal of all the recipes in this book: to inspire cooks to embrace them, understand them, and ultimately tweak them to be their own.

just pasta

2 to 3 tablespoons
kosher salt

1 pound **dry pasta** or **Fresh Pasta** (page 118)

save that pasta water

Don't pour that pasta water down the drain! Seasoned with salt and loaded with starch, the water you cook your pasta in is a valuable ingredient for pulling your dish together. It has some pasta flavor, and the starch helps the sauce stick to the noodles.

Use it warm to temper eggs and build the base sauce for Pasta alla Carbonara (page 126), or drizzle a bit into the pot with Basic Marinara Sauce (page 117) to thin the sauce and help it cling to your noodles. Adding a splash of hot pasta water is also a great way to reheat a pasta dish before serving.

We love our pasta cooked al dente, which means until it's tender but still has a nice amount of chewiness. Cooking it less results in firmer pasta, and more means softer pasta. This is just the basic method for cooking either dry pasta out of a box or fresh pasta, both store-bought or, hopefully, homemade! After cooking your pasta this way, it's ready to be dressed up with any of the sauces in this chapter—or any one you dream up.

1. Fill a large pot with water (4 to 6 quarts) and add the salt. Bring to a boil over high heat. (Use a stockpot, especially if you're cooking dry long-strand pastas like spaghetti, to ensure that the pasta will fully submerge in the water.) If you're using dry pasta, cook according to the package instructions for al dente, or 1 minute shy of the suggested cooking time. For fresh pasta, the cook time will be 1 to 3 minutes, depending on the pasta shape. (When the noodles float to the top and are tender but slightly firm, they are ready.)

2. For some pasta sauce recipes, you may want to reserve a cup of the pasta cooking water to incorporate into the sauce, so check your sauce recipe before draining the pasta water.

3. In most cases, the sauce should be hot in a separate pan, and you will combine the hot pasta with the hot sauce and serve right away.

basic marinara sauce

3 tablespoons **extra-virgin olive oil**

2 tablespoons minced **garlic** (6 to 8 medium cloves)

1 large can (28 ounces) **plum tomatoes** (San Marzano variety, if possible), or 2 pounds **fresh tomatoes**, chopped

¼ teaspoon **kosher salt**, plus more to taste

A few cracks of **freshly ground black pepper**, plus more to taste

Crushed red pepper flakes (optional)

10 **fresh basil leaves**, thinly sliced

1 pound **dry pasta**, or 24 ounces **Fresh Pasta** (page 118), cooked

Freshly grated **Parmesan cheese** to taste

Chopped **fresh flat-leaf parsley** to taste

This classic Italian tomato sauce couldn't be simpler—or more useful and versatile!

While it's sweet and fragrant with basil just as is, you can get creative with it and also add olives, capers, or other seasonings. And if you'd like to bulk it up with vegetables, feel free to add mushrooms, broccoli, or zucchini and cook your sauce for 10 to 15 minutes more, until the vegetables soften and their flavors meld with the sauce. We make marinara year-round with canned whole tomatoes (we seek out the sweeter, denser San Marzano varieties from Italy), but when tomatoes are in season, we always reach for fresh.

1. In a large saucepan, heat the olive oil over medium heat. Add the garlic and sauté for 1 minute, stirring constantly with a wooden spoon. Add the tomatoes and their juices and bring the mixture to a boil. Lower the heat to maintain a simmer and season with the salt, black pepper, and red pepper flakes (if using).

2. Break up the tomatoes with the back of a spoon and cook, stirring frequently, until thickened, about 15 minutes. Stir in the basil and cook for another few minutes, until the basil is wilted. Taste for seasoning and add more salt, black pepper, and red pepper flakes, if desired.

3. To serve, toss the cooked pasta with the sauce in the saucepan or in a large mixing bowl, adding a bit of reserved pasta cooking water if the marinara needs to be saucier.

4. Sprinkle with Parmesan and parsley and serve.

fresh pasta

*makes about 16 ounces

2 cups **all-purpose flour** (or a gluten-free substitute, such as Bob's Red Mill 1:1), plus more for dusting

4 large **eggs**

Kosher salt, for the water

Your favorite sauce, for serving

SPECIAL EQUIPMENT

Rolling pin or glass bottle with straight sides

Pasta machine (optional)

We all love dried pasta out of a box, but if you ask us—and our students—few recipes are more fun to make than fresh pasta dough. It might sound hard, but it's not—promise!

Marinara, pesto, and carbonara are all the more special when tossed with fresh pasta. What we love about this recipe is that it's made entirely by hand—even the rolling out and cutting of the noodles—so you get a real sense of the texture of the dough. It's a messy process, and your fingers will be entirely covered with a pasty, wet dough, but that's part of the fun!

You can opt to roll out and cut the dough using a pasta maker, but we prefer doing it by hand, nonna-style. In fact, one of our instructors, Sara, who hails from northeastern Italy (where fresh pasta is a specialty), says her grandmother rolls it thin enough that she can see the church steeple through it when she holds it up.

As with any dish where eggs are the star ingredient, go for the best quality you can find—we always seek out free-range farm-fresh eggs with bright yellow-orange yolks.

1. Mound the flour into a pile on a clean work surface. Use your fingers to make a deep well in the center of the flour. Crack one of the eggs into the well and, using a fork, gently whisk the egg, pulling in bits of flour as you go. Once there is more room in the well, add the second egg and continue to whisk and gradually pull in more flour. Repeat with the remaining 2 eggs.

2. Once it becomes difficult to mix with the fork, use your hands to knead the dough, pushing and pressing, until the mixture forms a cohesive ball and is no longer sticky. Wrap the dough tightly with plastic wrap and let it rest at room temperature for 20 to 30 minutes.

3. Bring a large pot of heavily salted water (it should taste like the ocean) to a boil over high heat. (If it comes to a boil before you are ready to cook the pasta, lower the heat.)

(RECIPE CONTINUES)

4. Unwrap the dough and cut it into 4 equal portions. Scatter a few pinches of flour evenly over your work surface until it looks like it's lightly dusted with snow. Place a portion of the dough on the work surface and rewrap the remaining portions.

5. Using a rolling pin or a glass bottle, roll it out into a long sheet of pasta, ideally 8 inches wide × 18 inches long and 1 millimeter thick. (You should almost be able to see through it, but not quite.)

6. Alternatively, if you have a pasta machine, turn the dial to the widest setting and use the crank to roll the pasta through it twice. Then turn the dial down 2 sizes and repeat. Keep doing this, going down in size, until the pasta is very thin (about 1 millimeter thick).

7. From the short end, roll the sheet of pasta into a log, dusting it with flour as needed to prevent the sides from sticking together, and slice it into noodles of your desired width. Flour another work surface and place the noodles on it. Coil them into little nests and dust them lightly with flour until you're ready to cook them; they'll keep in the refrigerator for up to 2 days. Repeat with the remaining portions of dough.

8. When you're ready to cook, turn the heat to high and let the water come back to a full, roiling boil, if necessary. Cook the noodles, a batch or two at a time, for 2 to 3 minutes, until they float to the top. Drain, reserving a cup of the cooking water, and toss the pasta in a hot pan with your favorite sauce (use a little of the reserved water, if necessary, to thin it out). Serve immediately.

summery one-pot mac and cheese

Kosher salt to taste

1 pound **dry short-cut pasta**, such as rigatoni, macaroni, penne, or cavatappi

3 tablespoons **extra-virgin olive oil**

2 teaspoons minced **garlic** (about 2 medium cloves)

1 cup (8 ounces) **whole-milk ricotta cheese**

1 cup (3 to 4 ounces) freshly grated **Parmesan cheese**

1 cup lightly packed **fresh basil leaves**, sliced into very thin strips (chiffonade)

1 tablespoon **freshly grated lemon zest** (from 1 small lemon)

¼ cup **freshly squeezed lemon juice**

A few cracks of **freshly ground black pepper**

Crushed red pepper flakes (optional)

Here's a classic way to get dinner done in one pot without a lot of fuss but with a lot of flexibility. Instead of making a full-on cheese sauce, we like to "sauce" the mac with ricotta cheese mixed with Parmesan and lots of basil ribbons. It comes out creamy but light—perfect for warm weather! You can also add another cheese, like fontina, asiago, or Gouda, for a sharper flavor. The real secret here is adding a half cup or so of starchy water reserved from cooking the pasta; the heat helps melt the cheese and the starch in the liquid gives the sauce a little heft.

1. Bring a large pot of heavily salted water (it should taste like the ocean) to a boil over high heat. Add the pasta and cook to a firm al dente, about 2 minutes shy of the package directions. Using a mug, scoop out and reserve about ½ cup of the pasta water. Drain the pasta in a colander and set it aside.

2. Work quickly! Set the same pot over medium heat, add the olive oil and garlic, and sauté until the garlic softens but does not brown, about 1 minute. Add the reserved pasta cooking water, the ricotta, and the Parmesan and stir until the cheeses melt.

3. Stir in the pasta, tossing well to coat. Add the basil, lemon zest, and lemon juice and season to taste with salt, black pepper, and a pinch of red pepper flakes (if using). Remove from the heat and serve immediately.

classic mac and cheese
with roasted broccoli

This is the ultimate comfort food dish, and once kids learn to make it from scratch, they'll never ask for the boxed version again. The creamy base is topped with seasoned bread crumbs to add crunch and a toasty flavor. So many dishes are more delicious with a little something crunchy on top!

And since we think everything is better with a bit of green, we toss in roasted broccoli. You can swap it with another vegetable; just make sure to cook whatever you're adding first so it doesn't seep liquid into the cheese sauce as it's baking in the oven.

1 pound **fresh** or **frozen broccoli florets**, cut into bite-size pieces

2 tablespoons **extra-virgin olive oil**

1½ teaspoons **kosher salt**, plus more as needed

½ teaspoon **freshly ground black pepper**, plus more as needed

12 ounces **dry elbow macaroni**

4 tablespoons (½ stick) **butter**, cubed

4 tablespoons **all-purpose flour** (or a gluten-free substitute, such as Bob's Red Mill 1:1)

2 cups **whole milk**, warmed

¼ teaspoon **freshly grated nutmeg**

Pinch of **dry mustard**

2½ cups (10 ounces) shredded **Cheddar cheese**

½ cup **panko bread crumbs** (optional)

2 tablespoons **fresh thyme leaves**

1. Preheat the oven to 425°F. On a large sheet pan, toss the broccoli with the oil, ½ teaspoon of the salt, and ¼ teaspoon of the pepper. Spread the broccoli out into a single layer. Roast in the oven, until browned in spots, 10 to 15 minutes.

2. Meanwhile, bring a large pot of heavily salted water (it should taste like the ocean) to a boil over high heat. Cook the macaroni until al dente, about a minute shy of the package instructions. Drain well.

3. In a large skillet, melt the butter over medium heat. Sprinkle the flour over the butter and whisk for 1 minute, until a paste forms and the mixture just begins to bubble. Be careful not to let the paste brown!

4. Gradually whisk in the warmed milk and, as soon as the mixture thickens, decrease the heat to medium-low. Whisk in ½ teaspoon of the salt, the remaining ¼ teaspoon pepper, the nutmeg, and the dry mustard. Stir in the cheese; when fully melted, remove from the heat, add the cooked macaroni and roasted broccoli, and stir well to combine. (It will look like too much sauce, but the macaroni will soak up the sauce as it continues to cook in the oven.) Transfer the macaroni mixture to a 9 × 13-inch baking dish, spreading it out evenly.

5. In a small bowl, combine the panko (if using), thyme, remaining ½ teaspoon salt, and pepper to taste. Sprinkle this evenly over the macaroni mixture. Bake uncovered until the sauce is bubbly on the sides and the panko is browned and crispy on top, about 15 minutes.

up-to-you seasonal pasta

While we're allergic to competitive cooking shows that turn the kitchen into a sports arena, we do love to challenge ourselves—and our students—to be creative with this improvisational seasonal cooking exercise. The mission: To create a beautiful peak-of-season pasta sauce with whatever ingredients you have on hand or discover at the market.

When we do our summer camps in Brooklyn, we go to the market around the corner and give each cooking group $10 to buy their ingredients and design their dish. Some splurge on special ingredients, like sugar snap peas or heirloom tomatoes; others buy a bit of sausage or bacon to season their sauce. While each group's pasta is different from the next, they all follow the same basic formula we teach here with this recipe. We can't wait to see what you create!

1 pound **dry short-cut pasta**, such as penne, farfalle, fusilli, or ziti

2 tablespoons **extra-virgin olive oil**, plus more as needed

1 medium **yellow** or **red onion**, thinly sliced

2 to 3 cups chopped, diced, or sliced mixed **fresh sturdy vegetables** and/or **leafy greens** (see pairing ideas opposite)

1 teaspoon minced **garlic** (about 1 medium clove)

1½ cups chopped **fresh tomatoes**, or 1 can (14 to 16 ounces) **diced**, **crushed**, or **whole peeled tomatoes** (optional)

½ teaspoon **kosher salt**, plus more as needed

A few cracks of **freshly ground black pepper**

½ cup packed chopped mixed **fresh tender herbs** (we like basil and parsley)

Large pinch of **crushed red pepper flakes** (optional)

½ cup grated or crumbled **cheese**, such as Parmesan, Grana Padano, ricotta salata, or goat cheese

1. Bring a large pot of heavily salted water (it should taste like the ocean) to a boil over high heat. Add the pasta and cook until very al dente (a few minutes shy of the package instructions). Using a large measuring cup or a mug, scoop out 1 cup of the pasta water and reserve. Drain the pasta, put it in a large bowl, toss with a generous drizzle of olive oil, and set aside.

2. Heat the olive oil in the pasta pot over medium heat. Add the onion and cook, stirring often, until translucent, about 5 minutes.

3. Add any sturdy vegetables, and cook, stirring, until softened, 3 to 10 minutes, depending on the vegetables. Add the garlic and cook, stirring, until aromatic, about 1 minute. Add the tomatoes (if using) or add more olive oil or a bit of the reserved pasta water.

4. Cover and cook until a sauce forms and the flavors come together, about 5 minutes. Add any leafy greens (if using) and cook until wilted. Season with the salt and black pepper. Stir in the fresh herbs and red pepper flakes (if using), then remove from the heat.

OPTIONAL GARNISHES

Crumbled **cooked bacon**, **prosciutto**, chopped **scallions**, additional chopped **fresh herbs, ricotta cheese**, crumbled **blue cheese, lemon zest**, toasted **bread crumbs**, toasted **nuts**

seasonal pasta pairing ideas

- Tomatoes, zucchini or yellow squash, fresh herbs, ricotta

- Tomatoes, broccoli, onions, grated Parmesan cheese

- Corn kernels, snap peas, scallions, fresh basil or mint, goat cheese

- Tomatoes, eggplant, bell peppers, basil, onions

- Fennel, spinach, lemon zest

- Broccoli, red peppers, onions

5. Add the cooked pasta to the vegetable sauce, stir, and add more pasta water if the sauce is too dry: it should coat the pasta without being too soupy. Heat over medium heat, stirring and adding a little more pasta water if the sauce gets dry. After about a minute, test one of the pieces of pasta. If it is cooked through without being mushy, remove the pot from the heat. Otherwise, keep cooking and adding pasta water, if necessary. Add the grated cheese and adjust the seasonings to taste. Serve immediately, topped with optional garnishes.

pasta alla carbonara

2 tablespoons **extra-virgin olive oil**

2 **garlic cloves**, smashed

6 ounces **pancetta** or **bacon**, cut into thin strips (optional; for a vegetarian version, substitute 8 ounces thinly sliced mushrooms)

1 pound **dry long-strand pasta**, such as bucatini or spaghetti

½ cup (about 2 ounces) grated **Parmesan cheese**, plus more for topping

2 large **eggs**

1 large **egg yolk**

Kosher salt and **freshly ground black pepper** to taste

2 tablespoons finely chopped **fresh flat-leaf parsley**, for garnish

Watching kids eat pasta alla carbonara for the first time is like watching them meet a new best friend. Watching them make it is even more fun. A simple concoction of eggs and Parmesan that's "cooked" with the heat of the warm pasta water, it comes together as a creamy, luxurious, bacon-y, cheesy sauce. The first step—sweating the garlic in oil, then discarding the clove—is a great lesson in infusing flavor without running the risk of burning the garlic and making the sauce bitter. The pancetta, which is more Italian and not smoked like bacon, or bacon gives it a deep flavor, but vegetarians can swap in umami-rich mushrooms. Either way, you can be sure the pasta bowl will be empty by the time dinner is done!

1. Bring a large pot of heavily salted water (it should taste like the ocean) to a boil over high heat.

2. Meanwhile, in a large skillet or Dutch oven, heat the oil over medium heat. Add the garlic and cook until golden brown and aromatic, about 1 minute. Remove and discard the garlic.

3. Add the pancetta and cook until crisp (alternatively, add the mushrooms and cook until they are soft and all the water they have released has cooked away, about 4 minutes). Remove from the heat. Using a slotted spoon, transfer the pancetta (or mushrooms) to a paper towel–lined plate. (If using pancetta, pour out and reserve the drippings for another use.)

4. Cook the pasta in the boiling water until al dente (about 1 minute less than the package instructions). Using a mug, scoop out and reserve about ¼ cup of the cooking water, then drain the pasta.

5. In a large bowl, whisk together the Parmesan, eggs, and egg yolk until smooth. Gradually whisk in the reserved pasta water (it should still be hot) to form a glossy sauce, then toss it with the cooked pasta and pancetta (or mushrooms). Season with salt and lots of pepper and top with parsley and more Parmesan.

up-to-you lasagna

8 ounces **spinach**, fresh and blanched (see page 282) or frozen and thawed, wrung dry, and chopped

3 cups (12 ounces) shredded **low-moisture mozzarella cheese**

¾ cup (about 7 ounces) **whole-milk ricotta cheese**

1 cup (about 3 ounces) freshly grated **Pecorino Romano** or **Parmesan cheese**

2 large **eggs**

2½ teaspoons **kosher salt**

2 teaspoons **freshly ground black pepper**, plus a few more cracks

2 tablespoons **extra-virgin olive oil**

1 pound **wild** or **cremini mushrooms**, thinly sliced

1 tablespoon minced **garlic** (about 3 medium cloves)

2 tablespoons chopped **fresh flat-leaf parsley**

5 cups **marinara sauce**, store-bought or homemade (see page 117), or canned **crushed tomatoes**

12 ounces **uncooked dry lasagna noodles**

Instead of no-boil lasagna noodles, we use regular uncooked noodles because they keep their shape and don't get mushy!

Lasagna is one of our favorite dishes because it can be completely different every time we make it. We've cooked this recipe with gluten-free, egg-free, and dairy-free kids, and also with kids who didn't want greens (of course we throw some in for that healthy vibe) or who wanted only mushrooms. It can be made with meat or without.

The other thing we love about it is that it allows us to work on our kitchen math and spatial relations as we divide ingredients between the layers (you have to portion out each element when building the lasagna layers). The best news is that this recipe is also forgiving, and if you run out of one of the layers before getting to the top, guess what? You'll still get lasagna! Perhaps the most heart-warming experiences we've had teaching kids to prepare lasagna is hearing how many students have made the dish for a friend or loved one as an offering of warmth and love.

1. Preheat the oven to 350°F.

2. In a large bowl, thoroughly mix the spinach, 2 cups of the mozzarella, the ricotta, ⅔ cup of the Parmesan, and the eggs; season with 2 teaspoons of the salt and 1 teaspoon of the pepper.

3. In a large skillet, heat the olive oil over high heat. Scatter the mushrooms in a single layer across the pan. Let the mushrooms sit in the pan undisturbed for about 30 seconds, then stir until they begin to sweat and shrink, about 2 minutes. Lower the heat to medium, add the garlic, parsley, and remaining ½ teaspoon salt and 1 teaspoon pepper, and cook until the mushrooms collapse and become soft, about 3 minutes. Transfer the mushrooms to a small plate.

4. In a 9 × 13-inch baking dish, spoon a thick layer of sauce (about 1 cup) over the bottom and cover it with a layer of uncooked noodles. Spread a third of the cheese mixture (about ¾ cup) on top of the noodles, evenly scatter a third of the mushrooms (about ½ cup), then top with a third of the remaining sauce (about 1 cup). Repeat to make two more layers of noodles, cheese, mushrooms, then sauce.

5. Add the final layer of noodles and top with the remaining sauce (about 1 cup). Sprinkle the remaining 1 cup mozzarella and ⅓ cup Parmesan across the top. Season with a few cracks of pepper.

6. Cover the baking dish tightly with foil and bake for 40 to 50 minutes, until the noodles are tender. (You will have crispy bits on the edges, so test a noodle toward the middle of the pan for doneness.) Remove the foil and cook for another 5 to 7 minutes to brown the cheese on top. Let the lasagna cool for at least 10 minutes before slicing and serving.

make it your own!

Don't love mushrooms? Or want to add more filling? Swap or add another vegetable or protein? Just make sure you precook raw vegetables so they don't add excess moisture to your lasagna. Here are a few swaps and additions we love!

- Sliced and sautéed zucchini or summer squash
- Thinly sliced, salted, and roasted eggplant
- Blanched broccoli florets
- Chopped roasted red peppers
- Caramelized onions
- Cooked ground sausage, turkey, or beef
- Thinly sliced salami

6

casseroles

One of the hardest working and most beloved vessels in our kitchen is the humble casserole dish. Whether it's a 9 × 13-inch Pyrex number or a vintage oval Le Creuset that's a family heirloom—or even the disposable aluminum pans we bring to potlucks—it's made for meals that you can prepare ahead and store in the fridge or freezer, pop in the oven to cook, and bring to the table to feed a crowd.

The recipes in this chapter couldn't be more different from one another, but the one thing that unites them all is that they're comforting one-dish meals—which also makes them great choices if you're cooking for a friend or neighbor in need or donating to a local charity. When we make a casserole at home, whether it's our Loaded Enchiladas (page 135) or Shepherd's Pie (page 132), we serve it with nothing more than a simple green salad, and dinner is done!

shepherd's pie
with potato-parsnip mash

On a cold winter night, we can't think of anything cozier than this shepherd's pie: a casserole of seasoned ground meat topped with fluffy potatoes (in this case with a secret ingredient for a touch of sweetness: parsnips!). A classic British dish that originated as a way to stretch leftovers from a Sunday roast, it makes a hearty one-dish meal that will warm you up from the inside.

It's also packed with some essential culinary lessons: evenly dicing vegetables to create a flavorful base called mirepoix (see page 283), browning and seasoning meat (or swap in cooked lentils for a delicious vegetarian version!), and creating a roux-thickened sauce to hold it all together.

FOR THE POTATO-PARSNIP MASH

2 pounds **russet potatoes**, peeled and cut into 1-inch pieces

1 pound **parsnips**, peeled and cut into 1-inch pieces

4 tablespoons (½ stick) **butter**, melted

Pinch of **freshly grated nutmeg**

½ cup **whole milk**

Kosher salt

1. Preheat the oven to 375°F.

2. **Make the potato-parsnip mash:** Rinse the cut potatoes in a colander until the water runs clear (this removes excess starch that can make the mashed potatoes gummy). Fill a large stockpot with heavily salted water (it should taste like the ocean) and add the potatoes and the parsnips.

FOR THE FILLING

2 tablespoons **extra-virgin olive oil**

1 medium **yellow onion**, diced

2 ribs **celery**, diced

1 large **carrot**, peeled and diced

4 teaspoons minced **garlic** (about 4 medium cloves)

1 pound **ground beef** or **lamb** (for a vegetarian version, substitute 4 cups cooked brown lentils)

2 tablespoons **all-purpose flour** (or a gluten-free substitute, such as Bob's Red Mill 1:1)

1 cup **chicken** or **vegetable stock**, store-bought or homemade (see page 262 or 264)

1 tablespoon **tomato paste**

1 tablespoon minced **fresh rosemary leaves**

1 tablespoon **fresh thyme leaves**

1 teaspoon **Worcestershire sauce**

1 cup **frozen peas**

Kosher salt and **freshly ground black pepper** to taste

¼ cup chopped **fresh flat-leaf parsley**, for garnish

3. Bring the water to a boil over high heat and cook until the potatoes and parsnips are tender, 15 to 20 minutes. (Test for doneness by pressing a piece against the side of the pot; it should easily break apart.)

4. Using a mug, scoop out and reserve about 1 cup of the cooking water, then drain the potatoes and parsnips and transfer them to a medium mixing bowl.

5. Add the butter and nutmeg to the potato-parsnip mixture. Using a masher or a fork, mash the potatoes and parsnips against the side of the bowl until chunky. Gradually add the milk, ¼ cup at a time, stirring and mashing until most of the lumps are gone and the mixture is fluffy and spreadable. Add some of the reserved cooking water, if needed. Season with salt and set aside.

6. **Make the filling:** In a large skillet or Dutch oven, heat the olive oil over medium heat. Add the onion and cook until soft and translucent, about 4 minutes. Add the celery, carrot, and garlic and cook, stirring occasionally, until the vegetables begin to soften, 4 to 5 minutes. If you're cooking with meat, add it now. Use a wooden spoon to mix it with the vegetables and to break up any large pieces, cooking until the meat has browned, 3 to 4 minutes.

7. Add the flour and stir until the meat and vegetables are fully coated, about 1 minute. Add a splash of the stock and use the wooden spoon to scrape up any browned bits stuck to the pan. Add the remaining stock, the tomato paste, rosemary, thyme, Worcestershire sauce, and peas (if cooking the vegetarian version, add the lentils now) and stir to combine. Reduce the heat to low and cook until the sauce thickens, about 5 minutes. Season with salt and pepper.

8. Transfer the filling to a 9 × 13-inch baking dish. Use a spoon or offset spatula to spread the potato-parsnip mash evenly over the top, making small peaks as you go. Top with pepper and bake for 30 minutes, until the sauce bubbles around the edges and the top starts to brown. (If you like a crispier top, place it under a broiler for a few minutes.) Let cool for 15 minutes before garnishing with parsley and serving.

cheesy cauliflower gratin

1 large head **cauliflower** (2½ to 3 pounds), florets and stems cut into bite-size pieces

2 cups **whole milk**

3 tablespoons **butter**

3 tablespoons **all-purpose flour** (or a gluten-free substitute, such as Bob's Red Mill 1:1)

1¼ cups (about 4 ounces) grated **Parmesan cheese** (see Note)

½ teaspoon **freshly grated nutmeg**

Kosher salt and **freshly ground black pepper** to taste

¼ cup **panko bread crumbs**

1 tablespoon **fresh thyme leaves**

> NOTE: If you prefer a cheesier, gooier version, you can substitute up to half the Parm with shredded Gruyère or mild white Cheddar cheese.

A gratin is just a fancy word for a casserole where the ingredients are baked in a creamy, often cheesy sauce. It's a great example of how to use a béchamel sauce (see page 113): tossed with cauliflower florets, spiked with nutmeg, and baked until the sauce is bubbly and the bread crumbs are golden brown and crisp on top.

This recipe is a good lesson in parcooking: We boil the cauliflower first to give it a jump start so the sauce doesn't overcook in the oven while the cauliflower is still getting tender. Parcooking allows every ingredient in the casserole to cook evenly and be ready at the same time.

This dish is so delicious that it's as worthy of a Thanksgiving side as it is a main-dish meal served with a salad. Either way, it can be made ahead, refrigerated, and then covered with the bread crumbs and baked right before serving. See the photograph on page 285!

1. Preheat the oven to 375°F.

2. Bring a large pot of heavily salted water (it should taste like the ocean) to a boil over high heat. Add the cauliflower and cook until just tender, about 5 minutes. Drain and set aside.

3. In a small saucepan, heat the milk over medium heat until small bubbles start to appear around the edges, then remove from the heat. In a large skillet with high sides, melt the butter over low heat. Whisk in the flour to form a paste and cook, whisking constantly, for 1 minute. Gradually whisk in the warm milk and bring to a simmer, then cook, whisking, until the sauce thickens, about 2 minutes.

4. Add 1 cup of the cheese and the nutmeg and whisk until the cheese is melted and the sauce is smooth. Remove from the heat. Season the sauce with salt and pepper, then add the cauliflower. Stir well to combine and transfer the mixture to a 9 × 13-inch (or 3- to 4-quart) casserole dish (alternatively, if your skillet is oven-safe, you can use that and wash one less dish!). Top the gratin with the remaining ¼ cup cheese, the bread crumbs, and the thyme and bake until bubbly along the edges and golden brown on top, about 15 minutes. Serve immediately.

loaded enchiladas

Ten 5- to 6-inch **corn tortillas**

4 tablespoons **olive oil**

1 large **yellow onion**, thinly sliced

2 tablespoons **all-purpose flour** (or a gluten-free substitute, such as Bob's Red Mill 1:1)

2 tablespoons **chili powder**

1 tablespoon **ground cumin**

½ teaspoon **dried oregano**

Pinch of **ground cinnamon**

¼ cup **tomato paste**

2 tablespoons **adobo sauce** (from a can of chipotle peppers in adobo; optional)

Kosher salt and **freshly ground black pepper** to taste

2 cups (8 ounces) shredded **Cheddar** and/or **Monterey Jack cheese**

1½ cups shredded **cooked chicken**, **pork**, or **beef** (optional)

1 cup canned or **cooked black beans** (see page 265), drained and rinsed (or 2 cups if not using meat)

¼ cup chopped **fresh cilantro leaves**, plus more for serving

TOPPINGS

Diced **onions, pickled jalapeños**, and **sour cream** or **plain Greek yogurt**

This classic Mexican one-dish meal is a cheesy, saucy favorite among our students and families. It's also a go-to when we're making meals to donate to shelters and community centers or to bring to neighbors or friends.

There are some fundamental cooking techniques baked into this recipe, like how to caramelize onions and making a roux-thickened sauce by toasting flour, spices, and tomato paste in fat and whisking in water. Feel free to replace the filling with leftover meat or vegetables.

1. Preheat the oven to 350°F. Stack the tortillas, wrap them in foil, and place in the oven to soften.

2. Heat 2 tablespoons of the olive oil in a large skillet over medium heat. Add the onion and cook, stirring often, until golden, 10 to 12 minutes. Transfer the onion to a large mixing bowl, leaving the oil in the skillet. Add the remaining 2 tablespoons oil to the skillet along with the flour and spices; whisk until aromatic, about 1 minute. Add the tomato paste and stir to combine, then whisk in 2½ cups water. Stir in the adobo sauce (if using). Simmer until the sauce thickens, stirring occasionally, about 5 minutes. Season with salt and pepper. Remove the sauce from the heat and set aside.

3. Add half the cheese and all the meat (if using), beans, and cilantro to the bowl with the onion. Add 1 cup of the enchilada sauce and stir to combine.

4. To assemble the enchiladas, spread ½ cup of the enchilada sauce over the bottom of a 9 × 13-inch baking dish. Remove the tortillas from the oven. On a cutting board, spoon a tablespoon of sauce onto a warm tortilla and spread it all over. Add a few tablespoons of filling in a long row across the center of the tortilla, then roll it up and place it seam-side down in the baking dish.

5. Repeat with the remaining tortillas, lining them up snug in the pan. Drizzle the remaining sauce on top, making sure to get it between each enchilada. Sprinkle with the remaining cheese and bake for 15 minutes, until the sauce is bubbly and the cheese is melted. Serve with the cilantro and all the toppings.

family-style chicken pot pie
with lattice crust

5 tablespoons **butter**

2 medium **yellow onions**, diced

2 medium **carrots**, peeled and diced

2 ribs **celery**, chopped

2 tablespoons minced **garlic** (about 6 medium cloves)

2 small or 1 medium **russet potatoes**, peeled and cut into ½-inch cubes

8 ounces **white button** or **cremini mushrooms**, sliced

2 tablespoons **fresh thyme leaves**

⅓ cup **all-purpose flour** (or gluten-free substitute, such as Bob's Red Mill 1:1), plus more for dusting

3½ cups **chicken** or **vegetable stock**, store-bought or homemade (see page 262 or 264)

Kosher salt and **freshly ground black pepper** to taste

3 cups chopped **cooked white** or **dark meat chicken** (see page 166 or use store-bought rotisserie chicken)

1 cup **frozen peas**

2 tablespoons chopped **fresh flat-leaf parsley**

One 10 × 15-inch sheet **frozen puff pastry**, thawed

This meal makes everyone happy: a casserole-size version of the classic comfort food of creamy chicken stew with a beautiful golden pastry crust. Take the time to learn how to dice all the vegetables the same size so they cook evenly. Sautéing onion, carrot, and celery (the combination is called mirepoix in French; see page 283) is a classic way to build a flavorful base for a dish. To that, we add flour to make a light-colored roux that thickens the stock we add to make the sauce. For a vegetarian version, substitute the same amount of peeled and chopped vegetables, such as sweet potatoes, parsnips, and/or mushrooms, for the chicken.

1. Preheat the oven to 400°F.

2. In a large skillet, melt the butter over medium heat. Add the onions, carrots, celery, and garlic and cook, stirring constantly, for 2 minutes. Add the potatoes, mushrooms, and thyme and cook, stirring often, until the vegetables are crisp-tender, about 5 minutes. (For a vegetarian pot pie, add additional peeled and chopped vegetables now; see headnote.)

3. Add the flour and stir until it is fully combined with the vegetables. Cook for 3 minutes, or until the flour is golden brown. Add the stock, stirring constantly, and bring to a boil. Reduce the heat to low and simmer until the filling thickens, 3 to 4 minutes.

4. Season the filling with salt and pepper. Add the chicken, peas, and parsley and stir to combine. Transfer the filling to a 9 × 13-inch baking dish and let cool for 10 to 15 minutes.

5. On a lightly floured work surface, slice the puff pastry lengthwise into 1-inch-wide strips. Weave a tight lattice pattern on top of the baking dish over the filling, pressing the ends of the pastry into the edges of the pan. (For an even simpler presentation, cut a few slits in a sheet of puff pastry to act as vents for steam and lay the whole thing on top of the filling.) Bake for 30 to 40 minutes, until the pastry is golden brown and the filling is bubbly.

7

soups & stews

When we first started The Dynamite Shop's after-school program, where kids made dinner for their families, it was a brisk fall. In Brooklyn that means some rain, turning leaves that eventually drop to the streets, and shortening days. Like most people, we had soup on the brain, not just for its cozy character but because many soups and stews are jam-packed with valuable lessons for beginning cooks, like basic knife skills. Some soups can be as simple as putting everything in a pot with water, but others can really help you develop your sense for seasoning and other techniques for adding more flavor to your food. Our chili (see page 146) became famous for feeding the neighborhood anytime we had an event or when our community gathered for activism like phone banking, climate-march sign making, or supporting the local women's shelter. We hope you also find great lessons and deep comfort in these recipes.

italian wedding soup

FOR TURKEY MEATBALLS (OPTIONAL)

12 ounces **ground turkey**

¾ cup **dried bread crumbs**

1 large **egg**

¼ cup (about 1 ounce) grated **Pecorino Romano cheese**

¼ cup (about 1 ounce) grated **Parmesan cheese**

1 tablespoon chopped **fresh oregano**, or 1 teaspoon dried

1½ teaspoons **kosher salt**

½ teaspoon **freshly ground black pepper**

3 tablespoons **extra-virgin olive oil**

"Wedding soup? I'm too young to get married!" Believe us, we've heard that more than once! But yes, the classic name for this dish is "wedding soup"—it's named for the marriage of flavors!

But the point of this lesson is how to make a soup-finishing mix of cheese and eggs that cooks into flavorful bits: stir eggs into the soup while it's cooking and watch them break up. (It's the same way you'd make Chinese egg drop soup, only without the cheese in that case.)

Also in this recipe is a great meatball flavored with salty Parmesan and pecorino and amped up with earthy oregano. Vegetarians can instead make a meatless version called canederli, a bread dumpling from northern Italy (and we've heard from some meat lovers that they even prefer the vegetarian version, so try it out!). If you can't find escarole, try any green that wilts well in hot broth: spinach, kale, chard, and so on.

1. **To make turkey meatballs (if using):** Combine the ground turkey, bread crumbs, egg, both cheeses, oregano, salt, and pepper in a bowl. Mix thoroughly, then form small (1-inch) meatballs; you should have about 20 total. Wash your hands thoroughly with warm soap and water before moving on to the next step.

2. In a large skillet or stockpot, heat the olive oil over medium-high heat. Add the meatballs and cook, turning often, until browned all over, 5 to 6 minutes. Set aside on paper towels to absorb any excess oil.

FOR CANEDERLI (VEGETARIAN VERSION; OPTIONAL)

12 ounces **day-old** or **stale bread**, cut or torn into ½-inch pieces

1 cup **whole milk**

2 large **eggs**

¼ cup (about 1 ounce) grated **Pecorino Romano cheese**

¼ cup (about 1 ounce) grated **Parmesan cheese**

1 tablespoon chopped **fresh oregano**, or 1 teaspoon dried

1½ teaspoons **kosher salt**

½ teaspoon **freshly ground black pepper**

¼ cup **all-purpose flour** (or a gluten-free substitute, such as Bob's Red Mill 1:1), plus more as needed

FOR THE SOUP

1 tablespoon **extra-virgin olive oil**

1 medium **yellow onion**, diced

4 teaspoons minced **garlic** (about 4 medium cloves)

2 quarts **chicken** or **vegetable stock**, store-bought or homemade (see page 262 or 264)

1 bunch (12 to 15 ounces) **escarole** or other **greens**, trimmed and torn into bite-size pieces

2 large **eggs**

¼ cup (about 1 ounce) grated **Pecorino Romano cheese**

¼ cup (about 1 ounce) grated **Parmesan cheese**

Kosher salt and **freshly ground black pepper** to taste

3. **To make canederli (if using):** In a bowl, soak the bread in the milk for at least 30 minutes or up to 1 hour, until soft. Beat in the eggs and mix with both cheeses, the oregano, salt, and pepper. Gradually add the flour until the mixture is dry enough that you can shape 1½-inch balls; you should have 15 to 20. Place on a plate or sheet pan until ready to add to the soup.

4. **Make the soup:** In a large stockpot, heat the oil over medium-high heat. Add the onion and garlic and sauté until the onion is tender and the garlic is soft but not browned, about 5 minutes. Add the stock and bring to a boil. Add the escarole, reduce the heat, cover, and simmer for 5 minutes. Add the meatballs or canederli and simmer for another 2 minutes, or until the meatballs or canederli are cooked through.

5. Meanwhile, combine the eggs and cheeses in a small bowl and stir gently with a fork to blend. While stirring the soup constantly, slowly pour in the egg mixture. Cover and simmer just until the egg bits are set, about 1 minute. Season the soup with salt and pepper and serve.

up-to-you vegetable soup

2 tablespoons **olive oil**

2 ribs **celery**, chopped

1 large **yellow onion**, chopped

1 large **carrot**, peeled and chopped

2 tablespoons minced **garlic** (about 6 medium cloves)

3 cups chopped **vegetables** (see Note)

½ teaspoon **crushed red pepper flakes** (optional)

Kosher salt and **freshly ground black pepper** to taste

6 cups **chicken** or **vegetable stock**, store-bought or homemade (see page 262 or 264)

1 teaspoon **dried thyme, oregano**, or **Italian seasoning**

1 **bay leaf**

1 or 2 **Parmesan cheese rinds** (optional; see opposite)

1 can (15 ounces) **white beans**, drained

⅔ cup **Any-Herb Pesto** (page 109) or store-bought

Grated **Parmesan** or **Pecorino Romano cheese**

SUGGESTED ADD-INS

Cooked chicken, cooked small pasta, tortellini, or **grains**

Who says vegetable soup has to be boring? The way we teach it, you get to decide which vegetables, grains or pastas, beans, and seasonings to add to the mix.

Everyone's bowl turns out so beautifully different and delicious! We've seen so many versions: kale/cannellini/barley; squash/ditalini/chickpea; chard/red pepper/brown rice. No matter which direction you go in, start the soup by sautéing chopped celery, onion, carrot, and garlic to build a strong foundation of flavor in the pot (see Mirepoix, page 283). A simmer with the other ingredients combines all their flavors; if you taste the mixture when you put the ingredients in and then again after you've cooked them together for a while, you'll see how the flavors come together after they get friendly!

Then we finish our soup with one more fresh blast of flavor from a dollop of pesto, another lesson in how to make food taste great—you can always add a condiment or a sauce to the bowl right before serving!

1. In a large stockpot, heat the olive oil over medium heat. Add the celery, onion, and carrot and cook, stirring often, until the onion turns translucent and the carrot is soft, about 6 minutes. Add the garlic, any sturdier chopped vegetables (such as zucchini, squash, or peppers) and red pepper flakes (if using). Cook until the garlic is fragrant and the vegetables begin to soften, about 4 minutes. Season with salt and black pepper, then stir in the stock. Bring to a simmer and add the thyme, bay leaf, Parmesan rinds (if using), and beans.

2. Simmer until the flavors combine, about 15 minutes, then stir in the leafy greens or chopped vegetables (if using), and any desired add-ins and cook until the greens are wilted and everything is hot, just a few minutes more.

3. To serve, ladle into bowls and top with a spoonful of pesto and some Parmesan.

no-waste parmesan rinds

Hey, wait! Don't toss those Parmesan rinds! We (like most cheese-loving people) adore Parmesan: It's all over this book! Grated on top of pastas, stirred into soups, snuck into meatballs, and gracing the tops of salads. We always buy Parmesan in chunks rather than pre-grated, because the flavor keeps better when the cheese is left whole until you use it. That means we end up with lots of Parmesan rinds: those hard edges around the outside of the hunk of cheese. The rind is actually still cheese, just dried out and hard, so it's full of flavor even if you can't really bite into it. You just need to break it down a bit to extract the flavor. There is a solution! We drop the rinds into simmering liquid to give a rich depth to our soups and stocks.

When you get down to the rind (or if a piece of Parm dries out in the refrigerator), store it in an airtight container, and when you're making stock (see pages 262 and 264), drop in the cheese rind. You can even make a stock *just* out of Parmesan rinds (maybe add a little garlic, too). We like to plop one or two rinds into this Up-to-You Vegetable Soup as it cooks or even into our Basic Marinara Sauce (page 117). They lend a rich salty flavor that really rounds out the dish. Just remember to fish out and discard the rinds before serving the dish, since they're still too hard to eat.

NOTE: Use any mix of sturdy vegetables like zucchini, summer squash, green beans, mushrooms, and red or yellow bell peppers, and leafy greens like kale, spinach, or chard . . . or anything else you like.

miso magic

Just what is miso, anyway? A traditional Japanese paste made from fermented soybeans, this pantry staple has many more applications than just miso soup (though we *are* big fans of miso soup!).

Miso comes in a range of colors and flavors (lighter-colored miso tends to be more mild and sweet in flavor, while darker colors have had longer fermentation times that yield bolder flavors).

Experiment with adding milder miso to sweets (we love it in chocolate chip cookies and salted caramel sauces) or using it as a dairy-free substitute in dishes where you want a punch of umami flavor (we sometimes swap in miso for Parmesan in pesto). Or try adding bolder miso to dressings, marinades, and pan sauces!

quick "ramen" noodle soup

2 tablespoons **toasted sesame oil** or **vegetable oil**, plus more if desired for the noodles

1 tablespoon peeled and coarsely chopped **fresh ginger** (a 1- to 2-inch piece)

2 teaspoons coarsely chopped **garlic** (about 2 medium cloves)

1½ quarts (6 cups) **chicken** or **vegetable stock**, store-bought or homemade (see page 262 or 264)

2 tablespoons **miso paste** (we use white/shiro miso)

2 tablespoons **soy sauce** (substitute tamari for gluten-free)

4 ounces **shiitake mushrooms** (6 to 8), cleaned and sliced into ¼-inch-wide strips

2 ounces (about 2 cups) **baby spinach**, washed

8 ounces **semi-firm tofu**, drained and cut into ½-inch cubes

12 ounces **fresh ramen noodles**, or 9 ounces dried (skip the flavor packet; substitute rice noodles for gluten-free)

Many of our students call ramen their favorite meal, so this is always a fun lesson. If you're used to the instant packages, you can learn how tasty fresh ramen can be, and if you're used to ordering it out, you can get excited about choosing all your toppings—from frilly mushrooms and bamboo shoots to seaweed and soft-cooked eggs (see page 48).

While making a traditional ramen broth can take days, this recipe is about getting dinner done, so we offer some quick shortcuts—the flavor heroes here are a few choice vegetables and the power-packed duo of miso and soy sauce. Taste after you add them to the broth and season with more if you'd like!

1. In a large stockpot, heat the oil over medium heat. Add the ginger and garlic and sauté until fragrant but not browned, about 1 minute. Add the stock and bring to a low simmer (do not boil). Add the miso and stir to dissolve. Add the soy sauce, mushrooms, and spinach and stir until the spinach wilts. Drop in the tofu.

2. Bring a separate large pot of water to a boil over high heat. Add the noodles and cook according to the package directions. Drain the noodles and either add them to bowls right away and top with the soup or, if the soup isn't ready yet, toss them with a few drops of oil to keep them from sticking, then divide them among the bowls when the soup is ready.

3. Garnish with your favorite toppings (if desired) and serve.

> TOPPINGS make ramen even more fun! Add bean sprouts, chopped scallions, crumbled dried nori, and halved soft-boiled eggs.

vegetarian three-bean chili with all the toppings

There's nothing like a pot of chili to feed friends, family, and neighbors. And that's exactly what we would make when community events were held at our school, anything from holiday cookie swaps to phone-banking events.

Our meat-free three-bean chili was always a hit with our students and families. There is a little bit of heat from the chili powder, so this is a great recipe to practice seasoning to taste. Start with 1 tablespoon, stir it in, then taste it and see if you want more.

Also, don't forget all the toppings! Setting those out lets everyone make their own bowl, and you'll see how all those different toppings add different flavors and textures.

2 tablespoons **extra-virgin olive oil**

1 large **white** or **yellow onion**, sliced

Kosher salt to taste

2 large **carrots**, peeled and cut into small chunks

4 teaspoons minced **garlic** (about 4 medium cloves)

3 tablespoons **tomato paste**

2 tablespoons **ground cumin**

2 tablespoons **smoked paprika**

1 teaspoon **ground cinnamon**

1 to 2 tablespoons **chili powder**, or to taste

1 can (28 ounces) **whole peeled tomatoes**

1 can (15 ounces) **black beans**, drained and rinsed

1 can (15 ounces) **pinto beans**, drained and rinsed

1 can (15 ounces) **garbanzo beans**, drained and rinsed

Up to 2 cups **stock** (any kind) or water, as needed

2 tablespoons **apple cider vinegar**

Freshly ground black pepper to taste

1. In a large heavy-bottomed pot, heat the olive oil over medium heat. Add the onion and a big pinch of salt and cook, stirring occasionally, until the onion is caramelized and deep golden brown, 15 to 20 minutes.

2. Add the carrots and garlic, then stir in the tomato paste; cook for 5 minutes, until the carrots are softened.

3. Add the cumin, paprika, cinnamon, and as much chili powder as you want to start with, stirring to coat the vegetables.

4. Pour the canned tomatoes into a large mixing bowl. Use your clean hands to break them into small pieces and release their juices, then add them to the pot.

5. Add the beans and 1 cup of the stock, bring to a boil, then reduce the heat to low and cook, stirring occasionally, until the flavors meld and the chili thickens, about 45 minutes. About midway through, check to see if it needs more liquid, depending on your desired consistency. Taste for spice level and add more chili powder, if desired. Stir in the vinegar and season with salt and pepper.

6. Serve immediately with your choice of toppings (if desired).

TOP with your favorite garnishes: sour cream or plain yogurt, shredded cheese, pickled jalapeños, roasted corn, scallions, diced onion, fresh cilantro, or lime wedges.

family-style french onion soup

½ cup (1 stick) **butter**

3 pounds **sweet onions** (like Vidalia), thinly sliced

1 teaspoon **granulated sugar**

A few cracks of **freshly ground black pepper**, plus more to taste

3½ teaspoons **all-purpose flour** (or a gluten-free substitute, such as Bob's Red Mill 1:1)

2 quarts **chicken, beef,** or **vegetable stock,** store-bought or homemade (see page 262 or 264)

10 sprigs **fresh thyme**, plus fresh leaves for garnish

3 **bay leaves**

Kosher salt to taste

8 to 10 **baguette slices** (1 medium baguette), toasted

2 cups (8 ounces) grated **Gruyère cheese** (or a mix of Parmesan, low-moisture mozzarella, and Swiss)

When you want to serve something that inspires oohs and aahs, make French onion soup from scratch. And what a great lesson this is on the magic of caramelized onions. Most of the flavor in this soup comes from the simple process of slowly cooking down onions over low heat until they're supersweet, glossy, and golden brown. It takes time and patience—the key is really to cook them gently for a long time, stirring often so the bottoms don't burn. This cooks the water out of the onions (which has no flavor, because it's water!) and concentrates their natural sugars; when you see them changing color, that's all the sugar turning into caramel!

You can serve the soup the traditional way in individual crocks blanketed with gooey cheese, but we think serving it family-style—in one big pot, topped with crusty bread slices and cheese that's broiled until molten and bubbly—is way more fun. Get ready for the gooey cheese pulls!

1. In an ovenproof stockpot or Dutch oven, melt the butter over medium heat. Add the onions, sugar, and pepper and cook, stirring regularly, until the onions are deeply golden (but not dark brown), about 40 minutes.

2. Sprinkle the onions with the flour, stir for 1 minute, then add the stock, thyme, and bay leaves. Stir, scraping up all the oniony browned bits at the bottom of the pan. Bring to a boil over high heat, then reduce the heat to low and simmer for 30 minutes, until the flavors have melded. Remove and discard the thyme sprigs and bay leaves. Season with salt and more pepper to taste.

3. Preheat the broiler.

4. If your broiler is part of your main oven and your pot will easily fit, lay the baguette slices on top of the soup, pressing down slightly to submerge them, and sprinkle with the cheese. Broil until the cheese is fully melted and bubbly. (Alternatively, if you have ovenproof bowls, you can place them on a sheet pan, ladle some soup into each, add the bread and press down to submerge it, top with the cheese, slide the pan under the broiler, and broil until the cheese is melted and bubbly.)

5. If your broiler is a separate unit (usually a drawer below the oven) that won't fit a big soup pot, place the baguette slices on a sheet pan, sprinkle with the cheese, and broil until the cheese is fully melted and bubbly, about 1 minute, but keep a close eye on it! Immediately lay the bread on top of the soup, cheesy-side up, pressing down slightly to submerge them.

6. Garnish with fresh thyme and freshly cracked pepper. To serve, bring the pot to the table and let everyone ladle their portion into bowls.

coconut curry noodle soup

1 tablespoon **vegetable oil**

1-inch piece **fresh ginger**, peeled and minced

2 **shallots**, minced

1 tablespoon minced **garlic** (about 3 medium cloves)

½ teaspoon **kosher salt**, plus more to taste

2 tablespoons **Thai Red Curry Paste** (recipe follows)

2 teaspoons **ground turmeric**

8 ounces **chicken breast** or **thighs**, cut into bite-size pieces, or semi-firm **tofu**, drained and cut into ½-inch cubes

2 cans (14 ounces each) **unsweetened full-fat coconut milk**

1½ cups **chicken** or **vegetable stock** store-bought or homemade (see page 262 or 264)

2 teaspoons **fish sauce**, plus more to taste (optional)

2 tablespoons **freshly squeezed lime juice**, plus more to taste

8 ounces **baby spinach**

8 ounces fresh **Chinese egg noodles** (or rice noodles for gluten-free)

Our students have a lot of love for this soup. It has a sweet, bright flavor from coconut milk and lime juice, nice chunky noodles, and lots of protein thanks to chicken or tofu. With the addition of big handfuls of spinach that wilt in the silky broth, this is really a one-bowl meal.

This is inspired by the classic Thai dish khao soi. Practically speaking, it is our intro lesson to curry. So many different cultures have dishes called curries: India, Pakistan, China, Japan, Malaysia, Indonesia, Vietnam, and many more! The thing that they have in common is a flavorful mix of spices (or ground-up aromatics and spices) that form a super-fragrant base for a saucy dish. This recipe uses a homemade Thai red curry paste but you can also use one from a grocery store.

1. Heat the vegetable oil in a large, heavy pot over medium heat. Add the ginger, shallots, and garlic and sauté until tender, stirring frequently, about 5 minutes. Stir in the salt.

2. Stir in the curry paste and turmeric and cook for 1 minute; it will have a strong aroma! And if the curry paste is spicy, it may sting your eyes or nose a little bit. Don't worry, it will fade.

3. Add the chicken (or tofu) and sauté until coated in the paste. Pour in the coconut milk, scraping up any caramelized bits from the bottom of the pot with a wooden spoon. When the mixture is bubbling, add the stock, fish sauce (if using), and lime juice. Let it cook for a minute or so, then add the spinach and stir until wilted, about 1 minute more. Taste and add more salt, fish sauce, and/or lime juice if desired.

4. Bring a large pot of water to a boil over high heat and cook the noodles according to the package instructions. Drain well.

5. For each serving, place a portion of the cooked noodles in the bottom of a wide bowl, top with a ladleful of soup, then garnish with plenty of toppings (if desired).

> TOP with red onion, cilantro, Thai basil leaves, chili oil, or lime wedges.

thai red curry paste

makes ½ cup

4 large dried long **red Thai chiles** or **guajillo chiles**, stemmed, halved, and seeded

Boiling water

3 medium **shallots**, halved

8 **garlic cloves**

2-inch piece **fresh ginger**, peeled and sliced

2 stalks **lemongrass** (use the bottom 2 to 3 inches and discard the hard outer layer; see page 33), bruised and sliced

½ cup chopped **fresh cilantro stems**

Peel of 1 **lime**, preferably makrut lime (reserve juice for soup)

1 tablespoon **ground coriander**

1 tablespoon **ground turmeric**

2 teaspoons **ground cumin**

2 teaspoons **freshly ground black pepper**

Up to 3 tablespoons **unsweetened full-fat coconut milk**, as needed

1. Place the chiles in a small heatproof bowl, add boiling water to cover, and let soak until softened, about 30 minutes.

2. Drain the chiles, reserving the soaking liquid. In a blender or food processor, combine the chiles, shallots, garlic, ginger, lemongrass, cilantro stems, lime peel, coriander, turmeric, cumin, pepper, and 2 tablespoons of the reserved soaking liquid. Puree, adding coconut milk by the spoonful as needed, until it forms a thick, smooth paste.

3. Store in a sealed jar in the refrigerator for up to 2 weeks.

Below are some of our favorite vegetables to add to this curry, with suggestions on how to cut and when to add them to the pot.

STURDY VEGETABLES

Peel and cut into ½-inch pieces, unless noted otherwise, and add with the spices:

Broccoli (cut into florets, the stem thinly sliced)

Butternut squash

Carrots

Cauliflower (cut into florets)

Parsnips

Potatoes, waxy varietals like new or red

Sweet potatoes

SOFT VEGETABLES

Prepare as indicated and add with the coconut milk:

Bell peppers (seeded and cut into 1-inch pieces)

Eggplant (diced into 1-inch pieces)

Green beans (trimmed and cut into 1-inch lengths)

Mushrooms (thinly sliced)

Zucchini (cut into ½-inch-thick rounds)

curry with all the vegetables

3 tablespoons **curry powder**

1 teaspoon **ground cumin**

1 teaspoon **fennel seeds** (optional)

3 tablespoons **extra-virgin olive oil**

1 large **yellow onion**, diced

2 teaspoons minced **garlic** (about 2 medium cloves)

2 pounds **mixed vegetables** (see opposite)

2 cans (14 ounces each) **unsweetened full-fat coconut milk**

2 cups packed stemmed and chopped **hearty leafy greens**, such as kale, chard, or collards

Kosher salt and **freshly ground black pepper** to taste

2 cups **cooked white, brown,** or **basmati rice** (see page 269 for a cooking guide), for serving

OPTIONAL TOPPINGS

Fresh cilantro and/or **basil sprigs, lime wedges,** thinly sliced **hot peppers,** such as Scotch bonnet

Some curries use fresh pastes made from aromatic vegetables and herbs (see page 152), and some use a mix of dried spices. Most traditional spice-based curries are made with spice mixes unique to the area or to the individual cook, but store-bought curry powder is a kind of shortcut.

Whatever spices you use, dry-toasting them before mixing them into a dish brings out their flavors, and that's a big part of this recipe's lesson. In this dish, we toast the spices and then sauté them with onion and garlic to make a base for a rich coconut milk sauce.

What you add to that sauce is up to you! Load it with your favorite vegetables, add some chicken or chickpeas or tofu or whatever you like, and top with a handful of fresh herbs!

1. In a large heavy-bottomed soup pot or Dutch oven, toast the curry powder, cumin, and fennel seeds (if using) over medium heat until you can really smell them and they turn just a bit darker, about 2 minutes. Be careful not to burn the spices. Transfer to a plate to cool.

2. In the same pot, heat the olive oil over medium heat. Add the onion and sauté until soft, about 3 minutes. Add the garlic and sauté for another minute, until fragrant. Add the toasted spices and any sturdy vegetables (see opposite) and cook, stirring often, until softened, 5 to 7 minutes.

3. Stir in the coconut milk and bring to a simmer. Stir in any soft vegetables (see opposite), along with the leafy greens. Reduce the heat to medium-low, partially cover, and simmer until the flavors combine and all the vegetables are tender, 20 to 25 minutes. Season with salt and pepper. Serve over rice, garnished with any desired toppings.

garden gazpacho

1 large can (28 ounces) **whole peeled tomatoes**, or 2 pounds **ripe tomatoes**, cored and chopped

1 small **jalapeño** or **Anaheim pepper**, stemmed, seeded, and cut into chunks (optional)

1 medium **cucumber**, peeled and roughly chopped

1 small **white onion**, cut into chunks

¼ cup roughly chopped **fresh cilantro leaves**

2 teaspoons **freshly squeezed lime juice**, plus more as needed

⅓ cup **extra-virgin olive oil**, plus more for serving

Kosher salt and **freshly ground black pepper** to taste

When it's too hot to turn on the oven, soup doesn't always seem like the first choice. That is, until you remember gazpacho!

Gazpacho—the cold soup of Spain—is always a star. Tangy, tomatoey, simple, and delicious, it's a soup you don't even have to cook. There are lots of variations on this dish—some are thickened with almonds and others with bread, among other differences. Ours is a simple blend of tomatoes, cucumber, onion, herbs, a splash of citrus, and, of course, lots of good oil.

This is a great lesson in using the blender to puree and also emulsify a chilled soup with oil: students can practice pulsing the gazpacho until chunky, then whirling it as the olive oil streams in until it's fully liquefied and almost creamy. We serve it with some Garlicky Bruschetta (page 281) on the side.

1. Using a blender or food processor and working in batches, if necessary, combine the tomatoes, jalapeño (if using), cucumber, onion, cilantro, and lime juice and begin blending on low speed, gradually increasing to high speed, until the mixture is smooth. Stop the blender a few times and scrape down the sides with a rubber spatula.

2. Increase the blender speed to medium and slowly drizzle in the olive oil until the mixture emulsifies and becomes creamy. Season with salt, pepper, and lime juice and chill for at least 10 minutes. Serve with olive oil drizzled on top.

green pozole

12 ounces **fresh tomatillos**, or 1 can (14 ounces) **whole tomatillos**

2 tablespoons **vegetable oil** or **extra-virgin olive oil**

1 medium **white** or **yellow onion**, roughly chopped

1 to 2 fresh **jalapeño peppers**, stemmed, quartered, and seeded (for less heat, if desired)

4 **garlic cloves**, smashed

1 teaspoon **kosher salt**, plus more to taste

½ teaspoon **freshly ground black pepper**, plus more to taste

½ teaspoon **dried oregano** (preferably Mexican), crumbled

3 cups **chicken** or **vegetable stock**, store-bought or homemade (see page 262 or 264)

¾ cup lightly packed chopped **fresh cilantro leaves**

¼ cup **pepitas**, toasted (see page 280)

2 cans (15 ounces each) **white hominy**, drained and rinsed

OPTIONAL TOPPINGS

Thinly sliced **radishes**, sliced **avocado**, shredded **romaine lettuce** or **cabbage**, chopped **red onion**, **lime wedges**, **tortilla chips**, **ground dried chile**, **dried oregano**

Pozole is a rich, nourishing stew made from hominy (dried field corn kernels)—the same kind used to make corn tortillas. This recipe is a green pozole, flavored and tinted by tomatillos, which look similar to green tomatoes, but have a milder, less-tart flavor.

Corn and tomatoes are a natural pairing in the summer, but this combination of corn and tomatillos is perfect for the winter. In Mexico, pozole is traditionally served on Christmas Eve, but it can be enjoyed any time you're craving coziness and warmth.

If you can't find fresh tomatillos, you might find them in the canned aisle. Hominy can be found dried (and you can prepare it just liked dried beans; see page 265), but it's also commonly sold in cans. If you don't have hominy, try the recipe with beans, chickpeas, or sweet corn. It won't be pozole, but it will be good!

1. Peel off and discard the papery husks of the tomatillos, wash the fruit in water, and cut them into quarters. (If using canned, just drain and quarter them.)

2. In a large stockpot or Dutch oven, heat the oil over medium heat. Add the tomatillos, onion, jalapeño, garlic, salt, pepper, and oregano and sauté for 3 to 5 minutes, until the onion starts to brown slightly. Pour in the stock. Bring the mixture to a boil over high heat, then reduce the heat to maintain a low simmer and cook for 30 minutes, skimming off any foam that rises to the top.

3. Using a slotted spoon, remove the cooked tomatillos, onion, and jalapeño and transfer them to a blender. Add ½ cup of the cilantro, the pepitas, and 1 cup of the broth and blend until completely smooth.

4. Return the blended mixture to the pot and add the hominy. Cook over medium heat for another 5 to 10 minutes, until the hominy is tender. Taste and adjust the seasoning with more salt and pepper, if desired.

5. Stir in the remaining ¼ cup cilantro and serve in shallow, wide bowls with your desired toppings.

phở
(vietnamese noodle soup)

Phở (rhymes with "duh") is a Vietnamese noodle soup. It has a clear broth, slippery rice noodles, and toppings galore—like herbs and crunchy beans sprouts—for flavor and texture. There are lots of different versions of it all over the country, and ours wouldn't be considered traditional (for the real deal, you simmer bones for hours or even days to make the broth), but it's tasty and satisfying and you can get it on the table tonight.

One of the key sources of flavor in this broth is the whole "sweet" spices: the cinnamon sticks, star anise pods, and cloves won't dissolve, so you'll have to strain them out after they've flavored the liquid. You'll also use the broiler to char—we mean really get the edges black!—onions and ginger, which gives the broth a rich depth.

Our spin adds thinly sliced mushrooms that flavor the dish beautifully. (Traditionally, you might add thinly sliced raw beef right to the bowl so it cooks in the hot broth.) Once kids fall in love with this dinner, we tell them it's time to try it for breakfast!

FOR THE BROTH

2 large **onions**, quartered

4-inch piece **fresh ginger**, quartered lengthwise

Two 3-inch **cinnamon sticks**

2 **star anise pods**

3 **whole cloves**

2 teaspoons **coriander seeds**

6 cups **beef** or **vegetable stock**, store-bought or homemade (see page 264)

1 tablespoon **soy sauce** (substitute tamari for gluten-free)

1 tablespoon **fish sauce** (optional)

3 **carrots**, peeled and chopped

FOR SERVING

8 ounces dried flat **rice noodles** (known as bánh phở; use up to ¼-inch width)

6 to 8 **shiitake mushrooms**, cleaned and very thinly sliced

TOP with sliced scallions, paper-thin sliced Thai bird or other chiles, lime juice, bean sprouts, fresh herb sprigs like cilantro, mint and/or Thai basil, hoisin and/or sriracha sauce.

1. Preheat the broiler. Arrange the onions and ginger on a sheet pan and place it under the broiler. Char the onions and the ginger until slightly blackened, 6 to 8 minutes on each side. Transfer to a colander and rinse with water, then set aside.

2. In a large pot, toast the cinnamon, star anise, cloves, and coriander seeds over medium-low heat for about 1 minute, stirring to prevent the spices from burning. When the spices are aromatic, add the stock, soy sauce, fish sauce (if using), carrots, and charred onions and ginger. Bring the mixture to a boil, cover, reduce the heat, and simmer for 30 minutes. Set a fine-mesh strainer over a clean pot and strain the broth through it. Discard the solids. Keep the broth hot.

3. Bring a large pot of water to a boil and cook the noodles according to the package instructions. Drain well.

4. Divide the cooked noodles among deep serving bowls. Scatter the mushrooms over the noodles. Ladle about 1½ cups of hot broth into each bowl. Serve with toppings as desired.

gumbo

1 can (14 to 16 ounces) **whole peeled tomatoes**

3 tablespoons **extra-virgin olive oil**

1 large **white onion**, diced

1 tablespoon minced **garlic** (about 3 medium cloves)

1 rib **celery**, diced

1 **red**, **yellow**, or **green bell pepper**, diced

1 teaspoon **Creole seasoning**

¼ cup **all-purpose flour** (or gluten-free substitute, such as Bob's Red Mill 1:1)

4 cups **chicken** or **vegetable stock**, store-bought or homemade (see page 262 or 264)

1 teaspoon **dried oregano**

½ teaspoon **filé powder** (optional)

1 **bay leaf**

1 cup chopped **okra** (frozen is fine)

¾ pound **smoked sausage** or **kielbasa**, sliced into coins

½ pound **medium shrimp**, peeled but tails left on

Kosher salt and **freshly ground black pepper** to taste

3 cups **cooked brown rice** (see page 269), for serving

New Orleans's signature stew is a delicious amalgam of Native American, French, West African, Caribbean, and other influences that contribute to the city's melting-pot cuisine.

This recipe makes use of a unique technique: a dark roux. Roux thickens sauces and soups. Most of the roux in this book are just quickly cooked combinations of butter and flour, but you make a dark roux by cooking your basic roux so long that you actually brown the flour. Be very, very careful with that step, since the dark roux is *extremely* hot.

Gumbo is one of those recipes that every cook puts their own spin on. We skirt the questions of whether to use okra or filé powder (ground dried sassafras leaves) to further thicken the stew, whether to flavor it with smoked sausage or shrimp, and whether to use or omit tomatoes. Often, making gumbo is a multi-hour affair. This version comes together pretty quickly, but the flavor does get better the longer it simmers.

1. Pour the tomatoes into a large mixing bowl and use your clean hands to break them into small pieces and release their juices. Set aside.

2. In a large heavy-bottomed pot, heat the olive oil over medium heat. Add the onion and cook, stirring until golden and translucent, about 3 minutes. Add the garlic, celery, bell pepper, and Creole seasoning and cook until fragrant, about 1 minute. Add the flour and mix well to combine with the oil and vegetables. Cook, stirring, until it's the color of milk chocolate, 5 to 7 minutes. It's fine for the roux to stick to the bottom of the pot, but don't let it burn.

3. Whisk in the stock and scrape up any roux from the bottom of the pot. Add the crushed tomatoes, oregano, filé powder (if using), bay leaf, okra, and sausage. Simmer until the gumbo thickens, about 10 minutes, then add the shrimp and simmer for 5 to 10 minutes more, until the shrimp turn pink and the flavors meld. Season with salt and black pepper and serve in bowls over cooked brown rice.

8

salads

Okay, so salads aren't usually kids' favorite foods, but hear us out. Our salads are built to entertain and impress. Each of these salads either has a surprise lesson in it (learn how salt breaks down tough kale leaves in the Massaged Kale Salad on page 182), or is super fun to make (ready to smash some cucumbers?) or has pops of flavor and color that will convert any salad skeptic into a fan. We can't pick favorites, but the Tangy Carrot and Cucumber Salad (page 170), Fattoush Salad (page 184), and Apple Cranberry Salad with Balsamic Vinaigrette (page 173) are all gorgeous and pack a tasty punch.

Luckily for both the cooks and the dinner guests, many of these salads count as a whole and hearty meal, like our Cobb Salad (page 164) and Rainbow Grain Bowl with Tahini Dressing (page 167). Don't worry, we also squeeze in some classics like a Caesar (see page 188—and hold the anchovies if you wish!) and a classic of Japanese American restaurants (all-time kids' favorite): Iceberg Wedge Salad with Carrot-Ginger Dressing (page 174).

cobb salad

FOR THE SALAD

4 slices **prosciutto**, or 8 slices **bacon** (optional)

3 large **eggs**, at room temperature

1 tablespoon **distilled white vinegar**

½ teaspoon **kosher salt**

2 large **romaine hearts**

1 ripe **Hass avocado**, halved, pit removed peeled, and sliced (see page 105)

6 ounces **grape** or **cherry tomatoes**, halved lengthwise

4 ounces **blue cheese**, such as Roquefort, crumbled

1 **Poached Chicken Breast**, sliced (recipe follows; optional)

FOR THE VINAIGRETTE

1 small **shallot**, minced

3 tablespoons **extra-virgin olive oil**

3 tablespoons **apple cider vinegar**

1 tablespoon **Dijon mustard**

Kosher salt and **freshly ground black pepper** to taste

When we're craving a main dish salad, Cobb is our go-to. With its chopped chicken, eggs, bacon, avocado, tomato, and cheeses lined up in neat rows atop a bed of lettuce, it's as satisfying as it is pretty. And what a fun history: It's named after Bob Cobb, the owner of Hollywood's famed Brown Derby restaurant. It was there, legend has it, that this salad came to be when Mr. Cobb threw together everything left in the refrigerator to make a late-night dinner for his guests. The last-minute salad became the hot spot's signature dish.

It's also a great lesson in knife skills, since all the toppings should be chopped to about the same size. You'll also make your own vinaigrette and practice poaching, which is a great way to make very tender chicken. So many lessons in one salad!

And there are so many ways to customize it. The classic recipe calls for crumbled bacon, but we think oven-crisped prosciutto (a lean, dry-cured Italian-style ham) is a healthier, crunchier, and tastier alternative. Bonus: It can be crisped days ahead and stored in an airtight container. You can also try using soppressata, salami, and other cured meats. Their flavor really intensifies in the oven!

For vegetarians, leave out the prosciutto and chicken and add more eggs. For vegans, skip the eggs and omit the cheese, but add toasted nuts, seeds, and/or crispy chickpeas.

From the choices of ingredients to how they are laid out on the bed of lettuce, you can make this your own way. We've seen stripes, circles, hearts made from cherry tomatoes—you name it. Have fun with it!

1. Make the salad: If using prosciutto, preheat the oven to 400°F. Place the pieces of prosciutto in a single layer on a baking rack set over a sheet pan. Bake until crispy, 8 to 10 minutes. Set aside to cool.

2. Place the eggs in a small saucepan with a lid and cover with water by 1 inch. Add the white vinegar and salt to the water to help prevent the shells from cracking

(RECIPE CONTINUES)

and the whites from running if they do. Bring the water to a boil over high heat. Once the water boils, remove the pan from the heat, cover, and set a timer for 10 minutes. Prepare an ice bath in a bowl that will hold the eggs. When the timer goes off, use a slotted spoon to remove the eggs from the pan and submerge them carefully in the ice bath. Allow them to chill for at least 30 seconds. Peel the eggs (sometimes doing this in a bowl of water or under cold running water is easier) and slice them in half lengthwise.

3. Slice the romaine hearts crosswise into thin ribbons, discarding or composting the root end. Arrange the romaine in the bottom of a wide salad bowl.

4. If using, crumble the cooked prosciutto and arrange it in a line or circle across the romaine. Arrange the avocado, tomatoes, blue cheese, chicken (if using), and halved eggs in a similar manner.

5. **Make the vinaigrette:** Combine the shallot, oil, apple cider vinegar, and mustard in a small lidded jar. Shake vigorously, then add salt and pepper, adjusting as needed for balance.

6. Just before serving, drizzle the dressing on top of the salad and toss.

poached chicken breast

makes 1

1 **boneless, skinless chicken breast** (about ½ pound)

2 tablespoons **kosher salt**

A few cracks of **freshly ground black pepper**

2 **bay leaves** (optional)

4 **garlic cloves**, smashed

1. Place the chicken breast in a saucepan with a lid and add the salt, pepper, bay leaves (if using), and garlic. Cover the chicken with water and bring to a boil over medium-high heat. Reduce the heat to low so that the water is barely bubbling. Cover the pan. Begin checking the chicken after 8 minutes; it is done when an instant-read thermometer inserted into the thickest part of the meat reads 165°F, or if the meat is completely white when you cut through the thickest part.

2. Using a slotted spoon, transfer the chicken to a plate or cutting board. When it's cool enough to handle, slice thinly, dice, or tear it into bite-size pieces.

rainbow grain bowl
with tahini dressing

6 small **lacinato kale leaves**, tough stems removed and discarded, leaves shredded

1 cup **cooked grains**, such as rice, bulgur, quinoa, millet, buckwheat, couscous, or farro (see page 269)

1 small **beet**, roasted (see page 64), peeled, and cut into bite-size pieces

⅓ ripe **avocado**, sliced

½ small **sweet potato**, roasted (see page 64) and cut into bite-size wedges

Handful of **broccoli** or **cauliflower florets**, roasted (see page 64)

Small handful of chopped **fresh cilantro leaves**, **flat-leaf parsley**, or a generous pinch of **sprouts**

1 to 2 tablespoons **Tahini Dressing** (recipe follows)

1 to 2 tablespoons **Grain Bowl Sparkles** (recipe follows)

Hot sauce or **tamari**, for serving (optional)

Have you heard the phrase "eat the rainbow"? A bowl of brightly colored vegetables—some cooked and some raw—tossed with hearty grains and a sesame-flavored tahini dressing, is a superfood meal because the natural pigments in the vegetables contain powerful good-for-you phytonutrients.

This dish is so customizable. We teach it as an "up to you" dish, in which everyone can pick their own toppings. You can decide how much of your chosen grains to cook, how many veggies, whether you want to roast them or keep them raw, and on and on. Not only is this recipe incredibly healthy, it is a good one to prepare ahead, too, storing each of the components separately in the refrigerator and using them to assemble lunches and dinners throughout the week. Feel free to add eggs, meat, cheese—whatever you want! But don't forget the "sparkles," a sweet, crunchy topping that adds flavor and texture to the dish.

1. In a medium saucepan, heat 4 cups water over medium-high heat until it starts to simmer. Add the kale and stir to submerge the leaves, then cook until bright green, about 1 minute. Drain, run under cold water for 10 seconds, then set aside to drain and cool.

2. Place the grains in the bottom of a shallow, wide bowl. Arrange the beet, avocado, sweet potato, kale, broccoli, and herbs around the bowl. Offer tahini dressing, sparkles, and hot sauce or tamari (if using) to season.

tahini dressing

makes about 1 cup

6 tablespoons **tahini paste**

¼ cup **freshly squeezed lemon juice**

½ teaspoon **kosher salt**

¼ cup **warm water**

Mix the tahini paste, lemon juice, and salt in a small cup. Pour in the warm water and whisk until the ingredients are blended, creamy, and a pourable consistency. If the dressing sits around for more than a few minutes, you may have to add more warm water to thin it.

grain bowl sparkles

makes ½ cup

⅓ cup **unsweetened shredded coconut** or **coconut chips**, lightly toasted (see page 280)

2 tablespoons **sesame seeds**, lightly toasted (see page 280)

¼ teaspoon **kosher salt**

¼ teaspoon **freshly ground black pepper**

¼ teaspoon **freshly grated lime zest**

Pinch of **cayenne pepper**

Combine all the ingredients in a small bowl. Sprinkle as desired on top of grain bowls, roasted vegetables, and salads.

tangy carrot and cucumber salad

2 large **cucumbers**, peeled, halved lengthwise, seeded, and cut into ¼-inch pieces

1 tablespoon **kosher salt**

¼ cup **rice vinegar**

2 tablespoons **toasted sesame oil**

2 tablespoons **granulated sugar**

2 large **carrots**, peeled, then shaved into ribbons with the peeler

1 **Thai red chile** or **jalapeño pepper**, seeded and chopped (optional)

¼ cup chopped **fresh cilantro leaves**

½ cup chopped **peanuts** (optional)

While you might not find this exact recipe on family dinner tables in Thailand, its flavors remind us of some of our favorite features of Thai food: tanginess, chile heat, and crunchy peanuts. We often enjoy it with some of our Thai-inspired main courses, like our Coconut Curry Noodle Soup (page 150) or our Laab Moo Lettuce Wraps (page 80). But, of course, enjoy it anytime you want a refreshing, sweet-tart crunchfest of a salad!

Salting cucumbers draws out their water, which gives you crunchier cucumbers with more concentrated flavor. And did you know you don't need a knife to cut carrots? Use a vegetable peeler to take off that rough outer layer, compost those peelings, and then just keep using the peeler to slice ribbons of carrot!

Finally, in most vinaigrettes, we use three times as much oil as we do acid (meaning the vinegar or lemon juice). But that is not the only way to mix up a salad dressing! This one uses twice as much vinegar as oil to give a much tangier result.

1. In a colander set over a bowl, toss the cucumbers with the salt. Set aside to drain for at least 10 minutes.

2. In a large bowl, whisk together the vinegar, sesame oil, and sugar. Add the drained cucumbers, carrots, chile (if using), and cilantro and toss to combine. Garnish with chopped peanuts, if desired, and serve.

apple cranberry salad
with balsamic vinaigrette

When apples are in season, we eat them every which way, but one of our favorite ways is in this hearty salad, where they add a sweet, refreshing crunch to go with chewy dried cranberries, sharp red onion, crisp romaine, creamy goat cheese, and toasty pumpkin seeds. The big lesson here is learning how important different textures are to a dish: food gets boring fast if it's all one texture—all soft, all mushy, or all crunchy. But a mix keeps things fun!

FOR THE SALAD

1 head **romaine**, chopped, or 6 cups **arugula** or **mixed greens**

½ cup thinly sliced **red onion** (about 1 small)

2 **apples**, cored and sliced

3 ounces **goat cheese**, crumbled (optional)

¼ cup **pepitas, sunflower seeds, walnuts**, or **pecans**, toasted (see page 280)

¼ cup **unsweetened dried cranberries**

FOR THE VINAIGRETTE

⅓ cup **extra-virgin olive oil**

3 tablespoons **balsamic vinegar**

1 scant tablespoon **Dijon mustard**

1 teaspoon **honey**

Kosher salt and **freshly ground black pepper** to taste

1. **Make the salad:** In a large mixing bowl, combine all the salad ingredients.

2. **Make the vinaigrette:** In a container with a tight-fitting lid, combine the olive oil, vinegar, mustard, and honey and shake until emulsified. Season with salt and pepper.

3. Drizzle the vinaigrette over the salad and toss well to combine. Serve immediately.

iceberg wedge salad
with carrot-ginger dressing

2 medium **carrots**, peeled and roughly chopped

½ **white onion**, roughly chopped

2 teaspoons peeled and finely chopped **fresh ginger** (about a 2-inch piece)

½ cup **vegetable oil**

⅓ cup **rice vinegar**

2 tablespoons **soy sauce** (substitute tamari for gluten-free)

1 head **iceberg lettuce**, trimmed and cut into small wedges

The recipe for this salad came about when a student in one of our sushi workshops asked about "that amazing salad with the yummy dressing you can get at Japanese restaurants." And we instantly knew what she meant, even without knowing which Japanese restaurants she's been to. (That simple salad with its iconic carrot-ginger dressing, it turns out, isn't traditionally Japanese at all and was actually invented in America.)

Iceberg is a little bit of an ignored lettuce, but in this case, it's the perfect choice for this crunchy and refreshing salad. We also love how vibrant the color is and how nutrient-packed this dressing is. Kids love it in their lunch as a dip for vegetables or drizzled on roasted vegetables, fish, or chicken at home.

1. Place the carrots, onion, ginger, oil, vinegar, and soy sauce in a blender and pulse for about a minute, until emulsified and creamy looking. You should have about 1½ cups of dressing.

2. On a platter, arrange the lettuce wedges and drizzle the dressing on top. Serve immediately.

garlicky smashed cucumbers

1 pound **cucumbers** (peeled if their skins are thick or waxy)

1 tablespoon **kosher salt**

1 tablespoon **granulated sugar**

1 tablespoon minced **garlic** (about 3 medium cloves)

2 tablespoons **rice vinegar**

1 tablespoon **soy sauce** (substitute tamari for gluten-free)

½ teaspoon toasted **sesame oil** (optional)

½ teaspoon **chili oil** or thinly sliced **fresh chiles** (optional)

Pinch of **ground Sichuan peppercorns** (optional)

2 or 3 sprigs **fresh cilantro leaves**, roughly chopped, for garnish

Our students enjoy making this spicy, refreshing Chinese-style salad as much as they love eating it: we break out rolling pins and mallets and whack the heck out of the cucumbers to soften them up and crack their skin before chopping them. If you like to bash things, it's a ton of fun!

And it's fun to eat, too. The crunchy, cooling cucumbers are tangy from the vinegar; savory from the soy sauce; garlicky from the, um, garlic; and spicy from the chili oil and the special ingredient—Sichuan peppercorns. This Chinese spice is often used with chile peppers but isn't hot on its own—in addition to a fruity flavor, Sichuan peppercorns make your tongue tingle and go a little numb. (If you don't like heat, you can skip the chili oil, and if you don't like the way the Sichuan peppercorns make your mouth feel after trying them, you can skip them, too.)

Salting the cucumbers and letting them sit for a few minutes draws the water out of them, which keeps it from diluting the dressing, so the salad is more flavorful.

1. On a cutting board, smack the cucumbers all over with a mallet or rolling pin to soften them and crack the skin (if they're unpeeled). Slice the cucumbers lengthwise into quarters, then cut them into 1-inch pieces. Transfer to a colander set over a bowl and toss with the salt and sugar.

2. Let the cucumbers sit for 10 minutes to drain their excess water. Pour off and discard the water and then put the cucumbers in the bowl. Toss with the garlic, vinegar, soy sauce, sesame oil (if using), chili oil (if using), and the Sichuan peppercorns (if using). Garnish with the fresh cilantro and serve.

antipasto salad

There's something for everyone on those big platters that come to the table at Italian American restaurants before the pizza or pasta: fresh and crunchy iceberg lettuce topped with a variety of canned and jarred vegetables like olives, roasted red peppers, and artichoke hearts.

Yes, we're a cooking school and we encourage cooking from scratch as much as possible, but we think this salad is better (and faster to make!) with roasted peppers from a jar and artichoke hearts from a can. Sure, you could use some fancy French olives, but the basic canned black olives are the true winners in this case. The dressing is what pulls it all together. Season it to taste, but we recommend lots of freshly ground black pepper!

FOR THE SALAD

1 cup canned pitted **black olives**, drained and halved lengthwise

½ cup very thinly sliced **red onion** (about ½ medium onion)

½ cup quartered canned **artichoke hearts**

1 rib **celery**, with its leaves, chopped

⅓ cup thinly sliced **marinated roasted red peppers** (about 1 piece from a jar or can)

2 tablespoons **extra-virgin olive oil**

1 tablespoon **red wine vinegar**

½ teaspoon **kosher salt**

½ teaspoon **freshly ground black pepper**

1 head **iceberg lettuce**

FOR THE DRESSING

½ cup plus 2 tablespoons **extra-virgin olive oil**

¼ cup **red wine vinegar**

½ teaspoon **kosher salt**, plus more to taste

½ teaspoon **freshly ground black pepper**, plus more to taste

1. **Make the salad:** In a large bowl, combine the olives, onion, artichokes, celery, and roasted peppers. Toss with the olive oil, vinegar, salt, and black pepper to thoroughly coat the vegetables. Set aside.

2. Remove the outer leaves and any wilted or brown leaves from the lettuce. Tear the remaining leaves into bite-size pieces. Wash and dry the lettuce.

3. **Make the dressing:** Combine the olive oil, vinegar, salt, and pepper in a lidded jar. Cover the jar and shake until well combined. Taste for seasoning, add more salt and pepper, if desired, and shake again. (The oil and vinegar will separate if the dressing sits for a while, so shake it again right before serving if needed.)

4. When you're ready to serve, add the lettuce and dressing to the marinated vegetable mixture in the bowl and toss.

arugula salad
with parmesan and zesty lemon dressing

¼ cup **extra-virgin olive oil**

1 to 2 teaspoons **freshly grated lemon zest** (from 2 medium lemons)

2 tablespoons **freshly squeezed lemon juice**

Kosher salt and **freshly ground black pepper** to taste

4 cups packed **baby arugula**

2 ounces **Parmesan cheese**, shaved (about ½ cup)

We often mix peppery arugula into salads with milder greens, like spinach or mixed baby lettuces, to tone down its assertive flavor, but in this case, it takes the spotlight, and its boldness is the point. This salad, traditionally served in Italy alongside steak, offers a great lesson in extremes. All the ingredients, from the lemon juice to the Parmesan, are big flavors, but when you put them together, the whole thing is well balanced, bright, and delicious.

You can buy shaved Parmesan in the store, but it's fun (and fresher) to make your own shavings with a vegetable peeler—just run a clean peeler over the hunk of cheese and watch little ribbons fall off. Not only do the shavings look pretty, they hold up better than grated cheese when the salad is dressed.

In a jar with a tight-fitting lid, combine the olive oil, lemon zest, lemon juice, salt, and pepper. Shake it up, then taste for seasoning and adjust if necessary. In a large mixing bowl, toss the arugula with the dressing and sprinkle with the cheese.

massaged kale salad

¼ cup **extra-virgin olive oil**

2 tablespoons **freshly squeezed lemon juice**

1 tablespoon **Dijon mustard**

2 teaspoons minced **shallot** (about ½ small shallot)

1 teaspoon minced **garlic** (about 1 medium clove)

Kosher salt and **freshly ground black pepper** to taste

1 bunch (about ½ pound) **curly** or **lacinato kale**, leaves stemmed

½ cup (about 1½ ounces) grated **Parmesan cheese**

¼ cup **pepitas**, toasted (see page 280) and lightly salted

We always tell kids that "when we were young, there was no kale." Okay, that isn't *totally* true, but in grocery stores, kale was mostly used as a decoration and pretty much never sold as a food! Now it's one of the most popular vegetables—it is amazingly nutritious, has great sturdy texture and powerhouse flavor, and takes to cooking any which way . . . or not being cooked at all!

This salad is *all* about the kale. And there's a special trick. Sure, you can dress it like any salad, but by massaging the leaves with your hands, you soften them and make them more pleasant to eat raw. Lemon helps brighten up the earthy flavor of the kale, although you could use any other acid, like our beloved apple cider vinegar or even rice vinegar. Pepitas (pumpkin seeds) are a nice alternative to nuts for adding a crunchy texture. We top this salad with a mountain of grated Parmesan that looks like snow atop the deep-green mountain of kale, or keep it vegan by using a sprinkle of nutritional yeast in place of the cheese.

1. In a jar with a tight-fitting lid, combine the olive oil, lemon juice, mustard, shallot, and garlic and shake until emulsified. Season with salt and pepper.

2. Use your hands to tear the kale leaves into smaller pieces and place them in a large bowl. Pour the dressing over the kale and use your hands to massage and lightly scrunch the leaves until they get slightly darker in color and more tender. Toss in the Parmesan and pepitas and serve.

save those stems!

Kale stems can be a bit tough and fibrous to eat raw, so we usually tear off the tender leaves. But don't toss the stems into the trash or compost bin. They're packed with flavor and nutrients and need just a little work before they're ready to eat!

Try these ideas:

- Add them to your scrap bag for Vegetable Scrap Stock (page 264).

- Soften them by blanching (see page 282) and then add to your favorite stir-fry. We love them with Up-to-You Fried Rice (page 84)!

- Make Quick Fridge Pickles (page 272). We love eating pickled kale stems as a snack, piled onto a sandwich, or as a topper for grain bowls, salads, and more!

fattoush salad

Fattoush (fah-TOOSH) is a Middle Eastern bread salad made with pita and usually featuring cucumbers, tomatoes, and sometimes cheese. The dressing includes sweet-tart pomegranate molasses (which you can make yourself if you want!), and the salad is finished with a sprinkling of sumac, a lemony spice that comes from the bright red berries of the sumac shrub, which actually grows by the side of the road in many parts of the United States.

We like this salad all on its own as a light summer dinner, but it is also a great side dish for Skillet-Roasted Whole Chicken (page 63) or Spiced and Marinated Kebabs (page 77). Obviously, when planning for how many pita chips to buy (or make!), we encourage students to budget for extra because inevitably the chefs end up snacking quite a bit!

FOR THE DRESSING

3 tablespoons **extra-virgin olive oil**

1 tablespoon **freshly squeezed lemon juice**

1 teaspoon **pomegranate molasses**, store-bought or homemade (recipe follows)

¼ teaspoon **ground sumac** (optional, but encouraged, as it gives the salad its distinct tang)

Pinch of **kosher salt**

A few cracks of **black pepper**

FOR THE SALAD

1 large **romaine heart**, root end trimmed, leaves chopped

1 small **Persian cucumber**, halved lengthwise and sliced crosswise

1 ripe **tomato**, chopped, or a handful of **cherry** or **grape tomatoes**, halved lengthwise

½ small **red onion**, very thinly sliced

3 tablespoons roughly chopped **fresh mint leaves**

3 tablespoons roughly chopped **fresh flat-leaf parsley**

1 large handful (about 2 ounces) **pita chips**, store-bought or homemade (see opposite)

½ cup (2½ ounces) crumbled **feta cheese**

¼ teaspoon **ground sumac**, for sprinkling (optional)

1. In an 8-ounce lidded jar, combine all the dressing ingredients and shake until emulsified and fully combined.

2. In a large bowl, combine the romaine, cucumber, tomato, onion, and herbs.

3. Just before serving, shake the dressing again, then drizzle as much as you want on the salad. Toss the salad, taste, and add more dressing if desired. Top with the pita chips and feta, toss the salad again, and sprinkle sumac on top, if desired, then serve.

pomegranate molasses

makes about 1 cup

1 cup **pomegranate juice**

1 tablespoon **granulated sugar**

2 teaspoons **freshly squeezed lemon juice**

Combine all the ingredients in a small saucepan and simmer over low heat for at least 30 minutes, stirring occasionally, until thick and syrupy.

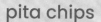

pita chips

This is more a technique than a recipe, so you can make as much as you want.

Preheat the oven to 400°F. Cut fresh pita breads into wedges and drizzle them with a little olive oil (it's up to you how much—you can get a few drops on each piece or lightly coat them). Sprinkle on a little kosher salt and freshly ground black pepper (you can also add ground spices—we love za'atar, the earthy and tangy spice blend with oregano, sumac, and toasted sesame seeds). Spread the wedges out on a sheet pan in a single layer and bake until crispy, about 10 minutes. Start peeking at 8 minutes or so, and don't let them burn!

chopped cucumber and radish salad
with honey-lime vinaigrette

This super-refreshing salad is the recipe we reach for when we're looking for a light counterpoint to something hearty, like our Loaded Enchiladas (page 135) or Vegetarian Three-Bean Chili with All the Toppings (page 146). Crunchy with radishes, cucumbers, and iceberg lettuce, tangy with fresh lime juice, and sweet with honey, it's a great lesson in teaching balance between extremes in tastes and textures. Like all chopped salads, it's important for the ingredients to be cut to about the same size, so that everything can mix and meld together and each bite is balanced.

2 tablespoons **freshly squeezed lime juice** (from 1 medium lime)

2 tablespoons **extra-virgin olive oil**

1 tablespoon minced **shallot** (about ½ small shallot)

1 tablespoon **Dijon mustard**

1 tablespoon **honey**

Kosher salt and **freshly ground black pepper** to taste

1 small to medium head **iceberg lettuce**, chopped (about 6 cups)

1 medium **cucumber**, peeled, quartered lengthwise, and chopped

5 or 6 **radishes**, sliced into thin rounds

3 tablespoons chopped **fresh cilantro leaves**

1. In a small jar with a tight-fitting lid, combine the lime juice, olive oil, shallot, mustard, and honey and shake until emulsified; season the dressing with salt and pepper and shake again.

2. Put the lettuce, cucumber, radishes, and cilantro in a large bowl. Drizzle some of the dressing over the salad and toss well to combine. Taste and, if needed, add more dressing, salt, or pepper.

cheater's caesar salad

Tangy, rich, and refreshing all at the same time, Caesar salad is a real crowd-pleaser. Making the dressing totally from scratch usually means slowly whisking oil into egg yolks, but there's no harm in a time-saving shortcut!

We use store-bought mayo, which provides an already-emulsified base for the garlic/lemon/anchovy–spiked dressing that coats the crunchy leaves and garlicky croutons. About those anchovies: They add another layer of umami to this flavor bomb of a salad, but many kids—and adults—are suspicious of these little fish. Give the recipe a shot and try to recognize the mild depth of flavor they add. By the end of the lesson, you'll probably be licking the dressing off the spoon! If not, no sweat, skip them next time. And if you're vegetarian, the Worcestershire sauce is optional, because it also contains anchovies.

1 large **romaine heart**, root end trimmed, leaves chopped

2 oil-packed **anchovy fillets**, roughly chopped (optional)

2 teaspoons minced **garlic** (about 2 medium cloves)

Kosher salt to taste

¼ cup **extra-virgin olive oil**

2 tablespoons **mayonnaise**

1 tablespoon **Dijon mustard**

1 tablespoon **freshly squeezed lemon juice**

½ teaspoon **Worcestershire sauce** (optional)

¼ cup (about 1 ounce) grated **Parmesan cheese**

Freshly ground black pepper to taste

3 cups **croutons**, store-bought or homemade (see page 281)

Freshly grated lemon zest, for topping (optional)

1. Wash and dry the romaine, then roll the leaves in paper towels and refrigerate until ready to use (this crisps up the leaves and ensures that they're dry).

2. In a large bowl using a whisk, mash the anchovies (if using), garlic, and a pinch of salt. Stir in a few tablespoons of the olive oil to form a paste. Whisk in the mayonnaise, mustard, lemon juice, and Worcestershire sauce (if using). Slowly whisk in the remaining olive oil until smooth and emulsified, then whisk in 2 tablespoons of the Parmesan. Season with salt and pepper.

3. Add the romaine to the bowl and toss well to coat the leaves. Add the croutons and toss to combine. Garnish with the remaining Parmesan, lots of freshly ground black pepper, and lemon zest, if desired.

9

breads & baking

One of the best toys to hand our kids when they were toddlers was a mixing bowl and a wooden spoon. There is something so natural to children about the motion of mixing and kneading. While some recipes, like the Sleepover No-Knead Bread (page 199), take practice to get professional-looking loaves, what's wonderful about bread is that at the end of the day, you're just combining flour (or gluten-free flour mix) with water and a few other ingredients, and you end up with something substantial and universally understood.

There is a reason the term "breaking bread" means sharing food of any kind. Mixing those ingredients and cooking them is a human act that goes back thousands of years. Each time we teach these lessons in bread and baking, we are reminded of that beautiful fact.

monkey bread

We wanted to give you something dazzling to make with yeasted dough, and nothing compares to monkey bread—pillowy dough balls rolled in melted butter and sugar, then baked together in a pan to make a gooey, sweet pull-apart treat.

FOR THE DOUGH

¼ cup **warm water** (between 100°F and 110°F)

1 envelope (2¼ teaspoons) **active dry yeast**

1¼ cups **whole milk**

2 tablespoons **butter**, plus more for greasing

1 large **egg**, lightly beaten

¼ cup **granulated sugar**

1 teaspoon **kosher salt**

4 cups **all-purpose flour** (or a gluten-free substitute, such as Bob's Red Mill 1:1), plus more as needed

½ teaspoon **ground cinnamon** (or a mix of ground cardamom, allspice, nutmeg, and/or cinnamon)

FOR THE STICKY COATING

½ cup packed **dark brown sugar**

1½ teaspoons **ground cinnamon** (or a mix of ground cardamom, allspice, nutmeg, and/or cinnamon)

Pinch of **kosher salt**

6 tablespoons (¾ stick) **butter**, melted

FOR THE ICING

1 cup **powdered sugar**

2 to 3 tablespoons **whole milk**

½ teaspoon **pure vanilla extract**

1. **Make the dough:** Place the warm water in a small dish and stir in the yeast. Let it sit until foamy, about 10 minutes.

2. Meanwhile, in a heavy saucepan, heat the milk and butter over medium-low heat until the butter is just melted. Remove from the heat and let cool to between 105°F and 110°F. Pour the warm milk into a large mixing bowl or the bowl of a stand mixer fitted with the dough hook. Stir in the egg, sugar, and salt. Add the yeast mixture and stir.

3. Add 2 cups of the flour and the spice(s) to the milk mixture and mix with a wooden spoon, or on medium-low speed if using a stand mixer, until the flour has been absorbed. Add the remaining 2 cups flour and mix, then switch to kneading with your hands in the bowl, or if using a stand mixer, continue mixing on medium-low. Knead or mix until the dough is shiny and smooth, 5 to 7 minutes with the stand mixer and a few minutes longer by hand. If after 8 minutes the dough does not pull away easily from the sides of the bowl, add more flour, a tablespoon at a time, until it does.

4. Grease a clean large bowl with a little butter. Transfer the dough to the greased bowl, cover with plastic wrap or a plastic bag, and let rest in a warm place for 30 minutes to 1 hour, until it has doubled in size.

5. **Make the sticky coating:** In a medium bowl, stir together the brown sugar, spice(s), and salt. Have the melted butter ready in a shallow bowl.

6. **Make the dough balls:** Grease a 10-inch skillet, cake pan, or 9 × 13-inch baking pan or line a muffin tin with paper liners.

(RECIPE AND INGREDIENTS CONTINUE)

Up to 1 teaspoon **freshly grated lemon** or **orange zest, ground cinnamon, cardamom, allspice, nutmeg**, or a combination

7. Lightly dust a clean work surface with flour. Turn the dough onto the surface and use your hands to pat it into a rough, flat slab about 1 inch thick. Using a bench scraper or knife, cut the dough into 1-inch chunks, or slightly smaller pieces if you're baking in a muffin tin.

8. Roll each piece of dough into a ball and dunk each ball into the melted butter, then roll it in the sugar-spice mixture until coated evenly. Layer the balls in your pan, staggering the rows as you build. (If using a muffin tin, you will probably get only 4 to 6 dough balls in each cup.) Cover the pan tightly with plastic wrap and refrigerate overnight. (If baking on the same day, cover with plastic wrap and let the dough rest again in a warm place for an additional hour, or until it has doubled in size. Continue with the baking instructions below.)

9. **Make the icing:** Sift the powdered sugar into a small bowl. Whisk in the milk, 1 tablespoon at a time, until the mixture is a smooth and pourable consistency. Whisk in the vanilla and any desired flavorings. Store the icing in an airtight container in the refrigerator until ready to use.

10. At least 1 hour before you plan to bake, remove the dough from the refrigerator and allow it to rise in a warm place, still covered. Remove the icing from the refrigerator and whisk until smooth.

11. Preheat the oven to 350°F.

12. Remove the plastic wrap and bake the monkey bread for 20 to 30 minutes (breads in the muffin tin will cook faster), until the top is deep golden brown and the caramel is bubbling. Cool the bread in the pan or muffin tin for no longer than 5 minutes (to prevent sticking), then turn it out onto a large serving platter. Cool for an additional 10 minutes, then use a spoon to drizzle the icing over the top. Serve immediately.

understanding leaveners

Leaveners are the ingredients that give baked goods a lift. Scientifically speaking, they create air pockets in batters and doughs that give shape and texture to cakes, cookies, breads, and other baked goods. (Next time you have a slice of bread or cake, take a look—it's filled with little holes! The leavener is what put those holes there.) There are a few different types of leaveners, each creating different results in texture and flavor in your final dish.

CHEMICAL LEAVENERS.
Have you ever done the science experiment that combines baking soda and vinegar to create a bubbling-over volcanic reaction? The baking soda is an example of a chemical leavener. Chemical leaveners react with acids (like the vinegar in your experiment) to produce carbon dioxide gas. There are two main types: baking soda (sodium bicarbonate) and baking powder. Baking soda reacts with acidic ingredients in your baked goods (think buttermilk, yogurt, even cocoa powder), while baking powder is the leavener you reach for when your ingredient list has no acid; it has the acid already built in and just needs a bit of water and heat to trigger the reaction. Chemical leaveners are what we reach for when we want a soft and crumbly texture (like in quick breads, cakes, and cookies).

MECHANICAL LEAVENERS.
Mechanical leaveners are ingredients that hold air in your dough or batter—but they need to be added manually. Egg whites and heavy cream act as mechanical leaveners when you whip them (think about how puffed up a meringue or whipped cream can get). Mechanical leaveners can deflate, though, so be careful when folding them into your batter. Do so gently, and you'll get a light and airy cake or pastry.

NATURAL LEAVENERS.
When we talk about natural leaveners, we're talking about yeast. Yeast comes in a few different forms, but essentially, it's a microscopic fungus that converts simple sugars into carbon dioxide gas. Yeast needs two things to do its work: a warm environment and plenty of time. But the payoff for your patience is a chewy, complex dough, like our Sleepover No-Knead Bread (page 199) or Overnight Pizza Dough (page 202).

mix-and-match muffins

2 cups **all-purpose flour** (or a gluten-free substitute, such as Bob's Red Mill 1:1), plus more if needed

2 teaspoons **baking powder**

½ teaspoon **salt**

¾ cup **granulated sugar**

⅔ cup **vegetable oil**, plus more (if needed) for the pan

⅔ cup **buttermilk** (see Note)

2 large **eggs**

Muffin Mix-Ins (see below)

If you're an experienced baker, this is a great muffin recipe to play around with, because it's tender and delicious and allows you to experiment with a wide range of flavors and textures to really make it your own. And if you're new to baking, this is a great place to start! It's simple to make and a great way to practice.

The first step in learning to bake well is learning to measure well. One thing that tends to separate baking from cooking—say, making a salad or a bowl of pasta—is that cooking tends to be more flexible. You can adjust seasonings as you go or stop or start cooking whenever. But when you're baking, often you have to mix the ingredients, put them in the oven, and just wait. So the key is putting the recipe together as intended, which means you have to break out your measuring cups and spoons to make sure you've got the right amount of each ingredient!

Once you've got that part down, the fun of these muffins is in their versatility: Choose which mix-ins you want to flavor your muffins—lemony coconut or berry. After you rock those two, use this same formula to experiment on your own with additions like chocolate chips, or pureed pumpkin and pumpkin pie spice, or orange zest and cranberries—you name it!

muffin mix-ins

BERRY

Dry mix-in: 1½ cups **frozen** or **fresh berries** (chop strawberries, if using)

Wet mix-in: ½ teaspoon **pure vanilla extract**

LEMONY COCONUT

Dry mix-in: 1 cup **unsweetened coconut flakes**, plus more for sprinkling on top before baking

Wet mix-in: 3 tablespoons **freshly grated lemon zest**

1. Preheat the oven to 400°F. Place paper liners in a 12-cup muffin tin. (If you don't have paper liners, you can use a pastry brush to lightly coat each cup in the tin with oil, then dust them with flour. Turn the whole tin over and tap it so any extra flour falls out.)

2. In a medium mixing bowl, combine the flour, baking powder, and salt; these are your dry ingredients.

3. In a large mixing bowl, whisk together the sugar, oil, buttermilk, and eggs; these are your wet ingredients. Add your desired mix-ins to their respective (dry or wet) bowls.

4. Gradually blend the dry ingredients into the wet ingredients until just combined. Stop mixing as soon as there are no more streaks of flour visible (this keeps your muffins from getting rubbery).

5. Spoon the batter into the prepared muffin cups, filling them two-thirds full. Don't fill it beyond that, or the muffins will spill over when baking! If making lemony coconut muffins, sprinkle additional coconut flakes on top.

6. Bake until a cake tester or toothpick inserted into the center of a muffin comes out clean, about 17 minutes. Remove the muffins from the oven and let them cool in the tin. Muffins are best enjoyed the same day, but you can transfer them to an airtight bag and freeze them for up to 2 months.

sleepover no-knead bread

1½ cups **warm water** (between 100°F and 110°F)

¼ teaspoon **active dry yeast**

3¾ cups (about 525 grams) **all-purpose flour** (or replace up to 1 cup/150 grams with whole wheat flour), plus at least another ½ cup for dusting

1 tablespoon (15 grams) **kosher salt**

SPECIAL EQUIPMENT

Dutch oven or lidded oven-safe pot that measures at least 8 inches across and 6 inches deep

preheat your pot!

This recipe is written with safety in mind, so you won't be preheating the bread pot. However, if you have help or can handle hot pots on your own, you will find that if you set your cooking vessel in the oven as it preheats, the bread's crust will be more crispy. Just be careful when you place the parchment paper and dough in the pot!

There might not be anything as satisfying as learning to bake your own bread from scratch. Our overnight method is fun because there's a slumber party involved! Some kids even take the resting dough into their bedrooms for the night.

While a lot of bread recipes ask you to knead the dough, this is a great recipe to start with because, like the name says, you don't need to knead it! Kneading is all about developing gluten. Gluten is the protein in wheat flour that gives bread and noodles made with wheat flour their firmness and chewiness. When you knead dough, you're basically unlocking the gluten in it. But another way of forming gluten is to let the just-mixed dough sit out overnight and allow it to happen by itself!

Here's the thing, though: When you're learning to make bread at home, you need a lot of patience. And you might not stick the landing on the first few tries. This is because there are a lot of variables to take into account, from the environment of the kitchen (humidity and temperature) to the type of flour used—plus the folding and shaping technique takes practice. The good news is, if you follow this recipe, we guarantee you'll get a delicious loaf of bread. Follow it a few times and you'll start making loaves that look professional . . . and then top a slice or two with homemade butter (see page 278) and homemade jam (see page 276) for the ultimate breakfast!

The recipe is forgiving, but it cannot predict the environment of your kitchen and thus cannot give you *exact* times for the proofings. If you mix the bread 3 hours or more before bedtime, then make sure it has its slumber party in the refrigerator (unless you have a very chilly kitchen!). But if you mix it just before bed, it can take its slumber on the counter—or your bedside table.

1. Place 2 tablespoons of the warm water in a small dish and stir in the yeast. Let it sit until foamy, about 10 minutes.

2. In a large mixing bowl, whisk together the flour and

(RECIPE CONTINUES)

measuring by volume vs. weight

There are two standard ways of measuring ingredients in a recipe: *volume* and *weight*.

Volume measures the amount of space an ingredient takes up. That's what you measure with your trusty measuring cups and spoons. For weight, use your kitchen scale.

While it's the American standard to measure by volume (and the way we wrote most of the recipes in this book), measuring by weight yields a more consistent result. This doesn't matter too much with small quantities for things like yeast, spices, and seasonings (which are difficult to weigh on a standard home scale), but it can make a difference when you're working with larger quantities where ratios are important, like in bread baking. This is a great recipe to illustrate this concept, so we give you both volume and weight measurements for the dry ingredients. (A cup of water always weighs the same, though, so it's not as necessary to have both measurements for that!)

Test it for yourself: Scoop a cup of flour using a measuring cup, and have a friend do the same. Weigh each of your scoops on a kitchen scale and see if they're the same!

salt. Add the remaining water and mix with your hands or a wooden spoon to combine. Tear off a walnut-size piece of the shaggy dough. Pour the yeast mixture on top of the dough in the bowl, then use the small piece of dough to wipe out the dish that held the yeast mixture and return it to the bowl with the rest of the dough. Mix with your hands or a wooden spoon to thoroughly combine. Wash your hands!

3. Cover the bowl with plastic wrap or a plastic bag and set aside. After 30 minutes, lightly stretch and fold the dough over onto itself a few times, as if folding a blanket. Squeeze the dough by pinching together the folded layers. Re-cover with plastic. It would be great to do this a second and even a third time spread out over the next couple of hours, but that's not totally necessary. After the final fold, leave the dough covered in the bowl at room temperature for the rest of the day. Just before bed, place the covered bowl in the refrigerator, unless you have only recently (within the last 3 hours or so) mixed the dough, in which case it can rest on the counter.

4. The next morning, take the bowl out of the refrigerator, set it on the counter, and let the dough come to room temperature, about 15 minutes.

5. Dust a smooth (not terry-cloth) kitchen towel or clean piece of fabric with about 2 tablespoons flour and nestle it into a medium mixing bowl. Dust a clean work surface with about 3 tablespoons flour.

6. Dust your hands with flour. Dump the loaf out of the bowl onto the prepared work surface; you may need a rubber spatula or dough scraper to get all the bits. Grab two opposite edges of the dough and stretch them away from each other (making an oblong shape), then fold them, overlapping, toward the center, as if folding a blanket into thirds. Repeat with the other two edges of the dough, creating a ball.

7. Lift the dough ball up and flip it over so the seam side is on the counter in front of you with about a foot of space between the dough and where your body meets the counter. Cup your hands around the sides of the ball and drag it toward your body while

be precise!

Here's something important to keep in mind when baking: Precise measuring is key for successful baking! When measuring dry ingredients, scoop or spoon the ingredients into your measuring cup and use a butter knife to push off any extra mounded over the rim; this is called leveling. For liquid ingredients, use a liquid measuring cup, making sure your eye is even with the cup to get an accurate pour!

simultaneously tilting the edge of the ball closest to you slightly into the counter. Pick up the ball and turn it 90 degrees and repeat three times until you have pulled all four sides. This tipped angle and dragging action help create a taut surface on the top of the bread.

8. Flip the shaped dough seam-side up into the floured, kitchen-towel–lined bowl and let it sit (this is called "proofing") for 30 to 60 minutes, covered loosely with the ends of the fabric, until a gentle finger poke creates a dimple that springs back slowly and incompletely.

9. Preheat the oven to 450°F.

10. When the dough is ready, place a circle of parchment paper on the top of it (still in its proofing bowl) and invert the parchment and dough onto the counter. Carefully lift the paper and dough and place it into a Dutch oven or an oven-safe pot that measures at least 8 inches across and 6 inches deep. Cover it with a fitted lid or a sheet pan. Bake, covered, for 20 to 25 minutes, until the top is showing some color. Remove the lid and continue baking until the loaf takes on a dark golden-brown color, 20 to 25 minutes longer.

11. Using oven mitts or long metal tongs, immediately remove the bread from the pot and set it on a wire rack to cool. If you can stand to wait until the bread cools completely, it will be easier to slice. If you can't wait that long, give it at least 20 minutes before slicing and serving.

overnight pizza dough

*15-ounce balls (enough for two 16-inch pizzas)

1½ cups **warm water** (between 100°F and 110°F)

¼ teaspoon **active dry yeast**

4 cups **all-purpose** or **"tipo 00" flour**

2½ teaspoons **kosher salt**

Neutral oil, such as olive or vegetable, for greasing

After we teach students this foolproof method for making their own pizza dough from scratch and they make their first homemade pie, we often hear squeals of joy, pronouncements of pride, and even sighs of relief (it can be stressful, but it always works out!). Like our Sleepover No-Knead Bread (page 199), the key here is to mix the ingredients, knead a bit, then let it all take a nice long nap. During that time, those precious gluten strands develop (we offer a GF version, too!) and the flavor deepens. Our go-to recipe has always been Ken Forkish's from his book *The Elements of Pizza*, and this recipe is our adaptation of his.

If you can find it in your grocery store, try using "tipo 00" flour, a finely ground Italian flour that yields a softer crust with a crispier bottom, although regular all-purpose flour will work just fine. What's beautiful about making pizza dough is the creative sense it presents, since it's essentially a blank canvas; the conversations about toppings are endless, and there are always surprises. Don't get us started about pineapple on pizza!

1. In a small bowl, mix 3 tablespoons of the warm water with the yeast until dissolved.

2. In a large mixing bowl, combine the flour and remaining warm water using a wooden spoon until a shaggy dough forms. Sprinkle the salt and the yeast mixture on top and, using a wet hand (this helps prevent the dough from sticking to you), stir the mixture by moving your hand around the inside of the bowl to mix the flour, water, salt, and yeast into a single mass. Then use your hands to squeeze the dough into a long, roughly formed rope, fold it in half lengthwise, and repeat, squeezing along the length of the dough and folding it over again. Make 2 or 3 folds in this manner and let the dough rest in the bowl for 20 minutes, covered loosely with a clean kitchen towel or plastic wrap.

3. Sprinkle some flour onto a clean work surface and scrape the dough out of the bowl onto the prepared surface. Knead it for about 1 minute, until smooth, by pushing the heel of one hand into the center of

timeline

This recipe has been designed so you can prepare your dough the day or night before class, but there are ways to adjust the timing to have perfect pizza dough without an overnight wait: you just have to make it the morning of the day you want to eat your pizza. Below are some alternative rise times for the initial fermentation (the rise that happens after you shape the dough and hold it in a bowl) and the second fermentation (after the dough has been divided and shaped). Next time you make pizza, try out a different timeline and see if you notice a difference in flavor or texture!

FIRST FERMENTATION

After shaping, let the dough rest for 2 hours at room temperature, then proceed to the next step.

SECOND FERMENTATION

After shaping, let the dough rest for at least 6 hours and up to 12 hours at room temperature.

After shaping, let the dough rest for 4 hours at room temperature, then hold it in the fridge for up to the next evening. (If you refrigerate the dough, let it come to room temperature for an hour or so before making your pizza.)

the dough ball, then scooping the elongated side of dough back onto itself, turning the dough a quarter turn, and repeating.

4. Spread a little oil to lightly coat the inside of a large airtight container. Place the dough ball seam-side down in the container. Cover with a tight-fitting lid or plastic wrap. Leave the dough at room temperature for 1 hour, then transfer the dough to the refrigerator to rest overnight. This is the initial fermentation. The next day, take the container out of the refrigerator 1 hour before baking and set it on the counter.

5. Clean, dry, and lightly flour the work surface. Remove the dough from the container and shape it into a slightly tightened ball. Using your hands, cup it on either side and pull the dough toward you while slightly pushing it against the counter to pull the ball taut. Turn the ball a quarter turn and repeat. Work the ball gently and be careful not to tear the dough.

6. Lightly sprinkle some more flour on the work surface. Place the dough ball on the flour, divide it with a knife into 2 equal pieces, sprinkle flour over the tops, cover with plastic wrap, and let rest at room temperature for at least 30 minutes for the second fermentation.

7. Make your pizza anytime within 4 hours following the second fermentation.

sheet pan pizzas

All-purpose flour, as needed

Two 15-ounce balls of **Overnight Pizza Dough** (page 202) or store-bought

1 cup **Tomato Pizza Sauce** (recipe follows)

16 ounces **fresh mozzarella cheese**, sliced

1 cup **toppings** (see Note)

A few **fresh basil leaves**, for garnish

> **TOPPINGS** can include anything you want, such as cooked sausage, pepperoni slices, sliced peppers, onions, or mushrooms. If you're using raw vegetables, be sure to slice them thinly so they'll cook through.

When it comes to baking your pizza, there's no need for a round pan or stressing over a perfectly round pie. We stretch the dough and place it in a large sheet pan to create a thin, misshapen Neapolitan-style pie, which develops a nicely charred crust in the oven. Be careful not to load up the pie with too much sauce, which will turn the dough soggy, or too many ingredients, which will prevent the thin dough from cooking quickly. We love to make pies pizza-party-style, where each person makes their own creation. We serve one pie at a time, so everyone gets a hot slice right out of the oven.

1. Preheat the oven to 475°F. Lightly flour two 13 × 18-inch half sheet pans.

2. Lightly flour a clean work surface and press 1 ball of pizza dough into a flat disk. Starting at the center and working toward the edges, use your fingertips to press the dough into a ½-inch-thick disk. Stretch the dough with your hands until it seems like it cannot stretch more without tearing.

3. Let the dough rest for a few minutes and then continue stretching until it is roughly a 12-inch diameter circle. It does not have to be a perfect circle! A good way of doing this is to hold up the dough by the edges like you're holding the top of a steering wheel, letting the dough hang and stretch, then turning the dough so that it stretches evenly by the time you put it back down. If you tear the dough, place it on the floured surface and pinch the torn spot back together to seal the hole.

4. Carefully set the dough on one of the floured sheet pans. Using a spoon, spread less than ½ cup of the pizza sauce very conservatively over the dough, leaving a ½-inch border. A thin layer is all you need and will make a better pie; you may not use the entire amount. Scatter up to half the cheese and up to half the toppings over the sauce. Be careful not to overload the pizza. A wet pizza will not crisp up.

(RECIPE CONTINUES)

5. Repeat with the second piece of dough and the remaining sauce, cheese, and toppings.

6. Bake the pizzas for 12 to 15 minutes, until the crust is lightly browned with bits of char. Remove the pizzas from the oven and transfer to a cutting board. Garnish with torn fresh basil leaves, slice, and serve immediately.

tomato pizza sauce

makes about 2 cups (enough for four 16-inch pizzas)

1 can (14 to 16 ounces) **whole peeled tomatoes**, preferably San Marzano, drained

2 **garlic cloves**

½ teaspoon **kosher salt**

Using a blender, puree the tomatoes, garlic, and salt until the large tomato pieces are just broken up. If you're working without a blender, use your hands to break up the tomatoes, finely mince the garlic, and mix both with the salt in a small mixing bowl. Use immediately or store in the fridge for up to 3 days.

skillet corn bread or corn muffins

*9-inch round loaf
or 12 muffins

1¼ cups fine, medium, or coarse **stone-ground yellow cornmeal**

1 cup **all-purpose flour** (or a gluten-free substitute, such as Bob's Red Mill 1:1)

5 tablespoons **granulated sugar**

1 tablespoon **baking powder**

½ teaspoon **baking soda**

½ teaspoon **kosher salt**

1 cup **buttermilk** (see Note on page 197)

4 tablespoons (½ stick) **butter**, melted and cooled, plus more for greasing

¼ cup **vegetable oil**

2 large **eggs**

1 cup **fresh**, thawed **frozen**, or drained canned **corn kernels** (optional)

This is our go-to accompaniment for Vegetarian Three-Bean Chili with All the Toppings (page 146), Gumbo (page 161), or any dish that benefits from having some buttery corn bread pieces crumbled in! Sometimes we bake it in a muffin tin, and other times we bake one big cast-iron skillet of corn bread.

This is a great lesson in the fundamentals of baking: measuring and mixing dry ingredients and wet ingredients. Also key to this recipe—and any recipe that uses baking soda—is using something acidic (in this case, buttermilk) to cause the baking soda to bubble up, giving the corn bread a good rise. The corn kernels are optional, but we love the texture they add; you could replace them with the same amount of cheese or a mix of cheese and pickled peppers, or you can skip it altogether.

1. Preheat the oven to 400°F. Grease a 9-inch cast-iron skillet or cake pan with butter. Alternatively, grease a standard 12-cup muffin tin or fit the cups with paper liners.

2. In a large bowl, whisk together the dry ingredients: cornmeal, flour, sugar, baking powder, baking soda, and salt. In another bowl, whisk together the wet ingredients: buttermilk, melted butter, oil, and eggs.

3. Pour the wet ingredients over the dry ingredients and stir just to combine. When blended but still lumpy, stir in the corn kernels (if using). Pour the batter into the prepared pan or divide it evenly among the lined muffin cups.

4. Bake the skillet corn bread for 20 to 23 minutes, or the muffins for 15 to 18 minutes, until the top is cracked and golden brown and a cake tester or toothpick inserted into the center comes out clean. Transfer to a baking rack and let cool for 5 minutes before slicing the corn bread into wedges or carefully removing each muffin from the tin mold to serve.

cornmeal types

You can use fine, medium, or coarse stone-ground cornmeal in this recipe. The finer the grind, the silkier the texture of the finished bread. (This isn't necessarily everyone's desired effect!)

buttery drop biscuits

2 cups **all-purpose flour** (or a gluten-free substitute, such as Bob's Red Mill 1:1)

1 tablespoon **baking powder**

1 teaspoon **salt**, plus a pinch for the top

½ cup (1 stick) **cold butter**, chopped into cubes, plus 1 tablespoon for greasing

¾ to 1 cup **whole milk**

Biscuits are one of those foods where there are all kinds of ways to make them. We like the method of "cutting in" the butter, combining the butter with the flour so that visible pieces of butter remain in the dough. When those bits of butter melt during baking, the water they contain turns to steam, pushing up and out of the dough. The result is a light and flaky biscuit.

And to help keep them light, resist the urge to work this dough too much! The less you work the dough, the more tender the biscuits will be.

These pair great with our homemade butter (see page 278) and jam (see page 276), and can become breakfast sandwiches when filled with scrambled eggs (see page 51). Or serve them with our Totally Adaptable Frittata (page 52), for a nourishing brunch menu. The best part is, they're ready in a flash, so anytime that biscuit craving comes on, this recipe is ready for it!

1. Preheat the oven to 450°F. Grease a 10-inch cast-iron skillet or round pan with 1 tablespoon butter.

2. Sift the flour, baking powder, and salt into a large mixing bowl. Using a pastry cutter or two table knives, cut the cubes of butter into the flour until they are pieces the size of black beans. Quickly rub the butter into the flour with your fingers until you have a bowlful of powdery-looking butter chips. Add ¾ cup of the milk and mix gently with a fork until a soft, shaggy dough forms. If it is too dry, add a little more milk.

3. Drop the dough by large spoonfuls into the greased pan, nestling the biscuits close together. Sprinkle a pinch of salt on top of the dough.

4. Bake for about 12 minutes, until the tops are lightly browned. Transfer to a baking rack. Serve warm.

5. The biscuits will keep in an airtight container at room temperature for up to 2 days, or wrap them tightly in foil and a layer of plastic wrap, or place in a zip-top plastic freezer bag or airtight container and freeze for up to 3 months. To reheat, wrap biscuits in foil and heat in a 300°F oven for 5 minutes.

banana bread
with brown sugar glaze

*9 × 5-inch loaf

5 very ripe small **bananas**

1½ teaspoons **pure vanilla extract**

1 cup lightly packed **dark brown sugar**

⅔ cup **vegetable oil** or **mild olive oil**, plus more for greasing

⅓ cup plain **whole-milk yogurt** or **full-fat buttermilk** (see Note on page 197)

2 large **eggs**

1½ cups **all-purpose flour** (or a gluten-free substitute, such as Bob's Red Mill 1:1)

1 teaspoon **baking soda**

1 teaspoon **baking powder**

½ teaspoon **kosher salt**

2 tablespoons **Demerara sugar** or other **coarse sugar** (such as Sugar In The Raw), for sprinkling (optional)

FOR THE BROWN SUGAR GLAZE

½ cup lightly packed **dark brown sugar**

½ cup **powdered sugar**, sifted

2 to 3 tablespoons **whole milk**, **half-and-half**, or **heavy cream**

Whether you realize it or not, you've probably eaten quick breads before. The most time-consuming bread to make is sourdough, which can take days or even weeks to get going. Then there are yeast breads, which are usually ready to bake in a day or even a few hours. But the quickest breads are—you guessed it—quick breads. They are usually made with baking powder or baking soda, which gives an instant rise to the bread as it bakes.

Even the youngest of cooks can whip up this banana bread practically blindfolded because there are very few points where you can make a mistake. But it has a showstopping flair in its presentation, with a shiny sliced banana on top.

Consider our banana bread a starting line for your own banana bread journey; add mix-ins or change the shape and bake it in a muffin tin. (Our favorite add-ins are toasted pecans, chocolate chips, and/or toasted coconut chips.) And definitely have a giggly debate with someone about whether banana bread is really cake in disguise! We say toast it for breakfast or drizzle it with melted chocolate for dessert.

1. Preheat the oven to 350°F. Grease a 9 × 5-inch loaf pan and line it with parchment paper.

2. Peel 1 banana and lay it on a cutting board. Slice it in half lengthwise so the cut sides are flat.

3. In a small bowl, mash the remaining 4 bananas with the vanilla (you'll have about 2 cups of mashed bananas).

4. In a large mixing bowl, whisk together the brown sugar, oil, yogurt, and eggs, making sure no dry clumps of brown sugar remain. Add the mashed bananas and stir to combine.

5. In a medium mixing bowl, whisk together the flour, baking soda, baking powder, and salt. Fold this into the banana mixture until just combined, then pour it into your prepared pan. Smooth the top with a spatula and place the halves of the sliced banana cut-side up, on the batter. Sprinkle with the Demerara sugar (if using).

It's best to bring your eggs to room temperature for baking because the yolks and whites will mix together more thoroughly.

6. Bake for about 1 hour, until a cake tester or toothpick inserted into the center comes out clean, the top of the banana bread is set, and the sugar has caramelized (if you used it). Let cool in the pan for at least 20 minutes, then remove from the pan and transfer to a wire rack to cool completely.

7. **Make the glaze:** In a small bowl, whisk together the brown sugar and powdered sugar. Whisk in the milk, 1 tablespoon at a time, until the mixture has a smooth and pourable consistency. Use a spoon to drizzle the glaze over the cooled banana bread. Slice and serve.

10

sweets

There is this idea out there that the only way to get kids to cook is to have them make desserts. We *know* that's not true! Still, we like to give sweets their fair share of the spotlight in our classes, because you can learn so much about cooking through making desserts.

Our lineup is filled with classics like cupcakes, birthday cake, brownies, pie, and cookies. Then we throw in some more sophisticated (but still very doable!) pastries like Olive Oil Orange Cake (page 223), Chocolate Pots de Crème (page 239), and Classic Cream Puffs with Raspberry Whipped Cream and Berries (page 246). What we love about making dessert is that it's often done with the goal of sharing it with other people at birthday celebrations, for holiday gifts, and for charity bake sales. See? There is so much goodness—beyond the sugar!—to be had with sweets.

buttermilk cupcakes

2 cups **all-purpose flour** (or a gluten-free substitute, such as Bob's Red Mill 1:1)

¾ teaspoon **baking soda**

½ teaspoon **salt**

½ cup (1 stick) **butter**, at room temperature

1 cup **granulated sugar**

2 large **eggs**

1 teaspoon **pure vanilla extract**

1 cup **buttermilk** (see Note on page 197)

2 cups **Buttercream Frosting** (page 217) or your favorite frosting

Sprinkles, crumbled **cookies**, or other toppings (optional!)

What youngster doesn't love a cupcake? Based on our data, very few!

Our go-to cupcake recipe is buttermilk-based and makes a great batter that's delicious on its own, but it's also perfect for customizing with different flavors, mix-ins, and even colors.

A couple things to take away from this recipe (beyond great cupcakes!): The buttermilk gives the batter a rich, balanced flavor and also provides the acid that the leavening agent (baking soda) needs to activate (see Understanding Leaveners, page 195). And when mixing the batter, alternating wet and dry ingredients ensures everything is evenly combined.

Put your own stamp on the way you decorate these cupcakes! Unicorn cupcakes, jelly bean cupcakes—you name it. We've included some suggestions for customizing, but we leave it to the kids to come up with the most original cupcakes!

suggestions for customizing your cupcakes

FOR CITRUS CUPCAKES: Add 1 tablespoon of grated zest from your favorite citrus (lemon, lime, or orange) while creaming the butter and sugar.

FOR CHOCOLATE CUPCAKES: Dissolve ¼ cup of cocoa powder in 2 tablespoons of hot water and add to the wet ingredients.

FOR SPICED CUPCAKES: Add up to 1 tablespoon of ground spices (such as cinnamon, cardamom, nutmeg, and/or cloves) to the dry ingredients.

OTHER FLAVORS: Swap out the vanilla extract for a different extract (such as almond, mint, or fruit).

MIX-INS: Stir in up to 1 cup of mix-ins (such as chocolate chips, butterscotch chips, toasted coconut flakes, chopped nuts, or sprinkles) after the batter has been mixed. Note that you will likely have extra batter for 1 or 2 additional cupcakes.

1. Preheat the oven to 350°F. Place paper liners in a standard 12-cup muffin tin.

2. In a medium bowl, combine the flour, baking soda, and salt. Whisk until combined.

3. Place the butter and sugar in the bowl of a stand mixer fitted with the paddle attachment and beat on medium speed until well combined, fluffy, and pale yellow, 3 to 4 minutes. Add the eggs, fully blending in the first one before adding the next one. Add the vanilla and beat until incorporated.

4. Turn the mixer to low speed and add half of the dry ingredients, then ½ cup of the buttermilk, then the remaining dry ingredients, then the remaining ½ cup buttermilk. Turn off the mixer to scrape down the bowl in between as needed to make sure all the ingredients are mixed in. Mix one final time until just incorporated.

5. Carefully fill each paper liner about two-thirds full. (If you want to add a swirl or marble effect to the batter, divide the batter between two bowls, add a small amount of coloring to each batch, and mix each until the color is even. Spoon a little of each color, alternating between colors, into the liners until they are two-thirds full. Put the tip of a knife or a chopstick into each cupcake and give it one turn to swirl the colors.)

6. Bake for 15 to 20 minutes, until a cake tester or toothpick inserted into the center of a cupcake comes out clean. When they're done, remove the tin from the oven and place it on a wire rack until cool enough to invert and free each cupcake. Let the cupcakes finish cooling in their liners on the rack.

7. Once cooled, decorate as desired. To frost cupcakes, dollop a few tablespoons frosting on each and smooth with a butter knife, or fill a piping bag with frosting to swirl and pile it high. Top with sprinkles, crumbled cookies, toasted coconut, or other desired toppings.

cupcakes for everyone!

Everyone deserves a cupcake, so even if you're gluten-free, dairy-free, or egg-free, we've got a recipe fix for you.

FOR GLUTEN-FREE

Substitute an all-purpose gluten-free flour for the flour. We like Bob's Red Mill 1:1.

FOR DAIRY-FREE

Substitute vegan butter baking sticks for the butter. We like Earth Balance.

Substitute unsweetened plant milk (we like oat or soy) plus 1 tablespoon lemon juice or white vinegar for the buttermilk.

Substitute coconut cream for the heavy cream.

FOR EGG-FREE

Substitute ½ cup unsweetened applesauce for the eggs.

buttercream frosting

1 cup (2 sticks) **butter**, at room temperature

Pinch of **salt**

3 cups **powdered sugar**

3 tablespoons **heavy cream**

1 teaspoon **pure vanilla extract**

OPTIONAL

A few drops of **food coloring**, or 3 tablespoons **unsweetened cocoa powder** (for chocolate frosting)

This is our go-to frosting recipe for cupcakes and layer cakes. It's so smooth, creamy, and delicious, you'll swear the baked good is just a vehicle for the frosting! There are lots of variations on the buttercream theme, but this version is the simple, classic, and foolproof American-style. The great lesson here is the importance of letting butter sit on the counter so it comes to room temperature and softens. Then you cream your softened butter with the sugar, incorporating air until it is pale yellow and takes on a fluffy, voluminous, spreadable texture. We won't blame you for licking the beaters!

This recipe makes enough for 12 cupcakes or our Classic Layer Cake (page 218).

1. Place the butter and salt in the bowl of a stand mixer fitted with the paddle attachment and beat on low speed for a few seconds, gradually increasing to medium speed. Beat until smooth, creamy, and pale yellow in color, about 5 minutes total.

2. Stop the mixer and add 1 cup of the powdered sugar. Start the mixer on low and gradually increase to medium speed, mixing until well combined.

3. Stop the mixer and scrape down the sides of the bowl and/or the paddle attachment if the mixture is clinging to either one and not incorporating. Then add another cup of the powdered sugar and continue with these steps until all the sugar has been incorporated. Each time you restart the mixer, start on low speed and gradually increase to medium speed.

4. Turn the mixer to low speed and add the cream and vanilla and food coloring (if using). Mix until everything is incorporated, again checking for unmixed ingredients stuck on the bowl or paddle.

5. Increase the speed to high and beat until the frosting is smooth and fluffy, about 5 minutes.

6. If you're not using this right away or the frosting is too soft to spread (which happens when it gets too warm), chill the frosting in the refrigerator and then whip again before using it to decorate.

classic layer cake

*6-inch double-layer cake

1½ cups **all-purpose flour** (or a gluten-free substitute, such as Bob's Red Mill 1:1)

½ cup **natural** (not Dutch-processed) **cocoa powder** (optional; for making a chocolate cake)

1 cup **granulated sugar**

1½ teaspoons **baking soda**

¾ teaspoon **baking powder**

½ teaspoon **salt**

¾ cup **buttermilk** (see Note on page 197)

½ cup **vegetable oil**, plus more for greasing

2 large **eggs**, at room temperature

1 teaspoon **pure vanilla extract**

⅓ cup **very hot water** (or coffee if you're making chocolate cake; see Note)

2 cups **Buttercream Frosting** (page 217)

Sprinkles or other **cake decorations** (optional)

In a world where bigger is too often thought of as better, here is the rarely sought-after but totally practical family-size birthday cake! It makes a beautiful double-layer cake with a moist, buttery-rich crumb that serves up to 8 people. It's a manageable size, the pans tuck into the back of your cabinet, and it's a fun cake to make as a gift. These cakes are less intimidating to decorate due to their petite size, and they are a great cake to bring to an event with other desserts. Okay, so "not huge is no fun" you say? Double it! (Check out our Cake Math on page 221.)

1. Preheat the oven to 325°F with a rack in the center. Smear a little oil all over the insides of two 6-inch round cake pans to grease them. Cut two circles of parchment paper that fit the pan bottoms and place them in the pans.

2. In a large bowl, whisk together the flour, cocoa powder (if using), sugar, baking soda, baking powder, and salt.

3. In a medium bowl, combine the buttermilk, oil, eggs, and vanilla. Beat vigorously until combined.

4. Slowly pour the wet ingredients into the dry ingredients and beat until just combined. Whisk in the hot water just until the batter has no dry lumps. Do not overbeat.

5. Divide the batter evenly between the prepared cake pans and place them in the oven. Bake for 30 to 40 minutes, rotating the pans 180 degrees halfway through cooking to ensure they bake evenly. The cakes are done when they pull away slightly from the sides of the pans and a cake tester or toothpick inserted into the center comes out clean.

6. Remove the cakes from the oven and let rest for 5 minutes on a wire rack. Turn the pans upside down to tip out the cakes. If the cakes stick, use a butter knife to free them from the pan. Allow to cool completely before frosting.

7. To assemble the cake, start with frosting that is set (chilled) but brought to room temperature. See how

(RECIPE CONTINUES)

the cakes puffed up a little in the center when baked? Carefully slice just the rounded tops off both cake layers using a long serrated knife (a bread knife) to make level, even cakes. (This is so that they can stack on each other without tipping.) Do so by placing the palm of your free hand on top of the cake, holding it steady while slowly shimmying the knife across the cake, keeping the blade parallel to the counter and tracing the lip of the cake so only the rounded top is removed. Repeat with the other layer.

8. Cut three 1- to 2-inch-wide strips of parchment paper (use the width of the roll to determine the length of the strips, usually 13 inches). Place them on a wide plate or cake stand so that they form a triangle. (These will keep the plate clean as you frost the cake.) Dollop a tablespoon of frosting in the middle of the plate to act as glue for the first cake layer.

9. Place one cake layer trimmed-side up on the plate. Spoon a few tablespoons of frosting across the top of the cake and spread it with the spatula as if buttering toast. This is called the "crumb coat," and it gets the cake ready for a more serious frosting layer by trapping any loose crumbs. Smooth another ½ cup of the frosting over the crumb coat to create the center layer of frosting and, using the spatula, move it evenly all the way to the edges of the cake.

10. Place the second cake layer on top, cut-side down. Spread another few tablespoons of frosting on top to form a crumb coat. Smooth about ¼ cup of the frosting on the sides to give them a crumb coat, too. Chill the cake for 30 minutes, but keep the frosting at room temperature.

11. Spread ½ cup of the frosting across the top of the chilled cake. Spread the remaining frosting on the sides, working the frosting first around the cake with the spatula perpendicular to the plate. Once it is evenly distributed, use the spatula to make the desired design, either waves or a very clean design, by continuing to turn the plate while keeping the spatula perfectly perpendicular to the plate. Finish smoothing the frosting on the top of the cake.

be gentle!

When combining the wet and dry ingredients, be careful not to overbeat the ingredients. Only mix until the mixture looks uniform and no dry lumps remain, no longer. Otherwise your cake will be tough and/or have big holes in it.

12. To decorate with sprinkles, place the cake plate or stand on a rimmed sheet pan to catch any rogue sprinkles. Hold a few spoonfuls in your hand and get close to the sides of the cake. In one motion, toss and press them gently into the cake. Collect the fallen sprinkles to continue decorating and minimize waste. Carefully remove the strips of parchment paper and serve the cake.

cake math

This recipe makes a 6-inch cake that, depending on how you frost it, can stand about 6 inches tall. If you want a bigger cake, or don't have a 6-inch pan but you do have a 9-inch pan, here's the math: A 6-inch cake pan holds 4 cups of batter. A 9-inch cake pan holds 8 cups, so if you're working with 9-inch pans, double the recipe. If you increase the recipe for a 9-inch pan, note that it will take a few more minutes to bake (test for doneness after 45 minutes). And don't forget to double the frosting!

olive oil orange cake

*9-inch cake

¾ cup plus 1 teaspoon **extra-virgin olive oil**

1 cup plus 1 tablespoon **granulated sugar**

1⅓ cups **all-purpose flour** (or a gluten-free substitute, such as Bob's Red Mill 1:1)

1 teaspoon **kosher salt**

½ teaspoon **baking powder**

¼ teaspoon **baking soda**

2 large **eggs**

¾ cup **whole milk**

1 tablespoon **freshly grated orange zest**

⅓ cup **freshly squeezed orange juice**

1 teaspoon **pure vanilla extract**

Whipped Cream (page 276) or **crème fraîche**, for serving (optional)

Don't worry, your olive oil cake won't taste like olives! When baked into a cake, olive oil actually imparts a very smooth, fruity flavor and incredibly moist texture. This dairy-free cake is super easy to make. You can adapt it for any type of citrus (grapefruit is amazing!).

Kids and adults both agree it's a top pick for the dessert course. You can eat it with your hands off a paper towel on the go, or serve it dusted with powdered sugar and a side of Whipped Cream (page 276) for something more elegant. You can even make a double layer and decorate it with our Buttercream Frosting (page 217) for a really dazzling special occasion cake!

1. Preheat the oven to 350°F. Grease a 9 × 2-inch round cake pan with 1 teaspoon of the olive oil and line the bottom with parchment paper cut to fit. Press the parchment into the pan and twist it in place to cover with oil then flip it over and nestle it into the pan. Sprinkle 1 tablespoon of the sugar all over the bottom and sides of the pan. Tap the pan to evenly distribute the sugar in the pan, focusing on the sides.

2. In a medium mixing bowl, whisk together the flour, the remaining 1 cup sugar, the salt, baking powder, and baking soda.

3. In a large mixing bowl, whisk the eggs until combined. Add the remaining ¾ cup olive oil, the milk, orange zest and juice, and vanilla and beat until well combined. Add the dry ingredients to the wet ingredients; whisk until just combined, making sure to break up any lumps.

4. Pour the batter into the prepared pan and bake for 50 to 60 minutes, until the top is golden, the middle is firm, and a cake tester or toothpick inserted into the center comes out clean. Transfer the cake to a wire rack and let cool for 30 minutes.

5. Run a knife around the edge of the pan, invert the cake onto a plate, and flip it back onto the rack to cool completely. To serve, slice it into wedges and plate with a dollop of whipped cream or crème fraîche, if desired.

rustic fruit galette

*10-inch galette

"Galette" is just a fancy word for an easygoing pie. Not that pies are uptight, but this method is so laid-back that it doesn't even need a pan. It's always fun to see one of these come out of the oven, each beautiful and unique. You can use just about any berry or stone fruit as a filling. (You can also use frozen fruit for this recipe; just don't defrost it before baking, otherwise you'll have a liquidy mess.)

FOR THE DOUGH

1⅓ cups **all-purpose flour** (or a gluten-free substitute, see Note), plus more for dusting

1 tablespoon **sugar**

½ teaspoon **kosher salt**

1 large **egg**

2 tablespoons **heavy cream**

½ cup (1 stick) **butter**, chilled and cut into ½- to ¾-inch cubes

1 to 3 tablespoons **ice water**

FOR THE FILLING

3 cups **summer fruit** (berries, stone fruit, figs), pitted (if necessary) and sliced (unless small)

½ cup plus 2 teaspoons **sugar**

Pinch of **kosher salt**

1 teaspoon **freshly grated lemon zest**

1 tablespoon **freshly squeezed lemon juice**

3 tablespoons **cornstarch**

NOTE: When using GF flour, the dough will be more crumbly, so roll the dough between two sheets of parchment paper.

1. In a large mixing bowl or a food processor, combine the flour, sugar, and salt. In a small bowl, beat the egg and 1 tablespoon of the cream.

2. Add the butter to the flour mixture and use a pastry cutter or your fingers to break up the butter, or pulse them briefly if using a food processor. Continue just until you have lumps of butter the size of a black bean. Add the egg mixture and mix or pulse until it just comes together; the mixture should look like slightly wet oats. If it is still too dry, drizzle in a tablespoon of ice water at a time, don't overmix the dough.

3. Put the dough on a lightly floured surface and form a disk. Wrap in plastic and chill for at least 30 minutes.

4. Preheat the oven to 400°F. Line a sheet pan with parchment paper or a baking mat. Roll the dough into a roughly 12-inch circle. Carefully transfer the dough to the pan, letting the edges of the dough hang over the sides of the pan, and refrigerate while you make the filling.

5. In a medium mixing bowl, combine the fruit, ½ cup of the sugar, the salt, lemon zest, lemon juice, and cornstarch. Take the dough out of the refrigerator and arrange the fruit in the center of the circle, leaving a 1- to 2-inch border. Carefully fold the pastry edge over until it just starts to cover the fruit, working around the circle, making pleats as you go to keep a round shape.

6. Brush the folded dough edge with the remaining 1 tablespoon cream. Sprinkle the remaining 2 teaspoons sugar over the crust.

7. Bake the galette for 35 to 45 minutes, until the filling bubbles up and the crust is golden brown. Transfer the pan to a wire rack. Serve warm or cooled.

blueberry-lemon hand pies

1 large **egg**

2 tablespoons **whole milk**

2 cups **frozen blueberries**

¼ cup **granulated sugar**

2½ tablespoons **cornstarch**

Pinch of **ground cinnamon**

Pinch of **kosher salt**

1 tablespoon **freshly grated lemon zest**

2 tablespoons **freshly squeezed lemon juice**

All-purpose flour, for dusting

Two 10 × 15-inch **frozen puff pastry sheets**, thawed

Demerara sugar or another **coarse sugar** (such as Sugar In The Raw), for sprinkling

Why have a slice of pie when you can have a *whole dessert all to yourself*? Hand pies are the perfect picnic, party, or bring-to-school treat, because there's no need to slice and serve: Everyone gets their own pastry packet wrapped around a fruity filling. If you're in the mood to make the pastry from scratch, go for it—we have a great recipe on page 224. But we'll just as soon applaud your smarty-pants resourcefulness for whipping up a homemade treat with store-bought puff pastry.

Feel free to be creative with this recipe: We love this filling's balance of sweet-tart and warm spice, but you can skip the cinnamon and add fresh thyme leaves or candied ginger to the berries before cooking, or swap the frozen berries for fresh-picked ones or sliced ripe peaches. It's dessert, not rocket science!

1. Preheat the oven to 400°F. Line a large sheet pan with parchment paper.

2. In a small bowl, whisk the egg and milk with a fork to make an egg wash. Set aside.

3. In a small saucepan, toss the blueberries with the granulated sugar, cornstarch, cinnamon, and salt. Heat over medium heat, stirring occasionally, until some of the berries burst and the mixture thickens slightly, about 5 minutes. Stir in the lemon zest and lemon juice. Remove from the heat and allow to cool. (The filling can be made 1 day ahead of time and refrigerated.)

4. Dust a clean work surface with a few big pinches of flour, roll out a sheet of puff pastry about ⅛ inch thick, and cut it into 8 equal rectangles each measuring about 3¾ × 5 inches. Repeat with the remaining pastry sheet, but with these rectangles, use either a knife to slice 3 small vents on top or a decorative cutter to cut out a shape like a star or a heart (it shouldn't be larger than 1 inch).

5. Place the 8 nonvented rectangles on your prepared sheet pan. Using a pastry brush, brush the edges of each with some of the egg wash. Add 3 tablespoons of the blueberry filling to the center of each rectangle. Cover each with a vented rectangle and use a fork to seal and crimp the edges; don't worry if some of the filling seeps out, but try to keep the whole berries in the center. Brush the entire tops of the hand pies with the egg wash and sprinkle with the Demerara sugar. Bake for 20 to 25 minutes, until golden brown. Let cool before serving.

puff pastry hacks

Our freezers are never without a package of puff pastry sheets, ready to use whenever we need a quick fix for sweet or savory dishes. Here are a few of our favorite ways to use it.

PIE OR GALETTE DOUGH: Roll out a sheet of puff pastry and swap it for pie dough or when making a galette (see page 224).

SWEET OR SAVORY TWISTS: Slice, twist, and bake sheets of puff pastry into a flaky, buttery snack. Butter and coat them with cinnamon sugar before baking for a sweet treat, or with Parmesan cheese for a savory one.

MINI TARTS: Cut puff pastry into small squares or rounds and top with poached fruit or vegetables, jam, meats, or cheeses for quick and beautiful tarts.

SOUP CRACKERS: Slice it into small squares and bake to make buttery crackers to top your favorite soup.

chewy brownies

*2-inch square brownies

½ cup (1 stick) **butter**, cubed, plus more for greasing

7 ounces **semisweet** or **bittersweet chocolate**, finely chopped, or **chocolate chips** (about 1 cup)

⅓ cup **granulated sugar**

⅓ cup packed **dark brown sugar**

3 large **eggs**

1 teaspoon **pure vanilla extract**

½ cup **all-purpose flour** (or a gluten-free substitute, such as Bob's Red Mill 1:1)

½ teaspoon **kosher salt**

¼ teaspoon **baking powder**

½ cup chopped **walnuts** (optional)

mix-ins and swirl-ins

Add up to 1 cup of mix-ins, such as nuts, butterscotch chips, or coconut flakes, after the batter has been mixed. Or dollop and swirl in up to 1 cup of sauce, such as salted caramel, tahini, or marshmallow spread, once the batter is in the pan.

If ever there was an essential baking recipe, it's the brownie. There are probably a million brownie recipes out there. Ours relies on melted bittersweet chocolate. Make it a few times with different types of chocolate, like semisweet, and compare the flavor and texture. That's how you learn! For some students, this will be the first time they've ever melted chocolate using the double-boiler method, which is setting a bowl on top of a pot of just-simmering water. It's a great technique for gently heating something without burning it and will come up often in your future baking adventures!

1. Preheat the oven to 350°F and place a rack in the center.

2. Line an 8 × 8-inch baking pan with parchment paper, leaving about 1 inch hanging over two sides. Lightly grease the pan and parchment with butter.

3. Fill a saucepan with a couple inches of water and bring it to a boil over high heat. When it boils, turn down the heat until the water is barely bubbling. Set a heatproof mixing bowl (metal or glass) over the saucepan, making sure that it fits well and that the bottom doesn't touch the water. Add the butter and chocolate to the bowl and heat, stirring frequently, until melted. Remove the pan from the heat and whisk in both sugars.

4. In a small bowl, beat the eggs with the vanilla until light and fluffy. Vigorously whisk the egg mixture into the chocolate mixture for about a minute, until smooth and glossy.

5. Stir in the flour, salt, and baking powder (and walnuts, if using). Pour the batter into the prepared baking pan and smooth the top with a silicone or offset spatula.

6. Bake the brownies for 25 to 30 minutes, until a cake tester or toothpick inserted into the center comes out with just a few crumbs attached. Do not overbake! The edges of the brownies should look firm and the center should be slightly moist. Remove to a wire rack to cool completely before slicing. To serve, first cut 4 strips, then cut each strip crosswise into 4 brownies.

7. Stored tightly in an airtight container, the brownies will keep for up to 4 days.

brown butter chocolate chip cookies

For sure, chocolate chip cookies are one of the all-time top recipes; they're also one of the treats that kids coming into our program have almost always made before. So our job was to develop a recipe that had all the things we love about chocolate chip cookies with a few new twists and lessons.

We made two important changes: we use browned butter—which is just butter you cook in a pan until you see brown, caramelized flecks—to give the cookies an even warmer, toastier flavor, and instead of chocolate chips, we use a chopped-up chocolate bar so that there is variety in the ooey-gooey chocolate pieces, which means there are also some really big ones in there! If you plan far enough ahead to give the dough a rest in the refrigerator (even a few hours are beneficial but overnight is ideal), your cookies will be even more delicious after a little time for the flavors to meld.

1½ cups **all-purpose flour** (or a gluten-free substitute, such as Bob's Red Mill 1:1)

1 teaspoon **salt**

¼ teaspoon **baking soda**

¼ teaspoon **baking powder**

¾ cup plus 2 tablespoons (14 tablespoons; 1¾ sticks) **butter**

¾ cup packed **light** or **dark brown sugar**

½ cup **granulated sugar**

1 large **egg**

1 large **egg yolk**

2 teaspoons **pure vanilla extract**

7 ounces **semisweet** or **bittersweet chocolate**, finely chopped, or **chocolate chips** (about 1 cup)

Flaky salt, for sprinkling

When making brown butter, use a pan with either a white or bright stainless-steel interior. That way you can monitor the changing color of the butter as it cooks. And freeze some preportioned dough balls to bake whenever you need a little treat!

1. Preheat the oven to 350°F. Line a sheet pan with parchment paper.

2. In a small mixing bowl, combine the flour, salt, baking soda, and baking powder. Set aside.

3. Cut 4 tablespoons (½ stick) of the butter into 1-inch cubes and place them in a large mixing bowl. Set aside.

4. Cut the remaining 10 tablespoons (1¼ sticks) butter into cubes and melt them in a medium skillet (preferably stainless steel or pale-colored) over medium heat. Cook the butter, stirring frequently and scraping the bottom of the pan, until the butter has browned (there will be brown flecks in the pan and the butter will have a nutty aroma), 5 to 6 minutes. Pour the browned butter over the cubed butter in the mixing bowl, using a rubber spatula to scrape the pan clean. Stir until the butter is fully melted.

5. Let the butter cool slightly, then whisk both sugars into the butter. Add the egg, egg yolk, and vanilla and whisk vigorously until the mixture is smooth and

(RECIPE CONTINUES)

glossy, about 1 minute. Use a spatula to fold in the flour mixture until just combined, then fold in the chocolate pieces.

6. Using a cookie scoop or tablespoon, portion and shape the dough into 1-inch balls and place them 2 inches apart on the prepared sheet pan. If you're not baking right away, place them on a plate or sheet pan, cover with plastic wrap, and chill in the refrigerator for at least 1 hour or up to 24 hours. To freeze the dough: Portion and chill individual balls of dough on a sheet pan, then transfer to a zip-top bag and freeze for up to 3 months. Thaw in the refrigerator and bake according to the instructions below.

7. Bake the cookies for 8 to 10 minutes (2 to 3 minutes longer if the dough was chilled), until they've just begun to brown around the edges. Immediately after baking, sprinkle a pinch of flaky salt on top of each cookie and cool completely on the sheet pan. Repeat to bake the remaining cookie dough.

8. To freeze the cookies: Place baked and completely cooled cookies in a zip-top bag, with parchment paper between each cookie. Thaw at room temperature.

mix-and-match holiday cookies

FOR THE BASIC SUGAR COOKIE

2¼ cups **all-purpose flour** (or a gluten-free substitute, such as Bob's Red Mill 1:1)

½ teaspoon **baking powder**

1 cup (2 sticks) **butter**, at room temperature

½ cup **granulated sugar**, plus more for rolling (or substitute decorative sanding sugar)

½ cup **powdered sugar**

¼ teaspoon **salt**

2 large **egg yolks**

1 teaspoon **pure vanilla extract**

Every holiday season we host a cookie swap as a fundraiser for a good cause. People pay what they can for entry and bring a few batches of their favorite holiday cookie, and they leave with a huge selection of different festive treats. Leading up to the big event in class, we spend the week baking several types of cookies—all with this one base recipe!

What we love about this lesson is that you can see the different roles ingredients play in a cookie batter. You can start with this basic sugar cookie recipe and sprinkle it with pretty sanding sugar, or you can see what happens when you add zest and make a jam-filled thumbprint, or when you replace some of the wheat flour with almond flour and swap out the vanilla for almond extract and toss with powdered sugar, or when you add chocolate and whole eggs to make a rich, gooey peppermint chew.

1. Preheat the oven to 350°F. Line three sheet pans with parchment paper.

2. In a medium mixing bowl, combine the flour and baking powder. Set aside.

3. In the bowl of a stand mixer fitted with the paddle attachment, beat the butter, both sugars, and salt on medium speed until pale yellow and fluffy, about 3 minutes. Add the egg yolks one at a time, scraping down the sides of the bowl between each addition. With the mixer on low speed, add the vanilla, then gradually mix in the flour mixture, ½ cup at a time, until thoroughly incorporated. Wrap the dough in plastic and chill for 20 minutes.

4. Unwrap the dough. Using clean hands, divide and roll the dough into 1-inch balls; you should have about 30.

5. Roll the balls in granulated sugar, place them 2 inches apart on the prepared sheet pans, and press down on them lightly with the bottom of a glass. Bake for 15 minutes. Let cool on the sheet pans for 5 minutes, then transfer to a baking rack to cool completely.

(RECIPE CONTINUES)

variations

Follow these tweaks to the recipe on page 233 to make three very different—and very delicious—holiday cookies!

lemon-raspberry thumbprints

1. Add the zest of 1 lemon (about 1 tablespoon) to the bowl of flour and baking powder.

2. After unwrapping the dough, roll 50 balls about ¾ inch in diameter and place them on the sheet pans, 1 inch apart. Use a small spoon to make an indentation in the center of every cookie, fill each with a little spoonful of raspberry jam, and bake for 15 minutes.

snowballs

1. Replace 1 cup of the all-purpose flour with almond flour.

2. Use ½ teaspoon pure almond or walnut extract instead of 1 teaspoon vanilla.

3. Add ½ cup crushed walnuts after the dough is mixed.

4. After unwrapping the dough, form 50 balls about ¾ inch in diameter and place them on the sheet pans, 1 inch apart.

5. When cool, toss in powdered sugar.

chocolate-peppermint chews

1. Add 1 teaspoon baking soda and an additional ½ teaspoon baking powder to the bowl of flour.

2. Add ½ cup unsweetened Dutch-process cocoa to the flour mixture.

3. Replace the powdered sugar with ¾ cup granulated sugar (for 1¼ cups granulated sugar total).

4. Add 2 more whole eggs when you add the egg yolks.

5. Replace the vanilla with ½ teaspoon pure peppermint extract.

6. Mix in ¾ cup semisweet or bittersweet chocolate chips or chopped chocolate once the dough is mixed.

7. After unwrapping the dough, form 40 balls about 1 inch in diameter and place them on the sheet pans, 2 inches apart. Press down slightly on each with the bottom of a glass to flatten them a bit.

8. Immediately after baking, sprinkle with crushed peppermint candies.

graham cracker pumpkin praline pie

*9-inch pie

Obviously Thanksgiving is one of our favorite holidays because of all the chances to cook and share food with the people we love . . . and because of the pumpkin pie! This one comes together quickly and has a little bonus on top—crunchy praline topping.

It's extra quick to make because we swap out a traditional pastry crust and instead use a pressed graham cracker crumb crust. Sure, it's a little different, but just watch—this might become your go-to Thanksgiving dessert!

FOR THE CRUST

1¼ cups finely ground **graham cracker crumbs** (about 5 ounces, from about 10 whole graham crackers)

6 tablespoons (¾ stick) **butter**, melted

3 tablespoons **granulated sugar**

¼ teaspoon **ground cinnamon**

Pinch of **kosher salt**

FOR THE FILLING

1 package (8-ounces) **cream cheese**, at room temperature

⅓ cup **granulated sugar**

2 large **eggs**, lightly beaten

1 cup canned **pure pumpkin puree**

½ cup **heavy cream**

1 teaspoon **ground cinnamon**

½ teaspoon **kosher salt**

½ teaspoon **ground ginger**

¼ teaspoon **ground cloves**

1. Preheat the oven to 350°F.

2. **Make the crust:** In a large bowl, combine the cracker crumbs, butter, sugar, cinnamon, and salt and stir until all the ingredients are evenly distributed. The mixture should look like wet sand.

3. Sprinkle the mixture evenly across the bottom of a 9-inch deep-dish pie plate. Using the bottom of a measuring cup or other flat-bottomed cup, press the mixture evenly over the bottom and up the sides of the pie plate.

4. Bake in the oven for about 8 minutes, until fragrant and beginning to brown. Remove from the oven and set aside to cool.

5. **Meanwhile, make the filling:** Either by hand with a wooden spoon or using a stand mixer fitted with the paddle attachment, beat the cream cheese and the sugar vigorously until well combined. Beat in the eggs until the mixture is uniform in texture. Add the pumpkin, cream, cinnamon, salt, ginger, and cloves. Mix until no white cream cheese flecks remain; this may take up to 3 minutes.

6. Pour the mixture into the cooled crust to about ¼ inch from the top, which allows for expansion as the pie bakes. (If you have leftover filling, you can bake it in ramekins until it's no longer jiggly; cook time depends on amount, but for a standard 6-ounce ramekin, start checking around 10 minutes.) Bake the pie for about an hour, or until the tip of a paring knife inserted into the center comes out clean. The center should jiggle

FOR THE PRALINE TOPPING

1 cup chopped **pecans** or **walnuts** (or pepitas for a nut-free pie—pumpkin seeds for pumpkin pie!)

⅔ cup lightly packed **light brown sugar**

4 tablespoons (½ stick) **butter**, melted

Pinch of **kosher salt**

slightly when moved, but it should not be wet. Let the pie cool for at least 1 hour.

7. When you're ready to finish the pie, preheat the broiler.

8. **Make the topping:** In a small bowl, combine the nuts, brown sugar, melted butter, and salt. Sprinkle the mixture evenly over the top of the pie, then place the pie under the broiler for 2 to 3 minutes, until browned and crisp, keeping a very close watch to ensure that it does not burn. Allow the pie to cool for a few minutes before serving.

separating eggs

While a whole egg is a perfect package, with a fatty, nutrient-dense yolk and lean white, there are times when a recipe calls for only one part or the other. You may need just the whites to add loft to an angel food cake or meringue, or just the yolks to add richness to fresh pasta or pudding.

Our process for separating eggs limits the risk of breaking the yolk: Have two bowls ready. Hold your hand out in a cup shape over one of the bowls. Crack an egg with your other hand and pour it into your cupped hand over one of the bowls. Slightly spread your fingers open so the white can pass through while the yolk stays intact in your fingers, then slide the yolk into the other bowl. Easy!

chocolate pots de crème

½ cup **heavy cream**

7 ounces **semisweet** or **bittersweet chocolate**, or **chocolate chips** (about 1 cup)

4 large **egg yolks**

½ cup **whole milk**

1 teaspoon **pure vanilla extract**

Pinch of **kosher salt**

Whipped Cream (page 276) or **crème fraîche**, for serving

Everything we teach at The Dynamite Shop has several culinary (and life!) lessons within it. Aside from being a "fancy French dessert," this creamy, chocolaty super-pudding recipe is a great way to learn how to separate eggs (see opposite). Puddings usually have a starch (like flour) doing the job of thickening, but pots de crème use eggs, which makes for a richer flavor and silkier texture.

Chopped chocolate is easier to melt than chocolate chips, because chips are engineered with less of the cocoa butter that gives chocolate that silky, melty quality; plus, there is a wider range of cacao strengths available in bar form, so if you really want to get fancy with it, you can experiment with semisweet and bittersweet chocolates.

1. Warm the cream in a small saucepan over medium heat, stirring frequently. When the cream just reaches a simmer, remove the pan from the heat and stir in the chocolate. Set it aside for a few minutes until the chocolate has melted completely, stirring once to confirm there are no chunks left.

2. In a blender, combine the egg yolks, milk, vanilla, and salt. With the blender running on medium speed, slowly stream in the warm chocolate cream and blend for 1 minute, until the ingredients are well combined.

3. Divide the mixture among four 6-ounce ramekins. Cover loosely with plastic wrap and chill until set, at least 4 hours.

4. Serve the pots de crème with small dollops of whipped cream. They will keep, covered, in the refrigerator without the whipped cream for up to 3 days.

banana pudding

Knowing how to make pudding or custard from scratch is an important life skill, if you ask us. The vanilla pudding is what makes this classic summery treat so special. Layered with banana slices, vanilla wafers, and whipped cream, this recipe is always the star of the potluck or backyard barbecue.

¾ cup **granulated sugar**

¼ cup **cornstarch**

Pinch of **salt**

4 large **egg yolks** (see page 238), beaten

3 cups **whole milk**

1¼ cups **heavy cream**

2 teaspoons **pure vanilla extract**

2 tablespoons **butter**

3 tablespoons **powdered sugar**

1 small box (11 to 12 ounces) **vanilla wafers** (or gluten-free cookies)

4 or 5 ripe (but not *too* ripe or mushy) large **bananas**, sliced into ¼-inch-thick rounds

1. In a medium saucepan, whisk together the granulated sugar, cornstarch, and salt until well combined. Gradually whisk in the egg yolks, milk, and ¼ cup of the cream until there are no lumps (if lumps remain, strain the mixture through a fine-mesh strainer into another bowl, then transfer the liquid back to the saucepan). Stir in 1 teaspoon of the vanilla.

2. Cook the mixture over medium-high heat, stirring constantly, until it begins to simmer, about 5 minutes. Do not let it boil. Reduce the heat to medium-low and cook, stirring constantly, until the pudding starts to thicken, about 5 minutes more. Remove from the heat and whisk in the butter until the pudding is smooth. Transfer the pudding to a bowl, cover with plastic wrap (pressing it directly against the surface of the pudding, to keep a skin from forming), and refrigerate until cool.

3. Use an electric mixer or a whisk to beat the remaining 1 cup cream and 1 teaspoon vanilla extract and the powdered sugar until stiff peaks form (this means the peak holds its shape and doesn't droop once the beater or whisk is lifted).

4. Assemble the banana pudding at least 2 hours before you're ready to serve. Set aside 5 vanilla wafers for the topping. Spread a layer of pudding to cover the bottom of a 3- to 4-quart baking dish. (You can also make individual banana puddings.) Add a layer of vanilla wafers, flat-side down, then a layer of bananas, then a layer of whipped cream.

5. Repeat until you've layered all the ingredients, ending with a layer of whipped cream. Crumble the reserved 5 cookies on top of the banana pudding and cover with plastic wrap; refrigerate for at least 2 hours and up to 1 day before serving so the cookies soften and the flavors meld. Store, covered, in the refrigerator for up to 2 days.

zesty lemon bars

Who invented the lemon bar, anyway? A shortbread cookie (to which we add extra lemon zest) with lemon curd on top? Genius! Lemon bars can be cloyingly sweet, so we set out to create a recipe that didn't feel like a tooth destroyer. We can't stress enough what a difference it makes to use pulpy freshly squeezed lemon juice rather than the store-bought kind in a squeeze bottle. That tangy citrus flavor will shine through without the acrid bitterness you sometimes get from bottled lemon juice. Can you make these with other citrus? You bet! Lime will be strong, so to get your ½ cup juice, do about half lime juice and half water. For orange bars we recommend decreasing the sugar in the curd to ¾ cup and increasing the zest to 3 tablespoons.

FOR THE CRUST

1¼ cups **all-purpose flour** (or a gluten-free substitute, such as Bob's Red Mill 1:1)

½ cup **powdered sugar**

½ teaspoon **freshly grated lemon zest**

¼ teaspoon **salt**

10 tablespoons (1 stick plus 2 tablespoons) **butter**, chilled and cut into ½-inch cubes, plus more for greasing

Ice water, as needed

FOR THE LEMON CURD

4 large **eggs**

1 cup **granulated sugar**

2 tablespoons **freshly grated lemon zest**

½ cup **freshly squeezed lemon juice**

¼ cup **all-purpose flour** (or a gluten-free substitute, such as Bob's Red Mill 1:1)

3 tablespoons **powdered sugar**, for serving

1. Position a rack in the center of the oven and preheat the oven to 325°F. Line a 9 × 9-inch baking dish with parchment paper, leaving about 1 inch hanging over two sides. Grease the exposed sides of the pan.

2. **Make the crust:** In a medium mixing bowl, combine the flour, powdered sugar, lemon zest, and salt. Add the chilled butter and, using a pastry cutter or two table knives to slice through the butter or working quickly with your fingers, mix the butter into the flour mixture until it resembles a coarse meal. You may need to add a tablespoon or two of ice water to help the dough come together.

3. Transfer the mixture to the prepared pan, scattering it in evenly, and use the flat bottom of a drinking glass to press the mixture evenly over the bottom all the way to the edges. Bake for 30 minutes, until golden. Remove the pan from the oven and set on a wire rack to cool slightly (keep the oven on).

4. **Make the lemon curd:** While the crust is baking, in a medium bowl, whisk together the eggs and granulated sugar until well combined and you see the color turn pale, which will take a few minutes. Stir in the lemon zest, lemon juice, and the flour until just combined. Pour the lemon curd over the warm crust. Return the pan to the oven and bake for 30 minutes, or until the center doesn't jiggle when you tap the pan.

5. Remove the pan from the oven and set it on a wire rack to cool completely, about an hour, then chill the lemon bars in the refrigerator for at least another hour. Remove the lemon bars by first running a sharp paring knife along the edges of the pan without parchment, then grasping the overhanging edges of the parchment and lifting the bars out of the pan. Cut into nine 3-inch square bars, or as desired.

6. To serve, place the powdered sugar in a fine-mesh strainer and dust the top of the bars. The bars will keep, covered, in the refrigerator for up to 3 days. To freeze the bars, wrap the completely cooled bars individually with plastic wrap and freeze. Thaw in the refrigerator, then dust with powdered sugar before serving.

why lemon juice *and* lemon zest?

Lemon zest has lots of flavorful oil that isn't as acidic as lemon juice and can stand up to the heat of the oven—a stronger fresh lemon punch!

buttermilk panna cotta
with choose-your-own compote

2 cups **whole-milk buttermilk** (see Note on page 197)

2½ teaspoons (0.25-ounce envelope) **unflavored powdered gelatin**

⅔ cup **granulated sugar**

1½ cups **half-and-half**, or ¾ cup **whole milk** plus ¾ cup **heavy cream**

Vegetable oil, for greasing (optional)

Fruit Compote, for serving (optional; recipe follows)

Panna cotta, which means "cooked cream" in Italian, isn't technically a custard or a pudding, but it's close. By using gelatin (or a vegetarian substitute like agar) to set it, the mixture tastes like a super-creamy pudding but is basically a milky Jell-O. While absolutely delicious on its own (or topped with a fruit sauce or compote), you can also flavor the base by infusing the milk with different spices and flavorings. You do this by "steeping," which is a fancy word for letting the flavoring sit in the hot mixture as if you were making tea. And because this recipe mimics Jell-O in that it conforms to its container, you can have good fun with the design. We like to use old-fashioned ramekins for a classic shape, but don't be afraid to play around with whimsical silicone molds. Unicorn panna cotta, anyone?

1. Pour 1 cup of the buttermilk into a large, heatproof bowl. Sprinkle the gelatin over the top and set it aside for 3 to 5 minutes to "bloom." The gelatin will absorb some of the milk and look like it's puffing up.

2. In a small saucepan, combine the sugar and half-and-half over medium heat and whisk until the sugar dissolves. Bring the mixture to a simmer, then pour the hot mixture over the buttermilk mixture. Whisk until the gelatin has dissolved. Stir in the remaining 1 cup buttermilk.

3. Strain the mixture through a fine-mesh strainer into a glass liquid measuring cup. Divide it evenly among six 6-ounce ramekins or glasses (greased with a thin layer of oil first if you intend to unmold them). Cover and refrigerate until completely set, at least 3 hours.

4. Serve the panna cottas in their ramekins or, to unmold, run a sharp knife around the edges of the ramekins and carefully turn the panna cottas out onto serving plates. We like them best topped with spoonfuls of fruit compote.

fruit compote

makes about 1½ cups

4 tablespoons (½ stick) **butter**

½ cup packed **light** or **dark brown sugar**, plus more to taste

¼ cup **freshly squeezed lemon juice**

1 pound **fresh** or **frozen fruit**, such as berries, chopped rhubarb, or pitted and sliced stone fruit

1. Melt the butter in a skillet over medium heat. Stir in the brown sugar and lemon juice and cook, stirring constantly, until the sugar completely dissolves. Add the fruit and cook until it begins to fall apart, 3 to 8 minutes, depending on the fruit. Taste for sweetness and add more sugar, if needed.

2. Before serving, allow the mixture to cool to room temperature. It will keep in an airtight container in the refrigerator for up to 1 week.

classic cream puffs
with raspberry whipped cream and berries

These whipped-cream–filled puffs are the way we introduce students to choux pastry—the dough used for éclairs, cheesy gougères, and more.

While making choux pastry isn't exactly difficult, it does require attention. Unlike most doughs that you mix in a bowl and then bake, you cook this one first in a saucepan and then bake it, where it puffs into big, airy bites.

4 tablespoons (½ stick) **butter**

½ cup **whole milk**

½ teaspoon **granulated sugar**

½ cup **all-purpose flour** (or a gluten-free substitute, such as Bob's Red Mill 1:1)

2 large **eggs**

1½ cups **fresh raspberries**

1 cup **heavy cream**

2 tablespoons **powdered sugar**, plus more for dusting

¼ teaspoon **pure vanilla extract**

1. Preheat the oven to 425°F. Line a large sheet pan with parchment paper.

2. In a medium saucepan, bring the butter, milk, and granulated sugar to a simmer over medium heat, then immediately remove the pan from the heat. Using a wooden spoon, add the flour and stir until fully incorporated. Return the pan to medium-low heat and stir vigorously until the dough pulls away from the sides of the pan and forms a ball. Remove from the heat and let cool for 2 minutes.

3. Add the first egg and, using the wooden spoon, beat vigorously until fully incorporated, about 1 minute. Add the second egg and keep beating until the dough is smooth and glossy, about a minute more.

4. Transfer the dough to a zip-top plastic bag and seal the bag. Squeeze the dough into one of the bottom corners and use scissors or kitchen shears to cut off the corner so you have a ½-inch-wide diagonal opening. Squeeze the dough into 6 evenly spaced golf ball–size rounds on the sheet pan. Bake until puffed and golden (but not brown), 20 to 30 minutes. Transfer to a wire rack to cool.

5. While the cream puffs are baking, make the whipped cream filling: Put ½ cup of the raspberries in a blender or food processor and puree to a pulpy liquid (alternatively, you can pulverize them in a bowl with a potato masher). Set a fine-mesh strainer over a small bowl and pour the raspberry puree into the strainer. Using a rubber spatula, stir and press the raspberry puree against the strainer until all the liquid has passed through (you should have about 2 tablespoons of raspberry juice). Discard the fruit pulp.

6. In a stand mixer fitted with the whisk attachment or in a chilled large bowl using a whisk or handheld mixer, beat the cream until soft peaks form (this means the peak doesn't hold its shape once the beater or whisk is lifted). Add the raspberry juice, powdered sugar, and vanilla and continue beating until stiff peaks form (meaning the peaks hold their shape and don't droop once the beater or whisk is lifted). Transfer the whipped cream to a pastry bag fitted with a rosette tip or to a zip-top bag and refrigerate until the cream puffs are ready to fill.

7. When the cream puffs are fully cooled, use a serrated knife to slice the top third off each; set the tops aside. Pipe the whipped cream into each cream puff, then add 3 raspberries and replace the top. Dust with powdered sugar. Serve immediately. (Alternatively, store the unfilled puffs and whipped cream in separate airtight containers, refrigerating the cream, for up to 1 day. Fill just before serving.)

11

drinks

A good meal isn't complete without a great drink. We'd never turn down a long, tall glass of water (maybe with a slice of lemon!), but it's special to have some Lemonade (page 255) made from scratch or a Shirley Temple (page 259) with homemade grenadine and maraschino cherries.

There's a ritual to making and serving good drinks, and it's one we observe in our Teen Supper Club, which is as much about the social experience of a meal as it is about the mechanics of cooking. These are those teens' favorite recipes, and they each involve great lessons. Whether it's making a flavored syrup for our Homemade Soda (page 250) or working with condensed milk for creamy sweetness in our Thai Iced Tea (page 254), we're always learning when we're cooking!

homemade soda

*16-ounce serving

1 cup **sparkling water**

¼ cup **flavored Simple Syrup** (recipe follows)

Ice, for serving

We like the "all things in moderation" approach to healthy living and certainly so for sugary drinks like soda, which can be so easy to gulp down. But wait! Did you know you can make your own soda? You can actually use less sugar in homemade soda than they use in the store-bought stuff, and it still tastes great. We promise! You start with simple syrup, which is made by dissolving sugar in warm water, using equal amounts of each. Simple! While you're at it, take total control of your sodas with the ability to make virtually any flavor you want, all from scratch and without anything artificial! We've seen blueberry, lemon, and even basil sodas. How many crazy flavors can you imagine?

Combine the water and syrup in a 16-ounce glass and stir to combine. Fill the glass to the top with ice and serve immediately.

---

simple syrup

makes about 1½ cups

1 cup **sugar**

1 cup **water**

Flavorings of your choice (see below; optional)

1. In a small saucepan, combine the sugar with the water. If you're making a flavored syrup, add any chosen fruit, herbs, spices, and so on.

2. Bring the mixture to a simmer over medium-high heat and then cook on low, stirring occasionally, for 10 to 15 minutes, until it's thick enough to coat a spoon. Remove the pan from the heat. If you added fruit, herbs, or spices, use a fine-mesh strainer to strain the syrup, then discard the solids (this is not necessary if you're making plain simple syrup). Let the syrup cool, then store in an airtight container in the fridge for up to 1 month.

make your own custom syrup flavors!

- **Fruit.** Frozen works great! We love strawberries, blueberries, peaches, pineapple, or mango. Use up to ½ cup sliced fruit (unless it's small, like blueberries).

- **Fresh herb sprigs** (mint, basil, or thyme). Add up to 1 cup leaves or 8 to 10 sprigs.

- **Whole spices** (cinnamon, peppercorns, cloves, or vanilla beans). Use 1 cinnamon stick or vanilla bean, or up to 1 teaspoon of smaller whole spices.

- **Fresh ginger or hot chile peppers** (for a little heat!). Thinly slice a 1-inch piece of fresh ginger or 1 to 2 peppers.

bubble tea

*16-ounce serving

1 **black tea bag** (caffeinated or decaffeinated)

2 teaspoons **Simple Syrup** (page 250)

3 tablespoons **whole milk**

Ice, for serving

⅓ cup cooked **Tapioca Pearls** (see opposite)

When we opened The Dynamite Shop in Park Slope, Brooklyn, we found ourselves near several Vietnamese restaurants, all selling bubble tea. Kids lined up around the block after school and on summer afternoons to buy cups of these sweet tea drinks with chewy tapioca boba (or "pearls") at the bottom, which are made with flour from cassava root. Bubble tea purveyors always have extra-large straws so that you can sip the boba through the straw without clogging it. During our first summer, we took our campers to meet the owners of one of the local bubble tea spots, Henry's. We tasted the different flavors (mango! black tea!), learned a bit about bubble tea's history (it became popular with kids in Taiwan in the 1980s), and then we went back to the shop and learned how to make our own. Ever since then, this simple recipe has been wildly popular. You can find dried boba—and special boba straws—online or at most grocery stores that specialize in Asian products.

1. In a small saucepan, bring ½ cup water to a boil. Add the tea bag to the water and let steep for at least 5 minutes, until the tea is dark brown. Remove the tea bag and stir in the simple syrup and milk. Let the mixture cool.

2. Fill a 16-ounce glass with ice and add the cooked tapioca pearls and cooled tea. Stir and serve immediately with a bubble tea straw.

---

almond bubble tea

*16-ounce serving

1 cup **almond milk**

¼ teaspoon **pure almond extract**

1 tablespoon **Simple Syrup** (page 250)

Ice, for serving

⅓ cup cooked **Tapioca Pearls** (see opposite)

1. In a small mixing bowl, whisk together the almond milk, almond extract, and simple syrup.

2. Fill a 16-ounce glass with ice and add the cooked tapioca pearls and the almond milk mixture. Stir and serve immediately with a bubble tea straw.

tapioca pearls (boba)

makes a heaping ⅓ cup (enough for one 16-ounce serving)

⅓ cup uncooked **tapioca pearls** (boba)

1. In a small saucepan, bring 3 cups water to a boil over high heat. Carefully add the tapioca pearls and stir to ensure they don't stick together. Reduce the heat to low and simmer for 5 minutes, or until the pearls puff up and become tender.

2. Drain the pearls, then transfer them to a bowl and cover with cold water. Set aside for 2 to 3 minutes, until cooled. Add them to your favorite tea.

mango-coconut bubble tea

*16-ounce serving

1 cup **pure mango juice**

2 tablespoons **unsweetened full-fat coconut milk**

1 tablespoon **Simple Syrup** (page 250)

Pinch of **kosher salt**

Ice, for serving

⅓ cup cooked **Tapioca Pearls** (above)

1. In a blender or a lidded jar, combine the mango juice, coconut milk, 2 tablespoons water, the simple syrup, and salt and blend or shake until smooth.

2. Fill a 16-ounce glass with ice and add the cooked tapioca pearls and the mango mixture. Stir and serve immediately with a bubble tea straw.

matcha bubble tea

*16-ounce serving

1 tablespoon **sweetened** or **unsweetened matcha (green tea) powder**

2 tablespoons **very hot water**

1 cup **whole milk**

1 tablespoon **Simple Syrup** (page 250; optional)

Ice, for serving

⅓ cup cooked **Tapioca Pearls** (see left)

1. Measure out the matcha powder into a small bowl, breaking up any clumps with your measuring spoon (or sift it, if it seems particularly clumpy).

2. Pour the hot water into the matcha bowl and whisk vigorously until the mixture is frothy and the matcha powder has fully dissolved, about 2 minutes.

3. Add the milk and, if using, simple syrup and whisk until combined. Let cool to room temperature.

4. Fill a 16-ounce glass with ice and add the cooked tapioca pearls and the matcha mixture. Stir and serve immediately with a bubble tea straw.

thai iced tea

*16-ounce serving

2 **black tea bags**, such as Ceylon or Assam (caffeinated or decaffeinated)

1 teaspoon **granulated sugar**

3 **star anise pods**

6 **whole cloves**

¼ teaspoon **cardamom seeds** (these are the small black seeds inside a green cardamom pod)

2 tablespoons **sweetened condensed milk**

¼ cup **evaporated milk**

Ice, for serving

There is a fair argument for putting this recipe in the dessert chapter rather than here with the drinks; this is a sweet one! Made with sweetened condensed milk, Thai iced tea is enjoyed in Thailand as a relatively recent creation, influenced by Western culture's penchant for sweet milky treats. We love recipes that teach us something about history and cultures . . . especially when they taste so good.

1. Bring 1 cup water to a boil in a kettle over high heat. Meanwhile, in a large heatproof container, such as a 2-cup (or larger) liquid measuring cup, combine the tea bags, sugar, star anise, cloves, and cardamom. Pour the boiling water into the cup and stir until the sugar dissolves. Let steep for at least 30 minutes, until the tea is dark brown and has cooled to room temperature.

2. Meanwhile, mix together the sweetened condensed milk and evaporated milk. Fill a 16-ounce glass with ice. Set a fine-mesh strainer over the glass and pour the cooled tea through it into the glass. Discard the tea bags and spices. Stir in the milk mixture and serve immediately.

lemonade

7 cups **cold water**

1 cup **granulated sugar**

1½ cups **freshly squeezed lemon juice** (10 to 12 lemons)

Ice, for serving

Fresh mint and **lemon wedges**, for garnish (optional)

Lemonade is one of the first recipes many of us remember making with our grandparents, with friends, and for our first lemonade stands. And it's so simple, with only three ingredients. But making it still offers plenty of culinary learning. The first big lesson is that with any fruit or vegetable, sweetness and the amount of juice vary a lot from fruit to fruit! Depending on the variety, time of year, and size, a lemon can give you a tablespoon of juice or up to ¼ cup. The juice can be unbearably tart, or it can border on mildly sweet, as with a Meyer lemon. So this lesson is a great way to teach the concept of "to taste" as kids decide how much sweetener their lemonade needs. We always say start low and add more, because you can always add more sugar, but you can't take it out!

1. In a medium pot, bring 1 cup of the water and the sugar to a simmer over medium heat. Stir occasionally until the sugar dissolves, then increase the heat to medium-high and bring to a boil. Continue boiling until the liquid reduces by a third and is thick enough to coat a spoon, 10 to 15 minutes.

2. Remove the pot from the heat and let the syrup cool completely.

3. Meanwhile, in a large pitcher or stockpot, combine the remaining 6 cups cold water and the lemon juice. Stir in the cooled syrup and serve over ice, garnished with mint and lemon wedges, if desired.

spicy chai

1-inch piece **fresh ginger**, chopped (no need to peel)

2 **star anise pods**

1 **cinnamon stick**

1 teaspoon **whole cloves**

1 tablespoon **whole green cardamom pods**, lightly crushed with a mortar and pestle or mallet

½ teaspoon **whole black peppercorns**

4 **black tea bags** (caffeinated or decaffeinated; we like PG Tips brand)

4 cups **whole milk** or your favorite **nondairy milk**

¼ cup packed **dark brown sugar**, or to taste

"Chai" means "tea" in Urdu, Hindi, and other languages, so properly you'd never say "chai tea"—it's just *chai*!

We've been making this sweet, milky, spicy chai from scratch for years, since moving to New York City and getting hooked on the tea from a little Pakistani deli in SoHo. When we opened The Dynamite Shop's little café, it immediately went on the menu, and kids often asked for some after class. So of course we taught them to make it themselves.

If you're unfamiliar with whole spices (spices that haven't been ground down to a powder), they're what making chai is all about. Our favorites are cinnamon, star anise, cloves, cardamom, and black peppercorns. (We also use fresh ginger, though not all chai experts agree on this.) We steep these spices in the milk, pretty much the same way you steep the tea leaves, and the flavors come alive and create a fragrant, sweet drink to get you going in the morning or send you off to sweet dreams. (Decaf tea bags for kids, of course!)

1. In a pot that can hold at least 3 quarts (12 cups), combine the ginger, star anise, cinnamon stick, cloves, cardamom, and peppercorns. Add 4 cups water and bring to a boil over high heat. Reduce the heat to medium-low, partially cover the pan, and simmer gently for 10 minutes, until fragrant. Add the tea bags and milk and simmer for another 20 minutes.

2. Discard the tea bags. Add the brown sugar and whisk to dissolve. Taste the tea for sweetness and adjust as necessary.

3. Strain the chai through a fine-mesh strainer into a teapot or individual cups or mugs and serve hot. Alternatively, bring it to room temperature, then refrigerate for iced chai.

italian hot chocolate

*enough for sixteen
4-ounce servings

8 ounces **semisweet** or **bittersweet chocolate**

¼ cup **granulated sugar**

¼ cup **unsweetened cocoa powder**

3 tablespoons **cornstarch**

1 teaspoon **salt**

In Italy, people drink a version of hot chocolate that is much thicker than what most of us are accustomed to in the States. It is extra rich, so a small portion goes a long way! Mixed into hot milk, this is a great treat to accompany cookies (dip them!) or to serve on its own as a small dessert after a big winter meal. Of course, any chocolate will work, but if you have some high-quality semisweet chocolate (60% cacao or higher), you will really notice the difference! This recipe makes a mix that you can store, then use a bit at a time to make cups of hot chocolate. The mix also makes a great gift packaged in decorative jars or bags.

1. Finely chop the chocolate into a rough powder and place in a small mixing bowl. Add the sugar, cocoa powder, cornstarch, and salt and stir to combine. (Alternatively, combine all the ingredients in a food processor and pulse until the chocolate pieces are finely chopped and the ingredients are well mixed.)

2. Store the hot chocolate mix in an airtight container in a cool place for up to 3 months.

3. **To make one 4-ounce serving of hot chocolate:** Heat ½ cup milk (or nondairy milk of your choice) in a small saucepan over medium-low until just warm and small bubbles form along the sides of the pan. Whisk in 2 tablespoons of the hot chocolate mix. Continue whisking over medium-low heat until the chocolate dissolves and the mixture thickens a bit. Remove from the heat and serve immediately.

shirley temple

6 ounces **ginger ale** (make your own with our Homemade Soda recipe on page 250)

Ice, for serving

1 tablespoon **high-quality grenadine**, store-bought (we like Bittermens) or homemade (recipe follows)

1 round **orange slice**

1 **high-quality maraschino cherry**, store-bought (we like Luxardo) or homemade (see page 274), or more to taste

The Shirley Temple is a classic drink for kids in restaurants. Made with ginger ale and bright red syrup (called grenadine), it can easily be made at home. But what's even more interesting is its history. Did you know that Shirley Temple was a child actress in the 1930s who grew up to become the US ambassador to Ghana and Czechoslovakia? The story goes that a bartender in Los Angeles invented the drink to serve to young Miss Temple, but she claimed she never liked the drink. "Too sweet!" We kind of agree! So learning to make this at home is all about flavoring to taste. Of course, you can buy the ingredients premade, but it's more fun to do it yourself!

Pour the ginger ale into a tall glass filled with ice. Stir in or "float" (which means to gently pour it on top) the grenadine, then garnish with a skewered orange slice and maraschino cherry.

grenadine

makes about ½ cup

1 cup **pomegranate juice**

½ cup **granulated sugar**

1 tablespoon **freshly squeezed orange juice**

1. Combine all the ingredients in a small saucepan. Bring to a simmer over medium heat and cook, stirring occasionally, until the liquid thickens and is reduced by half.

2. Store in the refrigerator in an airtight container for up to 1 week.

12

other things cooks do

Our mission isn't just to teach kids how to cook, but to teach them how to *think and act* like cooks, too. When our students start connecting the dots in their kitchen lives and realize that they can create a flavorful Vegetable Scrap Stock (page 264) with their produce trimmings, or whip up Easy Any-Fruit Jam (page 276) for their bread or crepes, or make Half-Sour Pickles (page 275) with the bumper crop of cucumbers in their garden, or make their pasta even better by adding some crunchy Zesty Bread Crumbs (page 277) on top; well, you can almost see them swelling with confidence. That's where these recipes come in: they're all things you could easily buy, but preparing them from scratch with your own two hands makes all the difference.

chicken stock

One of the beautiful things about roasting chicken is that the bones and the bits of meat left on them when you're done with the meal can be simmered into a rich, fortifying, super-flavorful stock that enriches everything from risotto to chicken potpie to vegetable soup—and is completely satisfying sipped from a mug on its own. We keep a zip-top gallon plastic bag in the freezer and store bones there after a roast chicken meal. Then, when you're ready to make the stock, pump up the flavor with carrots, celery, onions, and herbs.

Bones and carcass from 1 **roasted chicken**

2 **onions**, unpeeled, halved, and roughly chopped

3 or 4 **ribs celery**, including leafy tops, chopped

1 or 2 **carrots**, unpeeled, roughly chopped

2 **bay leaves**

4 or 5 sprigs **fresh thyme**

6 to 8 sprigs **fresh parsley**

1 teaspoon **whole black peppercorns**

Kosher salt to taste

1. Break the chicken carcass into a few smaller pieces.

2. Put the chicken bones, onions, celery, carrots, bay leaves, herbs, and peppercorns in a large stockpot and add 3 quarts (12 cups) water. Bring to a boil over medium-high heat, then reduce the heat to very low and cook for at least 1 hour or up to 3 hours for a richer stock, making sure to keep the pot at a very low simmer. You should see just a few bubbles here and there, a little movement in the liquid, and a bit of steam over the pot. Add more water if the bones become exposed. Skim off any foam or film that floats to the top of the stock.

3. After an hour, check the stock and season with salt, and when it has reached your desired flavor, strain it through a fine-mesh strainer into a large bowl (if you like a clearer broth, strain it again through cheesecloth). Use immediately or cool the stock quickly by placing the bowl in a large pan of ice, stirring frequently. When cool, evenly divide the stock among quart containers or zip-top freezer bags. Refrigerate for up to 1 week or freeze for up to 6 months.

alternate cooking methods

OVEN METHOD: Cover the pot and put it in a 225°F oven for 4 to 6 hours.

SLOW COOKER: Use the low setting and cook for 6 to 8 hours.

vegetable scrap stock

1-quart bag packed with **vegetable scraps** (about 4 cups; see Vegetable Scrap Stock Guide below), fresh or frozen

1 large **carrot**, halved and roughly chopped

1 **onion**, unpeeled, halved and roughly chopped

2 **garlic cloves**, smashed but not peeled

2 **bay leaves**

1 teaspoon **whole black peppercorns**

Kosher salt and **freshly ground black pepper** to taste

Vegetable stock is one of those recipes that is so easy you literally cannot mess it up, and yet so many people have never made it. It's a great way to put kitchen produce scraps to use instead of throwing them out. We keep a zip-top plastic bag in the freezer to fill with onion ends, carrot tops, celery root tips, celery leaves—you name it (we just make sure to add enough carrots for sweetness and onion and garlic for depth). Stock really is the golden trash can of the kitchen!

Once you've made your stock, you have the base for a great soup or sauce, or a liquid to cook rice in, or anything else you could use water for, but want more flavor.

1. Place the vegetable scraps, carrot, onion, garlic, bay leaves, and peppercorns in a large stockpot and add 3 quarts (12 cups) water. Bring to a boil over medium-high heat, then reduce the heat to medium and simmer for 10 to 15 minutes, until reduced by about a quarter.

2. Cover and continue to cook for another 15 minutes. Strain the stock through a fine-mesh strainer into another pot and season with salt and pepper (or leave it unseasoned until you use it). Use immediately or cool the stock quickly by placing the bowl in a large pan of ice, stirring frequently. When cool, evenly divide the stock among quart containers or zip-top freezer bags. Refrigerate for up to 1 week or freeze for up to 6 months.

vegetable scrap stock guide

All the random bits that end up in the vegetable drawer are game, *except* for cruciferous vegetables like broccoli and cauliflower, which lend a strong sulfuric flavor to your broth. (Kale can go in this direction as well, so it's also best avoided for stock.)

Here are the best vegetables to use for stock:

- Onion roots, tips, and skins
- Scallion roots and tips
- Leek roots and tips
- Carrot roots, tips, and skins
- Celery roots, tips, skins, and leaves
- Herb trimmings and leaves
- Radish tops
- Fennel fronds
- Lettuce or escarole roots and leaves
- Pea pods
- Zucchini ends

cooking dried beans

There is nothing wrong with popping open a can of beans and throwing together a quick dinner. We do it sometimes! But until you've made your own beans, you don't know what you're missing. There are three advantages to making beans from scratch (and by "from scratch," we mean soaking and cooking dried beans that are usually sold in a bag): it costs a lot less money, you can infuse the beans with the flavors of your choice, and you will get better beans. By cooking them slow and low, your beans will be super tender and creamy. And while the time investment is no joke (a few hours at least), the effort is minimal. This is definitely a back-burner recipe, meaning you can put it on the back burner and walk away (keeping safety in mind!). Here we provide a whole guide to making beans at home, but don't forget that when you have a last-minute craving for burritos or a rice-and-beans bowl, we give you full permission to open that can!

Soaking Beans

Soaking the dried beans before cooking helps them cook faster and more evenly. There are two methods for soaking beans.

OVERNIGHT METHOD

Put the beans in a bowl and fill the bowl with water to cover the beans by 2 inches. Add 1 tablespoon kosher salt per pound of beans. Cover and let them sit overnight at room temperature. When ready to cook, drain and rinse the beans.

QUICK METHOD

Put the beans in a medium pot and fill the pot with water to cover the beans by 2 inches. Over high heat, bring the water to a boil, then remove the pot from the heat. Let the beans sit for at least 1 hour, then drain and rinse them before cooking.

Cooking Beans

Once the beans have soaked, they're ready to cook. Put the beans in a large pot, cover with water by at least 2 inches, and add aromatics (this is optional, but we love adding garlic cloves, shallots, bay leaves, or herbs) and a large pinch of kosher salt. Heat the water over low heat, letting the beans stay at a low simmer and stirring occasionally. Depending on the type of bean, they will cook for 2 to 4 hours.

Test for doneness by tasting a couple beans. They should be tender all the way through, with no crunch.

Use the cooked beans immediately or let them cool, then transfer the beans and their cooking liquid to containers and store in the fridge for up to 1 week.

(RECIPE CONTINUES)

bean there, done that!

Once you cook your beans, you can use them every which way. Here are a few of our favorites!

- Mash them with minced garlic and herbs, slather on toast, and drizzle with good olive oil.

- Simmer with seasoning to use for tacos, Loaded Enchiladas (page 135), or Healthy Greens Quesadillas (page 92).

- Make Vegetarian Three-Bean Chili with All the Toppings (page 146).

- Toss with scallions, cucumbers, and radishes and dress with a vinaigrette for a chilled salad.

- Add to Curry with All the Vegetables (page 153).

- Bulk up Up-to-You Vegetable Soup (page 142).

cooking grains

NOTE: The following grains are gluten-free: buckwheat, millet, quinoa, and rice (but always check notes on the packaging about potential factory cross-contamination).

Oh, how we love grains! Rice, yes, but also there is a whole wide world of grains! Quinoa, millet, bulgur, buckwheat, couscous, farro—these grains have a variety of flavors and textures. And most of them cook up quickly, so you can get your meal on the table fast. One of our favorite ways to use grains is in our Rainbow Grain Bowl with Tahini Dressing (page 167)—it's a one-bowl dinner that's well-rounded and super nutritious. Once you find your favorite grains, experiment with doubling or even tripling the recipe so you have a healthy meal base on hand throughout the week. This guide should give you everything you need to become your household's grain expert!

This recipe yields 1 cup of cooked grains per serving. To get this amount, here are the ratios of grain to water or stock, with approximate cook times.

BULGUR >>> ⅓ cup bulgur + ⅔ cup water > Simmer 10 to 12 minutes

BUCKWHEAT >>> ⅓ cup buckwheat + ⅔ cup water > Simmer 15 to 20 minutes

COUSCOUS >>> ⅓ cup couscous + ½ cup water > Simmer 5 minutes

FARRO >>> ⅓ cup farro + 1 cup water > Simmer 30 minutes

MILLET >>> ⅓ cup millet + ⅔ cup water > Simmer 15 to 20 minutes

QUINOA >>> ⅓ cup quinoa + ⅔ cup water > Simmer 10 to 15 minutes

WHITE RICE >>> ⅓ cup rice + ⅔ cup water > Simmer 15 to 20 minutes

BROWN RICE >>> ⅓ cup rice + ⅔ cup water > Simmer 40 to 60 minutes

THE BASIC METHOD

1. Put the grains in a mixing bowl, rinse with cool water, swishing them around and pouring out the water, and repeat until the water runs clear. Drain the grains well.

(RECIPE CONTINUES)

2. Bring the measured amount of water or stock to a boil over high heat in a saucepan with a tight-fitting lid.

3. Add the grains to the water and allow the water to return to a boil.

4. Lower the heat to maintain a low simmer and cover the pan.

5. Cook until the liquid has been absorbed (see cook times on page 269).

6. Fluff the grains with a fork, replace the cover, remove from the heat, and let sit for a few minutes before serving.

coconut rice

makes about 3 cups

2 teaspoons **coconut oil**

1 cup **long-grain white rice**, rinsed

1 cup **unsweetened full-fat coconut milk**

1 teaspoon **kosher salt**

1 teaspoon **granulated sugar**

You can add flavor to rice by swapping the water for a flavorful liquid, in this case, coconut milk. We love the richness it adds to white rice and like to serve it alongside our Laab Moo Lettuce Wraps (page 80) and Curry with All the Vegetables (page 153). You can also follow this technique using stock or broth in place of the water–coconut milk mixture to make a slightly savory rice.

1. In a medium saucepan, heat the oil over medium heat. Add the rice and stir until toasted and slightly translucent, 1 to 2 minutes. Add ½ cup water, the coconut milk, salt, and sugar and stir to combine.

2. Bring to a boil, then reduce the heat to low, cover, and simmer for 15 minutes, until the liquid has been fully absorbed. Shut off the heat and let the rice steam, covered, for another 10 minutes. Fluff with a fork and serve.

sticky rice

makes about 3 cups

1½ cups **glutinous rice**

Often labeled "sweet rice" or "glutinous rice" (even though it doesn't actually contain gluten!), this Southeast Asian variety is made by steaming the rice over a hot pot of boiling water. With a spongy, sticky texture, it's traditionally eaten with your hands, which is exactly how we enjoy it: scooping up a little bit and using it to sop up marinades and curries.

1. Put the rice in a large mixing bowl and pour in water to cover, stirring. Pour out the water and repeat until the water runs clear.

2. Fill the bowl with water to cover the rice by at least 2 inches. Set aside to soak for at least 2 hours.

3. Fill a pot with a few inches of water, making sure a fine-mesh strainer can fit in the pot with at least 1 inch of space between the bottom of the strainer and the water.

4. Drain the soaked rice in the fine-mesh strainer and place the rice still in the strainer into the pot, balanced above the water. Bring the water to a boil over high heat, then cover the pot and strainer with a tight-fitting lid or a sheet of foil.

5. Lower the heat to medium-high and steam for 15 minutes. Using a rubber spatula, flip the mound of rice over and cook for another 15 minutes. Test for doneness: the rice should be soft but not mushy. Turn out into a bowl and serve immediately.

quick fridge pickles

*32-ounce jars

2 pounds **mixed vegetables**, root ends of thin vegetables such as asparagus, green beans, or okra trimmed, or vegetables such as cucumbers, radishes, carrots, peppers, or cauliflower florets, trimmed and sliced into ⅛- to ¼-inch pieces

1 small **red onion**, thinly sliced

6 to 8 **garlic cloves**, smashed

2 cups **vinegar**, such as distilled white, apple cider, or rice vinegar

2 tablespoons **granulated sugar** (optional)

2 tablespoons **kosher salt**

3 tablespoons **pickling spice** or **whole spices** like peppercorns, coriander seeds, and mustard seeds

OPTIONAL FLAVORINGS

A few sprigs of **fresh herbs** (dill, thyme, rosemary), 1 tablespoon minced **fresh ginger** (about a 1-inch piece), ¼ to 1 teaspoon **ground spices** (turmeric, smoked paprika, Aleppo pepper)

When cucumbers are in season in the summer, they can go crazy in the garden, and they are an obvious first stop for students on a pickling journey! But this recipe works just as well in the winter with vegetables like fennel, beets, or winter squash. (They'll just need a few days in order to get tender in the pickling juices.) Pickles are great as a snack on their own or added to sandwiches, salads, grain bowls, eggs, and more!

The reason these are called "Quick Fridge Pickles" (or "Quickles" for short!) is because they use a shortcut method in which vinegar preserves the vegetables (which is pretty much instant) as compared to fermenting in a salt brine (which can take days or weeks). After we make them, they last for a good while in the fridge. They have a tangier, less-funky flavor than fermented pickles, but they're crisp and refreshing!

1. Wash and thoroughly dry two widemouthed quart jars (or other 32-ounce sealable containers) and their lids.

2. Pack the mixed vegetables, onion, garlic, and any optional flavorings into the jars, leaving ½ inch of space at the top. Pack them as tightly as you can without smashing them.

3. Place the vinegar, sugar (if using), salt, pickling spice, and 2 cups water in a small saucepan. Bring the mixture to a simmer over medium-high heat. Stir the mixture until the sugar and salt dissolve. This is your brine.

4. Pour the brine over the vegetables, filling each jar to within ½ inch of the top. Carefully tap the jars on the counter to release any trapped air, then top them off with more brine if needed to cover the vegetables. Seal the containers with a tight-fitting lid.

5. Let the jars cool to room temperature. Store the pickles in the refrigerator; they will be ready after 12 hours. Refrigerator pickles will keep for about 1 month.

pickled red onions

*16-ounce jar

1 large **red onion**, thinly sliced (about 2 cups)

¾ cup **distilled white** or **apple cider vinegar**

Large pinch of **granulated sugar**

Large pinch of **kosher salt**

These sweet and tangy onions are so easy to make and great in tacos and sandwiches and on top of chili.

1. Wash and thoroughly dry a widemouthed pint jar (or other 16-ounce sealable container) and its lid.

2. Fill the jar with the onion slices, leaving ½ inch of space at the top.

3. Place the vinegar, sugar, salt, and ¾ cup water in a small saucepan over medium-high heat. Bring the mixture to a simmer, stirring until the salt and sugar dissolve.

4. Pour in enough hot brine to cover the onions. Carefully tap the jar on the counter to release any trapped air, then top off with more brine if needed to cover the onions. Seal the container with its lid.

5. Let the jar cool to room temperature. Store the onions in the refrigerator for up to 1 week.

maraschino cherries

*16-ounce jar

¾ cup **granulated sugar**

¼ cup **freshly squeezed lemon juice**

¼ teaspoon **pure almond extract** (optional)

Pinch of **kosher salt**

1½ cups (½ pound) stemmed and pitted **sweet cherries**, fresh or frozen

That neon red jar of cherries on the supermarket shelf isn't so tempting when you learn to make these yourself. Use them in Shirley Temples (page 259), plopped into a tall glass of lemonade, or atop an ice cream sundae.

1. Combine the sugar, lemon juice, almond extract (if using), salt, and ¾ cup water in a small saucepan and bring to a boil over high heat.

2. Reduce the heat to low and simmer for a minute or two until the sugar dissolves, stirring occasionally with a wooden spoon.

3. Add the cherries and simmer on low heat for 8 minutes, until the liquid has thickened slightly. Remove the pan from the heat and set aside to cool slightly. Carefully transfer the cherries and liquid to a 16-ounce glass jar and cover with the lid. When cooled to room temperature, place the jar in the refrigerator and let the cherries soak for at least 12 hours before eating. Store in the refrigerator for up to 2 weeks.

half-sour pickles

*32-ounce jars

¼ cup plus 1 teaspoon (33 grams) **kosher salt**

2 cups **warm water**

2 to 2½ pounds **Kirby cucumbers**

10 to 12 **garlic cloves**, smashed

2 sprigs **fresh dill** (if you can include a dill flower, even better!)

3 tablespoons **pickling spice** or **whole spices** like peppercorns, coriander seeds, and mustard seeds

Steeping something in vinegar isn't the only way to make a pickle! This recipe uses a method called "fermentation," which is the process of inviting friendly bacteria to set up shop and prevent bad bacteria while making foods delicious in the meantime! Just submerge your cucumbers in a salty brine and wait a few days. The salt will ward off any harmful bacteria and create a welcoming environment for friendly bacteria (in this case, lactobacillus, which also turns milk into yogurt) that will slowly eat the natural sugars in the cucumbers, fermenting and preserving them. A precise amount of salt is necessary for proper fermentation; we make a big batch of brine to ensure we have enough to submerge the cukes and then discard any that's left over.

These garlicky, crunchy, bright-green pickles are called half-sours because they don't ferment for as long as full sours, so they keep their crisp and don't get too funky!

It's natural for the brine to turn cloudy after a few days, but discard the jar if you discover any mold.

1. In a pitcher, dissolve the salt in the warm water, then refrigerate until cool. Wash and thoroughly dry two widemouthed quart jars (or other 32-ounce sealable containers) and their lids.

2. Thoroughly wash the cucumbers and cut them lengthwise into quarters to make spears.

3. Place the cucumbers, garlic, dill, and pickling spice into the jars, packing them as tightly as possible without smashing them, and pour in the cooled brine, leaving ½ inch of space at the top. The cucumbers should be fully submerged. Carefully tap the jars on the counter to release any trapped air, then top off with more brine if needed. Seal the containers with a lid.

4. Store the pickles in a cool, dark place. After 12 to 24 hours, unscrew the lid to let out any built-up gases (it's normal to see some fizz). Screw the lid back on tightly and transfer to the refrigerator to slow the pickles' fermentation and preserve their crunch. After 2 days, taste for readiness. Half-sours will continue to ferment and strengthen in flavor. Eat within 2 weeks.

easy any-fruit jam

¾ pound **fresh** or **frozen stone fruits** or **berries**, sliced if larger than a raspberry

¾ cup **granulated sugar**

1 teaspoon **freshly squeezed lemon juice**

It's a fun problem to have: too much delicious fruit. But it happens, and we have a solution. This quick jam transforms fruit that is on its way out into a great topping for your toast, or a stir-in for your yogurt, or even spooned over vanilla ice cream. This is not a jam to "put up," the old-fashioned term for holding on to seasonal fruit's flavor for the winter months on your shelf—there's a whole process for jam making that allows it to be shelf-stable. This is jam for right now. After all, what other kind of jam do you actually want?

1. Combine the fruit, sugar, and lemon juice in a medium saucepan. Cook over medium heat, mashing the fruit against the pan with the back of a wooden spoon. Bring the mixture to a rolling boil at high, then immediately lower the heat to medium and cook, stirring often, for 8 to 10 minutes, until thickened slightly, occasionally skimming any foam from the surface with a metal spoon.

2. Carefully transfer the jam to a clean 8-ounce jar and let it cool. Screw on the lid and refrigerate. The jam will keep for about 1 week in the refrigerator.

whipped cream

½ cup **heavy whipping cream**

1 tablespoon **powdered sugar**

¼ teaspoon **pure vanilla extract**

We always love an excuse to whip up some cream, whether it's summer's first berries or a bowl of pudding. And while you could certainly break out your handheld mixer or stand mixer to do the work, we love getting a workout and whipping cream by hand.

Place a medium metal bowl and metal whisk in the freezer for at least 10 minutes. Combine the cream, powdered sugar, and vanilla in the chilled bowl and whisk until the cream reaches stiff peaks (this means the peaks hold their shape and don't droop when the whisk is lifted). If you're not using it right away, store it in an airtight container in the refrigerator for up to 2 days. When ready to use, whisk for a few seconds to reaerate it.

zesty bread crumbs

¼ cup **extra-virgin olive oil**

1 teaspoon minced **garlic** (about 1 medium clove)

1 cup **panko bread crumbs**

Kosher salt and **freshly ground black pepper** to taste

OPTIONAL ADDITIONS

1 or 2 **anchovy fillets** or a pinch of **crushed red pepper flakes** (added with the garlic); 1 teaspoon **freshly grated lemon zest** or 1 tablespoon **fresh** or **dried herbs** (added with the salt and pepper)

Don't stop at garlic, salt, and pepper. Add a pinch of fresh or dried herbs, or citrus zest if you want!

Sure, you can buy seasoned bread crumbs at the grocery store, but why do that when you can season them yourself? Bread crumbs can be tossed on top of pastas and salads for extra crunch and pop.

For this recipe, we start with unflavored store-bought crumbs (we love the crisp, light ones called panko) and flavor them with garlic oil. But if you want to make your own bread crumbs from scratch, wait for a loaf of bread to go just a day or two past prime (stale, not moldy!), cut it up into chunks, and bake in a 250°F oven for about 20 minutes, or until dry and brittle all the way through. Whiz them in the food processor for a few moments and hello bread crumbs!

Heat the oil in a large skillet over medium heat. Once hot, add the garlic (and anchovies or red pepper flakes, if using) and cook until fragrant, about 1 minute. Add the bread crumbs and cook, stirring regularly, until the crumbs are toasted and golden brown. Season with salt and black pepper (and the lemon zest or herbs, if using). Transfer to a paper towel–lined plate to cool.

shaken butter

1 cup **heavy cream**

Pinch of **kosher salt** (optional)

There's an argument to be made that not *everything* homemade is "better." Butter might be on that list; after all, these days you can find fancy French butter, butter made from Irish grass-fed cows, local butter—you name it. But seeing how cream transforms into butter just by shaking or churning is a real-life magic trick. When we first started teaching this recipe in camp, it was one of the activities we did while our Sleepover No-Knead Bread (page 199) rested. By the end of a long day, you might have a lot of wiggles to shake out, so pump up some music and have a butter-shaking dance party. This might not be the most efficient way to make butter, but it's certainly the most fun!

1. Pour the cream into a 16-ounce jar or plastic pint container. It should fill the container halfway. Snap or screw the lid on tight.

2. Shake the jar vigorously until the cream thickens, then turns into a ball. Keep shaking until you see liquid separating out. Depending on how hard you shake, this could take several minutes. The ball is your butter, and the liquid remaining is essentially buttermilk (but since the kind of cream we start with is pasteurized, this buttermilk isn't the tangy, cultured buttermilk you buy in the store, so you can discard it).

3. If you aren't using your butter immediately, you need to "wash" out the remaining buttermilk that's still mixed into your butter. Place the ball of butter into a bowl of very cold water and knead it in your hands, changing the water every so often until you are kneading in clear water. You can also put the butter ball in a handkerchief-size piece of cheesecloth and squeeze to extract the liquid.

4. Add the salt, if using, and continue kneading.

5. Refrigerate the butter in a sealed container or wrapped tightly in parchment or plastic wrap for up to 3 days.

handmade corn tortillas

*5-inch tortillas

1 cup **masa harina**, preferably Maseca brand

¼ teaspoon **kosher salt**

¾ cup **hot water**

SPECIAL EQUIPMENT

Tortilla press or a rolling pin and parchment paper

> Make tortillas without a tortilla press by using a rolling pin to roll out the balls very thinly between two sheets of parchment paper.

Fresh tortillas hot off the griddle! Nothing quite matches it. We have many recipes in this book that would benefit from some fresh tortillas—Loaded Enchiladas (page 135), Healthy Greens Quesadillas (page 92), Salsa Fresca (page 104), and Classic Guacamole (page 105)—but to be honest, one of our favorite ways to eat these homemade corn tortillas is piping hot with melted butter and a little cinnamon sugar or grated cheese.

To make the dough, all you have to do is buy masa harina, which is a special type of corn flour used for tortillas, and mix it with water. Masa harina is gluten-free, and you only have to knead the mixture for a couple minutes. Maseca is the most popular brand, and you can find it in many supermarkets and definitely in any Latino grocery.

1. Cut a zip-top plastic bag open along the sides. Open a tortilla press and lay the opened bag inside. Alternatively, cut two 12-inch squares of parchment paper.

2. In a small mixing bowl, combine the masa harina and salt. Add the water and stir to combine. With clean hands, knead the dough in the bowl until smooth and no longer sticky, about 2 minutes. If the dough is still crumbly, add water, 1 tablespoon at a time, and knead until it comes together. If the dough still feels too sticky to handle, add more masa harina, 1 tablespoon at a time.

3. Cover the bowl with a clean kitchen towel and allow the dough to rest for 15 minutes.

4. Using your hands, form balls of masa about the size of a Ping-Pong ball. Put a ball in the center of the bag-lined tortilla press. Lower the top of the press down and flatten the dough into a ⅛-inch-thick tortilla. Peel the tortilla off the plastic and carefully set aside. Only press as many as will fit easily in your pan without overlapping, since the dough dries out super fast once pressed. Expect to do at least several rounds of pressing and cooking. (Alternatively, if you don't have

(RECIPE CONTINUES)

a tortilla press, place the masa ball in the center of a square of parchment, top with the other square, and flatten it into a circle with your hand or the bottom of a pot. Then use a rolling pin to roll it out to a thin 5-inch circle.)

5. Warm a large skillet over medium-high heat. When a few drops of water immediately sizzle when flicked into it, it is ready. Cook the tortillas, being careful that they don't overlap, for 1 to 2 minutes on each side, until lightly browned with dry edges. You might have to taste the corner of one to find out how long the tortillas should cook on your setup. Stack the cooked tortillas and wrap them in a clean kitchen towel to keep warm. If you have leftovers, keep them refrigerated in a plastic bag and reheat, wrapped in foil, for 10 minutes in a 350°F oven.

toasted nuts and seeds

This isn't really a recipe—it's just a method—but to get the most flavor and crunch out of your nuts and seeds, toast them!

Place the nuts or seeds in a small dry skillet set over medium heat and toast, stirring with a wooden spoon, until golden and fragrant, 3 to 5 minutes, keeping a close eye on them to make sure they don't burn. Let them cool, and they're ready to use!

garlicky bruschetta and croutons

10 to 12 slices **rustic bread** (sliced on the diagonal about 1 inch thick)

3 or 4 **garlic cloves**

Extra-virgin olive oil, for drizzling

Kosher salt to taste

Bruschetta are essentially garlic toasts and the perfect vehicle for other foods. We serve them with countless meals: on the side of our Garden Gazpacho (page 154) or Meatballs and Sauce (page 90), or topped with fresh ricotta or mozzarella. These are packed with quite the garlic punch, so for a less intense flavor, you can rub the garlic on just one side of the toast.

One they've cooled, you can crumble them by hand into croutons for salads like Cheater's Caesar Salad (page 188) or as a topping for soups.

1. Preheat the oven to 350°F.

2. Arrange the bread in a single layer on a sheet pan. Toast the bread in the oven for about 5 minutes, until golden brown and crispy, flipping halfway through; if you want the slices extra crisp, just toast them longer. Remove the pan from the oven and let the bread cool just enough that you can handle it.

3. Meanwhile, peel the garlic. Rub a slightly smashed clove of garlic on both sides of the bread; the crispy bits will grate the garlic directly onto the bread. Drizzle the bread with the oil and sprinkle with salt. Serve immediately.

If there's a word or a term you don't know in any of our recipes, it's probably here!

Against the grain

When you look at a piece of meat, you can see what direction the fibers are going—they are usually in a line. Cutting "against the grain" means to slice the meat so that you're cutting those lines shorter (as opposed to "with the grain," which means to cut alongside the lines, keeping them long). This makes the meat more tender by cutting the longer muscle fibers that otherwise would be chewy and get caught in your teeth.

Al dente

Italian for "to the tooth," al dente is what you're looking for when you're cooking pasta: it should be soft on the exterior but have a little chew when you bite through, and it usually requires cooking it a minute or two shy of the package instructions. Nothing is worse than mushy pasta! For recipes where the pasta will continue to cook in sauce on the stove or in the oven, it's important to cook the pasta for an even shorter time, or extra al dente.

Bake

We all know that baking means cooking something in the oven, but unlike roasting, baking is usually at a lower, gentler temperature and transforms a wet or soft batter or dough into a solid baked good.

Blanch

To blanch an ingredient is to boil it quickly to soften it up, then "shock" it by submerging it in an ice bath to stop the cooking process. This is a form of parcooking that's useful for preparing vegetables ahead of time in order to quickly sauté or stir-fry or use them in other cooked dishes. It also helps preserve the bright color of vegetables.

Brown butter

Butter is a magical ingredient that's delicious on its own, but when you cook it until it foams and the milk solids turn to brown specks and the aroma turns nutty, you're left with something even more amazing: brown butter, which brings a depth of flavor to anything it's added to. Drizzle it over vegetables, swap it out for regular melted butter in cookies. Once you make it, you'll turn to it again and again.

Deglaze

When you sear something, all the browned bits stuck to the pan are pure, concentrated flavor. Deglazing is when you pour liquid—it could be anything from water to cider to stock—into the hot pan and scrape up all the browned bits to release them and create a simple, flavorful sauce.

Drizzle

This means to pour just a little bit of a liquid on top of the dish, like a little bit of honey or olive oil or maple syrup.

Dust

When you dust a pan or your work surface, you're covering it with just a very thin layer (a dusting!) of flour, sugar, or whatever is called for.

Emulsify

This word refers to the process of mixing two liquids that normally don't easily combine, like oil and water or vinegar. When you whisk vigorously or shake them in a jar to force them to come together, they will look like a creamy sauce when you're done, but they'll usually separate again after a little while. It's often useful to have an emulsifying agent—something thick like mustard, honey, miso, tomato paste, applesauce—to help that process along and keep the mixture stable so it doesn't separate. You emulsify when you make vinaigrettes (where the emulsifiers could be any of those items listed) and mayonnaise (where the emulsifier is the egg).

Ice bath

An ice bath is just a big bowl of cold water with enough ice cubes added to make it super cold. You give ingredients a dip in an ice-cold water bath when you want to stop the cooking process.

Mirepoix

Many dishes start with a base of flavor built by cooking diced onion, celery, and carrots in oil, butter, or another fat. In French cuisine, this is called mirepoix; it's similar to the Italian soffritto and Spanish sofrito.

Mise

Mise is short for mise en place, a French term used in kitchens that translates into "everything in its place." It refers to a cook's setup: the lineup of prepared ingredients and tools that make up everything they need to prepare a meal. In home kitchens, having a proper mise requires looking through the recipe to assemble and prepare ingredients and placing them in small bowls or piles, organized in the order they're called for.

Parcook

Adding "par-" in front of words like "cook," "bake," or "boil" means to partially cook it so that it can continue to cook later. For example, you often parboil potatoes to give them a jump start if you're going to add them to another dish later.

Poach

Poaching is a gentle cooking method where ingredients that need to be handled carefully (like fish or very ripe fruit such as pears) are cooked in barely simmering water. You can add flavorings, like bay leaves or garlic, to the poaching liquid to infuse more flavor into the ingredients you're cooking.

Sauté

Sautéing is a method in which ingredients are cooked in a small amount of fat (like oil or melted butter) in a pan while stirring. Sauté comes from the French word *sauter*, meaning "to jump," so you can imagine the ingredients jumping in the pan.

Scant

Scant refers to slightly less than the unit of measurement called for. So, a scant tablespoon would be a little less than a tablespoon that is leveled at the top.

Season

To season something means to boost its flavor, usually with salt and pepper or other spices called for in the recipe. When a recipe says "season to taste" it means to taste the dish at that stage and adjust the seasoning by adding more, if necessary.

Sift

Sifting flour or powdered sugar, whether by using a handheld sifter or by passing it through a fine-mesh strainer, helps ensure there are no lumps. You often sift powdered sugar over baked goods before serving to make them even prettier and add a touch more sweetness.

Simmer

When you're heating a liquid, the stage when small bubbles form around the edge of the pan and continue to rise up to the surface is called "simmering." It's the stage right before boiling, and it's often the best stage for cooking soups and stews.

Sweat

Cooking ingredients, like garlic or spices, over low heat in fat infuses the fat with the flavor of the ingredients. You do this when you want to flavor the fat so that it disperses throughout the dish when other ingredients are added and carries that flavor with it.

Translucent

Almost-but-not-quite see-through. You will most often see this term in reference to onions, which means cooking onions until they turn from white to translucent and glossy.

Truss

Trussing a piece of meat, like a rolled pork loin or a whole chicken, means to use kitchen twine to tie it together so it holds its shape. It also helps the meat cook more evenly. When the meat is done cooking and resting, remove the twine before serving.

Toast

Toasting ingredients like nuts and spices means to heat them to intensify their flavor. Usually this is done in a dry pan, but you can also toast spices in oil.

ACKNOWLEDGMENTS

It is no small feat to write a book, let alone to do it while also running a business. We are old enough and wise enough to know to ask for help. Without the following people, this project would have not come to life at all, let alone so beautifully.

Clarkson Potter is a publishing house jam-packed with pros. Thank you to Doris Cooper for first seeing potential for a Dynamite Shop book. As busy business owners and parents, we have a lot of balls in the air, and sometimes it takes someone with vision who "gets it" through and through to say, "Hey, what about a book"? Thank you, Doris. Gratitude to Francis Lam, who thoughtfully edited our manuscript and helped guide the vision to completion, and Darian Keels, for managing the details so nothing fell through the cracks.

Our friend Aubrie Pick took the mission of The Dynamite Shop and brought it to life. The energetic and joyful photos you see here are all her vision and execution. World class! She worked with Claire Mack on props and Fanny Pan on food styling. They make a stellar team. We want to thank all the Dynamite kids (most of whom are longtime students) who signed on to demonstrate their cooking skills during the photo shoot: seeing you when we flip through the pages, and knowing that your love of cooking will inspire other kids, warms our hearts and makes us love this book even more. Stephanie Huntwork pulled all the art together with her design to create this gorgeous package. Thanks to you all for bringing to life a spirit of exuberance, confidence, and community that lives so deeply within us!

The role of a literary agent can take many forms, but in the case of Janis Donnaud, it is to be the smartest and most loyal guide in the business. Janis, our deepest appreciation for your fierce care.

At The Dynamite Shop we have been lucky to work with an amazing team. Brianne Ross helped keep our recipes organized, consistent, and, most importantly, successful. Brianne is not only an excellent teacher, she also tested and taught most of the recipes in the book. Sara Redeghieri kept the business buzzing when we were deep in writing. Known as a beloved Dynamite instructor, Sara also single-handedly kept the trains running behind the scenes. Thank you to instructors Kate DelCiampo, Josh Liebeskind, and Gabby Romero, who helped us keep the Dynamite spirit alive in kitchens across the world over the past few years.

Thanks to our life partners, Lindsay Bowen and Pete Ho, who make us feel 10,000% supported every day, and our kids, Jack and Ursula, who remind us why it's crucial to teach kids to make dinner.

Finally, our deepest gratitude to our Dynamite Shop families, who come to class day after day and entrust us to teach their children to take charge of their relationship with food and cooking. And to our young cooks specifically: You are on a path to unfolding the infinite joy and discovery ahead. We are so excited for you and so honored to be along for the journey!

DANA BOWEN
and
SARA KATE GILLINGHAM

Note: Page references in *italics* indicate recipe photographs.